Slow Cookers For Dummies®

Great Tips for Slow Coo...

Follow these tips for the best slow cook...

- **Brown meats and poultry first.** Although doing so may add a few extra minutes in prep time, food takes on a whole different look and flavor when first browned. Add a small amount of oil, like canola or olive, to a nonstick skillet large enough to hold the meat or poultry. Warm it over medium-high heat a couple minutes, add the food in small batches, and brown the food evenly on all sides.

- **Don't overdo the liquid.** Very little evaporation occurs in a slow cooker compared to stovetop or oven cooking. Most slow cooker recipes, with the exception of soups and sauces, call for 50 percent less liquid than conventional ones.

- **Always cook covered.** To maintain the proper balance between time and temperature, always cook with the cover on. If you must peek or stir, do so quickly; it can take up to 20 minutes to recover lost heat after the cover is removed.

- **Even pieces mean evenly cooked food.** Food should be cut into even, bite-sized pieces so that they cook evenly at the same time.

- **Season liberally.** Because slow cooker food cooks longer than other conventional methods, the flavor of herbs and spices can diminish. Fresh herbs should be added during the last 60 minutes of cooking. Also add a pinch or two more of dried herbs than you think is necessary. Season to taste with salt and freshly ground black pepper. Taste again and adjust as needed before serving. *Never* salt dried beans until they're cooked to the point of being almost tender. Salt hardens the outer coating of the bean when added too soon.

- **Never add dairy products in the beginning of the cooking process.** Slow cooking causes ... to curdle and aged ... to become oily. Either add dairy products the last 60 minutes of cooking or use canned sweetened, condensed, or evaporated milk. Substitute processed cheese for aged cheese.

- **Never use frozen ingredients.** For food safety, a slow cooker must reach at least 140° in four hours or less. Frozen food prolongs the cooking process, increasing the possibility of harmful bacteria growth. Large pieces of foods like meat and poultry should be safely thawed a day or two before in the refrigerator. Frozen vegetables and the like should be thawed before being added.

- **Take care with power outages.** Resume cooking in slow cooker if the outage has been for less than two hours — or remove food from the cooking container and continue cooking in a saucepan or ovenproof dish on the stovetop or in the oven. If the outage was longer than two hours and the food was still cooking, discard the food to avoid the possibility of food-borne illness.

- **Don't subject the ceramic cooking container or glass lid to extreme temperatures.** The ceramic cooking container and glass cover react to changes in temperature and can crack or break if cold ingredients are added when hot, or if placed on a cold surface when hot.

- **Do not overfill or underfill.** For best cooking results, fill your slow cooker at least halfway and no more than two-thirds.

- **Note that cooking times increase above an altitude of 4,000 feet.** Check with your local cooperative extension bureau for cooking time conversions.

For Dummies™: Bestselling Book Series for Beginners

Slow Cookers For Dummies®

Cheat Sheet

Temperature Conversions

Degrees Fahrenheit	Degrees Celsius
140	60
145	65
160	70
165	75
170	80
180	85
250	120
275	135
300	150
325	160
350	175
375	190
400	205
425	220
450	230
475	245
500	260

Cooking Temperatures

Food	Safe Cooking Temperature in Degrees F
Eggs	Cook until yolk and white are firm
Egg dishes	160
Ground Meat and Meat Mixtures	
Turkey, chicken	165
Veal, beef, lamb, pork	160
Fresh Beef	
Medium rare	145
Medium	160
Well done	170
Fresh Lamb	
Medium rare	145
Medium	160
Well done	170
Fresh Pork	
Medium	160
Well done	170
Poultry	
Chicken, whole	180
Turkey, whole	180
Poultry breasts, roasted	170
Poultry thighs, wings	180
Ham	
Fresh (uncured)	160
Precooked (ready to eat)	140

Determining cooking times

Most slow cooker recipes take 6 to 10 hours to cook. Use the following guidelines when converting favorite recipes to the slow cooker.

Cooking Times

Traditional Recipe	Slow Cooker Low Setting	Slow Cooker High Setting
45 minutes	6–10 hours	3–4 hours
50–60 minutes	8–10 hours	4–5 hours

When in doubt, the safest way to determine that food has safely finished cooking is to test it by inserting a meat or an instant-read thermometer into the thickest part of the cooked food. To get an accurate reading, do so without touching bone or the cooking container.

IDG BOOKS WORLDWIDE

Copyright © 2001 IDG Books Worldwide, Inc. All rights reserved.

Cheat Sheet $2.95 value. Item 5240-6.

For more information about IDG Books, call 1-800-762-2974.

For Dummies™: Bestselling Book Series for Beginners

TM

References for the Rest of Us!™

BESTSELLING BOOK SERIES

Do you find that traditional reference books are overloaded with technical details and advice you'll never use? Do you postpone important life decisions because you just don't want to deal with them? Then our ...*For Dummies*® business and general reference book series is for you.

...*For Dummies* business and general reference books are written for those frustrated and hard-working souls who know they aren't dumb, but find that the myriad of personal and business issues and the accompanying horror stories make them feel helpless. ...*For Dummies* books use a lighthearted approach, a down-to-earth style, and even cartoons and humorous icons to dispel fears and build confidence. Lighthearted but not lightweight, these books are perfect survival guides to solve your everyday personal and business problems.

> "More than a publishing phenomenon, 'Dummies' is a sign of the times."
> — The New York Times

> "...you won't go wrong buying them."
> — Walter Mossberg, Wall Street Journal, on IDG Books' ...For Dummies books

> "A world of detailed and authoritative information is packed into them..."
> — U.S. News and World Report

Already, millions of satisfied readers agree. They have made ...*For Dummies* the #1 introductory level computer book series and a best-selling business book series. They have written asking for more. So, if you're looking for the best and easiest way to learn about business and other general reference topics, look to ...*For Dummies* to give you a helping hand.

IDG BOOKS
WORLDWIDE

1/99

by Tom Lacalamita and Glenna Vance

IDG Books Worldwide, Inc.
An International Data Group Company

Foster City, CA ◆ Chicago, IL ◆ Indianapolis, IN ◆ New York, NY

Slow Cookers For Dummies®

Published by
IDG Books Worldwide, Inc.
An International Data Group Company
919 E. Hillsdale Blvd.
Suite 400
Foster City, CA 94404
www.idgbooks.com (IDG Books Worldwide Web Site)
www.dummies.com (Dummies Press Web Site)

Library of Congress Control Number: 00-106306

ISBN: 0-7645-5240-6

Printed in the United States of America

10 9 8 7 6 5 4 3 2 1

1O/RQ/RQ/QR/IN

Distributed in the United States by IDG Books Worldwide, Inc.

Distributed by CDG Books Canada Inc. for Canada; by Transworld Publishers Limited in the United Kingdom; by IDG Norge Books for Norway; by IDG Sweden Books for Sweden; by IDG Books Australia Publishing Corporation Pty. Ltd. for Australia and New Zealand; by TransQuest Publishers Pte Ltd. for Singapore, Malaysia, Thailand, Indonesia, and Hong Kong; by Gotop Information Inc. for Taiwan; by ICG Muse, Inc. for Japan; by Intersoft for South Africa; by Eyrolles for France; by International Thomson Publishing for Germany, Austria and Switzerland; by Distribuidora Cuspide for Argentina; by LR International for Brazil; by Galileo Libros for Chile; by Ediciones ZETA S.C.R. Ltda. for Peru; by WS Computer Publishing Corporation, Inc., for the Philippines; by Contemporanea de Ediciones for Venezuela; by Express Computer Distributors for the Caribbean and West Indies; by Micronesia Media Distributor, Inc. for Micronesia; by Chips Computadoras S.A. de C.V. for Mexico; by Editorial Norma de Panama S.A. for Panama; by American Bookshops for Finland.

For general information on IDG Books Worldwide's books in the U.S., please call our Consumer Customer Service department at 800-762-2974. For reseller information, including discounts and premium sales, please call our Reseller Customer Service department at 800-434-3422.

For information on where to purchase IDG Books Worldwide's books outside the U.S., please contact our International Sales department at 317-572-3993 or fax 317-572-4002.

For consumer information on foreign language translations, please contact our Customer Service department at 800-434-3422, fax 317-572-4002, or e-mail rights@idgbooks.com.

For information on licensing foreign or domestic rights, please phone +1-650-653-7098.

For sales inquiries and special prices for bulk quantities, please contact our Order Services department at 800-434-4322 or write to the address above.

For information on using IDG Books Worldwide's books in the classroom or for ordering examination copies, please contact our Educational Sales department at 800-434-2086 or fax 317-572-4005.

For press review copies, author interviews, or other publicity information, please contact our Public Relations department at 650-653-7000 or fax 650-653-7500.

For authorization to photocopy items for corporate, personal, or educational use, please contact Copyright Clearance Center, 222 Rosewood Drive, Danvers, MA 01923, or fax 978-750-4470.

About the Authors

Tom Lacalamita (Long Island, New York) is a bestselling author of five appliance-related cookbooks. Nominated for a James Beard cookbook award, Tom is considered a national authority on housewares and has appeared on hundreds of television and radio shows across the country. With a passion for food, cooking, and all sorts of kitchen gadgets, Tom is also a spokesperson for various food and housewares manufacturers.

Glenna Vance (Milwaukee, Wisconsin) is director of consumer affairs for a major ingredient manufacturer in the Midwest. A published author, Glenna has been involved in developing consumer recipe programs with major appliance manufacturers and ingredient companies. As a board member of the Milwaukee chapter of the American Institute of Wine & Food, Glenna is instrumental in bringing nationally renowned culinary professionals to Milwaukee for culinary programs and events.

ABOUT IDG BOOKS WORLDWIDE, INC.
AND CDG BOOKS CANADA, INC.

Welcome to the world of IDG Books Worldwide and CDG Books Canada.

IDG Books Worldwide, Inc., is a subsidiary of International Data Group, Inc., the world's largest publisher of computer-related information and the leading global provider of information services on information technology. IDG was founded more than 30 years ago and now employs more than 9,000 people worldwide. IDG publishes more than 295 computer publications in over 75 countries (see listing below). More than 90 million people read one or more IDG publications each month.

Launched in 1990, IDG Books Worldwide is today the #1 publisher of best-selling computer books in North America. IDG Books Worldwide is proud to be the recipient of eight awards from the Computer Press Association in recognition of editorial excellence and three from *Computer Currents'* First Annual Readers' Choice Awards. Our best-selling *...For Dummies®* series has more than 55 million copies in print with translations in 31 languages. In record time, IDG Books Worldwide has become the first choice for millions of readers around the world who want to learn how to better manage their businesses.

In 1998, IDG Books Worldwide formally partnered with Macmillan Canada, a subsidiary of Canada Publishing Corporation, to create CDG Books Canada, a dynamic new Canadian publishing company. CDG Books Canada is now Canada's fastest growing publisher, bringing valuable information to Canadians from coast to coast through the introduction of Canadian *...For Dummies®* and *CliffsNotes™* titles.

Every one of our books is designed to bring extra value and skill-building instructions to the reader. Our books are written by experts who understand and care about our readers. The knowledge base of our editorial staff comes from years of experience in publishing, education, and journalism — experience we use to produce books to carry us into the new millennium. In short, we care about books, so we attract the best people. We devote special attention to details such as audience, interior design, use of icons, and illustrations. And because we use an efficient process of authoring, editing, and desktop publishing our books electronically, we can spend more time ensuring superior content and spend less time on the technicalities of making books.

You can count on our commitment to deliver high-quality books at competitive prices on topics you want to read about. At IDG Books Worldwide and CDG Books Canada, we continue in the IDG tradition of delivering quality for more than 30 years. You can learn more about IDG Books Worldwide and CDG Books Canada by visiting www.idgbooks.com, www.dummies.com, and www.cdgbooks.com.

John Kilcullen
President and Publisher
IDG Books Worldwide, Inc.

Steven Berkowitz
Chairman and CEO
IDG Books Worldwide, Inc.

Hart Hillman
President
CDG Books Canada, Inc.

Eighth Annual Computer Press Awards ▷1992

Ninth Annual Computer Press Awards ▷1993

Tenth Annual Computer Press Awards ▷1994

Eleventh Annual Computer Press Awards ▷1995

IDG is the world's leading IT media, research and exposition company. Founded in 1964, IDG had 1997 revenues of $2.05 billion and has more than 9,000 employees worldwide. IDG offers the widest range of media options that reach IT buyers in 75 countries representing 95% of worldwide IT spending. IDG's diverse product and services portfolio spans six key areas including print publishing, online publishing, expositions and conferences, market research, education and training, and global marketing services. More than 90 million people read one or more of IDG's 290 magazines and newspapers, including IDG's leading global brands — Computerworld, PC World, Network World, Macworld and the Channel World family of publications. IDG Books Worldwide is one of the fastest-growing computer book publishers in the world, with more than 700 titles in 36 languages. The "...For Dummies®" series alone has more than 50 million copies in print. IDG offers online users the largest network of technology-specific Web sites around the world through IDG.net (http://www.idg.net), which comprises more than 225 targeted Web sites in 55 countries worldwide. International Data Corporation (IDC) is the world's largest provider of information technology data, analysis and consulting, with research centers in over 41 countries and more than 400 research analysts worldwide. IDG World Expo is a leading producer of more than 168 globally branded conferences and expositions in 35 countries including E3 (Electronic Entertainment Expo), Macworld Expo, ComNet, Windows World Expo, ICE (Internet Commerce Expo), Agenda, DEMO, and Spotlight. IDG's training subsidiary, ExecuTrain, is the world's largest computer training company, with more than 230 locations worldwide and 785 training courses. IDG Marketing Services helps industry-leading IT companies build international brand recognition by developing global integrated marketing programs via IDG's print, online and exposition products worldwide. Further information about the company can be found at www.idg.com. 8/24/99

Dedication

I dedicate this book to my mother, Frances Porretta, a woman of great culinary talent, who over the course of my life has given me her unconditional love and support.

— Tom Lacalamita

Dedicated with love to my mom, Mildred Weir, who has been a queen in her kitchen all these many years and a positive influence in my life.

— Glenna Vance

Authors' Acknowledgments

A book is never the work of a single person. There are many who contribute to its success, and this book is no exception.

We would like to especially thank IDG Books and Holly McGuire for asking us to write *Slow Cookers For Dummies*. We'd also like to thank Linda Ingroia for keeping things on track and Angela Miller for bringing us all together.

We are extremely grateful for our very patient and understanding project editor, Suzanne Snyder. It was Suzanne's wisdom, soothing voice, and firm stance that got us through each and every day. Every author should, at least once in their lifetime, have an editor as professional and caring as Suzanne!

It's amazing how even with a computer grammar and spelling checker, errors somehow still slip by. For making this book grammatically correct, we heartily thank Tina Sims, who made sure that each and every dangling preposition and missing comma were found.

We are thankful for the luxury of a competent recipe tester, Laura Penseiro, who tested, tasted, and tweaked our recipes with the same loving care we would bestow. We also thank her for checking to make no sure there were no technical blunders.

Since a picture is worth a thousand words, we hope that you enjoy as much as we do the quirky, wonderfully descriptive illustrations of artist Liz Kurtzman.

We also want to thank Pam Mourouzis, Emily Wichlinski, and the remaining crew at IDG for their expertise in getting this book to you.

Last but not least, we would be amiss for not thanking our families and friends for their support, understanding, and unconditional love, which we know was not always easy for them to provide as our deadlines approached!

Publisher's Acknowledgments

We're proud of this book; please register your comments through our IDG Books Worldwide Online Registration Form located at http://my2cents.dummies.com.

Some of the people who helped bring this book to market include the following:

Acquisitions, Editorial, and Media Development

Project Editor: Suzanne Snyder

Acquisitions Editor: Linda Ingroia

Copy Editor: Tina Sims

Acquisitions Coordinator: Erin Connell

Technical Editor and Recipe Tester: Laura Penseiro

Permissions Editor: Carmen Krikorian

Editorial Manager: Pam Mourouzis

Artist: Liz Kurtzman

Editorial Assistants: Carol Strickland, Melissa Bluhm

Production

Project Coordinator: Emily Wichlinski

Layout and Graphics: Amy Adrian, Beth Brooks, Brian Drumm, Kristin Pickett, Brent Savage, Kendra Span, Brian Torwelle

Proofreaders: David Faust, Betty Kish, Dwight Ramsey, Charles Spencer

Indexer: Anne Leach

General and Administrative

IDG Books Worldwide, Inc.: John Kilcullen, CEO; Bill Barry, President and COO

IDG Books Consumer Reference Group

Business: Kathleen A. Welton, Vice President and Publisher; Kevin Thornton, Acquisitions Manager

Cooking/Gardening: Jennifer Feldman, Associate Vice President and Publisher

Education/Reference: Diane Graves Steele, Vice President and Publisher; Greg Tubach, Publishing Director

Lifestyles: Kathleen Nebenhaus, Vice President and Publisher; Tracy Boggier, Managing Editor

Pets: Dominique De Vito, Associate Vice President and Publisher; Tracy Boggier, Managing Editor

Travel: Michael Spring, Vice President and Publisher; Suzanne Jannetta, Editorial Director; Brice Gosnell, Managing Editor

IDG Books Consumer Editorial Services: Kathleen Nebenhaus, Vice President and Publisher; Kristin A. Cocks, Editorial Director; Cindy Kitchel, Editorial Director

IDG Books Consumer Production: Debbie Stailey, Production Director

IDG Books Packaging: Marc J. Mikulich, Vice President, Brand Strategy and Research

◆

The publisher would like to give special thanks to Patrick J. McGovern, without whom this book would not have been possible.

◆

Recipes at a Glance

Master Meat Sauce Recipes

Master Roast Turkey Breast Recipes

Meat and Poultry

Meatless Main and Side Dishes

Sauces and Spreads

Snacks

Soups, Chowders, and Chili

Stews

Salads

Contents at a Glance

Cartoons at a Glance

By Rich Tennant

page 7

page 67

page 27

page 155

page 203

Fax: 978-546-7747
E-mail: richtennant@the5thwave.com
World Wide Web: www.the5thwave.com

Table of Contents

Introduction

• •

*M*any people don't like to cook, but for the most part, they sure do like to eat. As two people who like to do both, we think that people's aversion to cooking comes from the stress of day-to-day living and not having the time or the energy to cook dinner after a long, hard day of work or even play. That's probably why more and more people are once again discovering the benefits and advantages of slow cookers. Who wouldn't like to come home to a hot, homemade dinner at the end of a long day? We know we sure do!

Slow cookers were introduced 30 years ago and have undergone various improvements and innovations. So today's version of the appliance is not your mother's slow cooker, and the recipes you use don't have to be your mother's either. *Slow Cookers For Dummies* is a collection of our favorite foods along with some updated classics, all made in the slow cooker. But it's really much more than that. It also represents our collective experience and effort on how to get the best-tasting food from the slow cooker to the dinner table with the least amount of time and effort. We are going to share with you everything we've come to know and like about cooking in a slow cooker, as well as tips and suggestions for getting the best results. If you are as inquisitive as we are, you're in for a real treat because you also find out how slow cookers work and how to correct problems as they happen. Because food safety is a concern for everyone, you also discover how to use your slow cooker properly in order to avoid foodborne illness.

How to Use This Book

Although the beginning is usually a good place to start, books about cooking are different. You should be able to pick one up and start reading wherever you want, so that's exactly what we set out to do when we wrote this book. Looking for a great recipe for minestrone soup? Well, turn to Chapter 7 — which contains information about making soups and chowders in your slow cooker — and find everything you need to know to make it. Wondering how much liquid to use when making grandma's pot roast recipe? You find that information in Chapter 9 — the chapter on meats.

Naturally, we're proud of all the information we compiled for this book and hope that you will take the time to read most of it. If you don't initially, that's okay, too, because we know you'll like the recipes so much that before you know and even realize it, you will have ultimately read almost everything from cover to cover!

Conventions Used in This Book

For the most part, all the information in this book is straightforward and simple to grasp — even for people with a limited cooking background. Where necessary, we point out things at the beginning or end of the recipes that we think you should know. These items include time-saving tips and suggestions, or even information — such as how long you can store something in the freezer safely. Although some of these items may appear obvious, we'd still like for you to read them to avoid misunderstandings.

Here are two issues that require further clarification:

✔ **Time:** Time is an important issue for all of us. Naturally, you need to know how long the food must cook. We also feel that it is important that you know how much time is needed to prepare the food before the slow cooker takes over. Therefore, you will notice that every recipe gives you separate times for the preparation and cooking. Preparation time is how long we estimate it will take you to slice and dice, and perhaps brown or sauté, the food before it goes into the slow cooker. Cooking time refers to the amount of time needed for the prepared food to cook in the slow cooker. Both of these times are, at best, approximations.

The basic idea behind a slow cooker is to enable you to prepare a recipe from start to finish with no further intervention once the cover is in place and the unit turned on. Because most people work an 8-hour day and need approximately 1 to 2 hours more for commuting, a slow cooker needs to be able to cook and hold food safely for approximately 8 to 10 hours from start to finish, something that all these recipes do.

However, because our job as food authors entails staying in the kitchen and watching food cook as we develop and test recipes, we discovered that in most instances the food was ready much sooner than anticipated. Initially we saw this as a dilemma and were faced with two possible options: state all the cooking times as 8 to 10 hours — as the manufacturers do — regardless of whether the food was done sooner, or provide the cooking times that we determined to be the most accurate for the recipe being prepared.

After much consideration, we decided to go with the second option and provide cooking times without overstating them. We did so, knowing that foods like roasts, stews, chilis, and soups, hold up relatively well if cooked longer in the slow cooker. By providing you with the *actual,* shorter cooking times, you can get dinner on the table even sooner than you thought. If you happen to be home when the food is done cooking and are not ready to sit down to dinner yet, set the slow cooker to the warm setting until you're ready to eat. This way, the food stays at the perfect temperature for serving without drying out or overcooking.

✔ **Sodium:** As you will see, all the recipes in this book contain a complete nutritional analysis, including sodium content. Because some people watch their sodium intake for a variety of reasons, we want this information to be as accurate as possible. To do so, we decided to add into the total sodium calculation a small amount of salt, ½ teaspoon to be precise, whenever a recipe says to "salt and pepper" the meat or poultry.

Foolish Assumptions

Just because you're reading the introduction to a book about slow cookers, we can't necessarily assume that you already own a slow cooker. Some people use a book like this one as a guide to find out more about the product before purchasing it. If that's the case, we recommend you take a look at Chapter 2, where you're certain to find everything you need to know about slow cookers. You may also check the appendix for a list of slow cooker manufacturers.

How This Book Is Organized

The opening chapters go into detailed product information, as well as use and care information. Because food safety is such an important topic nowadays, we provide you with the latest information on safe cooking practices. You will find the recipes in Part III of this book organized in typical cookbook-menu sequence: snacks and beverages first, then soups and chilis, followed by meat and poultry entrées, and then desserts.

One of our favorite things about our slow cookers is that we can make extra-large batches of foods like tomato meat sauce and chicken broth, freeze them in small portions, and then use them to prepare stovetop entrées that we can serve in no time at all. We view this as an extra perk of the slow cooker. As an added bonus, we include these recipes in a separate part of this book — above and beyond the normal recipe section. We're certain that you will enjoy these recipes as much as we do.

Part I: Revving Up Your Slow Cooker

This is the place to find out all there is to know about how slow cookers work. Millions of consumers use them, so you're far from alone! We explain the differences between the types out there, as well as advise you on the latest innovations and features.

Part II: Making the Best and Safest Use of Your Slow Cooker

Slow cookers make great food and are safe to use if you know what you're doing. So let us share with you everything we know to make sure you get the best and safest results possible. Besides use and care and safe cooking practices, we give you the ins and outs of slow cooker cooking as well as how to adapt your favorite recipes to be made in the slow cooker. For illustration purposes, we take five of our all-time favorite dishes and show you how we adapted them for the slow cooker.

Part III: Basic and Delicious Recipes for the Slow Cooker

Quick, delicious, homemade food is what it's all about, and those are the results (not to mention compliments) you're bound to get when you make any of the recipes in this section. Part III contains 65 recipes — covering the gamut from snack foods, to savory stews and succulent roasts, to old-fashioned comfort food desserts like Apple Brown Betty and rice pudding.

Part IV: Jump-Starting Dinner with Your Slow Cooker

Imagine a freezer stocked with quarts of thick tomato sauce or rich chicken broth. Or think about what you could create from a juicy, tender roast turkey breast. If you had previously made these dishes in your slow cooker, they would be ready to be transformed into delicious dinner entrées in less than 60 minutes! Well, dream no more and get cooking with 34 quick and easy recipes to choose from!

Part V: The Part of Tens

Years ago it was common practice for people to pick up the phone and call Mom with their cooking questions. You can still call Mom today, but you'll probably get her answering machine (after all, she's got her food in the slow cooker and she's out on the town). Instead, check out our Part of Tens, where we give you invaluable tips, troubleshooting hints, slow cooker-related Web site addresses, and ten menus for any time of the year.

Appendixes

Someday, sometime, something may well go wrong, and you're going to need to contact the manufacturer with a question or for assistance. Rather than scramble through old drawers looking for the owner's manual, refer to Appendix A for a complete listing of the manufacturer's customer service phone numbers and Web sites, if available. See Appendix B for handy metric and other conversion information.

Icons Used in This Book

Icons are symbols or pictures that represent or convey an idea. We use three of them throughout this book where we think an idea or concept should be stressed for your benefit.

We've picked up these tips or shortcuts over the years and want to share them with you to make cooking less of a hassle and more fun.

This icon indicates a potential problem or pitfall that you may encounter. But rest assured because we also tell you how to avoid or overcome it.

Okay, we know you've heard it before. It's just too important not to repeat, so we mention it again with an icon.

A Few Guidelines Before You Begin

We learn to walk before we run. And so it goes with everything in life. Because you have taken the trouble to pick up this cookbook and read it to this point, we assume that you are interested in cooking and that you have at least some experience in the kitchen. With this in mind, we give you some pointers that should make life easier for you before you even get started. So please take the time to read them.

- ✔ Always read a recipe from beginning to end at least once before preparing a dish to make sure that you know how long it's going to take to prepare and cook, what steps and cooking utensils you will need, and what procedures are involved.

- ✔ Have all the ingredients on hand before you start cooking. In fact, just so you don't miss anything, you may want to place all the ingredients out on the counter.

✔ All dry ingredient measurements are level. Spoon into the appropriate sized measuring cup and level off with the blunt edge of a knife. There's no need to pat down because more is not necessarily better than less.

✔ Vegetarian recipes are marked with a tomato bullet instead of the usual triangle. Some vegetable recipes may call for chicken broth. This can be replaced with vegetable stock and the recipe made vegetarian.

✔ All of our recipes were developed and tested in the most popular 4- and 6-quart slow cookers, round and oval versions included. Unless indicated in a specific recipe, you can use either size or shape with equally good results. If we feel that a certain size should be used, we tell you.

✔ This book is about slow cookers, so we opted to prepare most recipes on the low setting unless we felt that the recipe benefited from being prepared on high, as indicated in the recipe.

✔ Most recipes, with the exception of the master recipes in Part IV, are for 4, 6, or 8 servings. Some recipes can be doubled, and we note that whenever appropriate. Because a slow cooker must be filled at least halfway and no more than two-thirds full, we do not recommend arbitrarily doubling or halving a recipe.

✔ Unless you're on a sodium-free or restricted diet, judiciously salt your food to taste as it cooks rather than at the end. We like to use kosher salt because it doesn't contain additives and therefore has a "cleaner" taste. Pepper should always be in the form of freshly ground black peppercorns for maximum flavor.

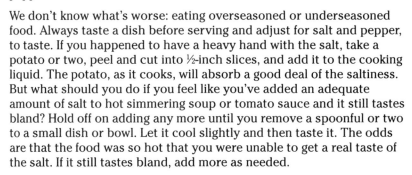

We don't know what's worse: eating overseasoned or underseasoned food. Always taste a dish before serving and adjust for salt and pepper, to taste. If you happened to have a heavy hand with the salt, take a potato or two, peel and cut into ½-inch slices, and add it to the cooking liquid. The potato, as it cooks, will absorb a good deal of the saltiness. But what should you do if you feel like you've added an adequate amount of salt to hot simmering soup or tomato sauce and it still tastes bland? Hold off on adding any more until you remove a spoonful or two to a small dish or bowl. Let it cool slightly and then taste it. The odds are that the food was so hot that you were unable to get a real taste of the salt. If it still tastes bland, add more as needed.

✔ Fresh milk tends to curdle during the long cooking time of most slow cooker recipes. Unless indicated, the recipes call for canned evaporated milk or sweetened condensed milk. Both are available in whole, lowfat, and fat-free varieties and work equally well.

✔ Oven temperatures are in Fahrenheit.

✔ Keep vegetable oil cooking spray on hand and spray the inside of the cooking container before you place the ingredients inside for cooking. Doing so prevents sticking. In most cases, we remind you to do this in the first step of the recipe.

✔ All eggs are large.

Part I
Revving Up Your
Slow Cooker

The 5th Wave   By Rich Tennant

"Can a slow cooker have a stir-fry setting?"

In this part...

We're going to tell you exactly what slow cookers are, who's using them, and why — as well as how they differ from other familiar cooking methods. We fill you in on how the slow cooker has changed over the past 30 years and what innovations you can expect to find in terms of new sizes, features, and configurations.

Chapter 1

Slow Cooking in the Fast Lane

*I*t's 5:55 p.m. and there you are — sitting in stalled traffic for the third night in a row. Work was a bear and your boss was beyond belief. The kids must have called you at least a half-dozen times since they got home from school, bellyaching that there was nothing good in the house to eat and asking you when you're going to be home. And just as you realize that the inspection sticker on your car expired last week, that nice police officer driving along-side of you asks that you pull over at the next intersection. So you're having a bad day.

But at least you did one thing right. You had the foresight to set up your slow cooker with a fantastic leg of lamb with roasted potatoes 20 minutes before heading out for work this morning. After the type of day you had, the last thing you want to worry about is what to make for dinner. Although slow cookers may not solve all your problems, they can at least make things a little more bearable!

The Hare and the Tortoise: Fast Food versus Slow Food

What we eat helps define us as a people, and sometimes how food is cooked defines us as a society and culture. Based on many Americans' preference for meals from drive-through windows, fast food establishments appear to have become surrogate mothers, at least when mealtime rolls around. Approximately 47 cents of every dollar spent on food in this country is spent on restaurant meals, with fast food restaurants outperforming full-service establishments. The reasons are simple to understand. For the most part, fast food tastes good.

Fast food is usually consistently prepared and provides good value for the dollar when all other issues are cast aside. Great for providing instant gratification for our tummies, fast food restaurants usually are nonthreatening, clean, and air-conditioned and have become the sanctums of our inner cities and the refuge of travelers the world over. Nowhere else can you be served a meal in two minutes or less at such an affordable price. Fast foods appeal to both young families and the retired, and many a baby's first solid food has been the humble French fry!

Nevertheless, we all know that reliance on a fast food diet leads to health concerns such as obesity and heart disease. Most people are aware that sitting down to a home-cooked, well-balanced meal is preferable to wolfing down a high-fat meal of little nutritional value and fiber, along with a sugary, carbonated drink, while driving to an appointment or working at our desks. Eating on the run, we lose track of how much we've eaten and tend to fall prey to impulse eating. Recent studies reveal that over 50 percent of the American population is overweight, with fast food and lack of exercise the main culprits. When it comes to fast food, moderation is the key word.

But because of these health concerns and a desire to maintain the traditions of old, 83 percent of all households still make an effort to get dinner on the table at least five nights a week, even though since 1969 we have on average 22 fewer hours a week to spend with our family because of professional and personal commitments. How we prepare dinner at home has undoubtedly changed, with such conveniences as salad in a bag, frozen heat-and-serve pizzas, and supermarket rotisserie chicken now available. Nevertheless, when given the opportunity, what we're doing can still be defined as preparing and cooking dinner.

Since its introduction in 1971, the slow cooker has been a way for Americans to get a home-cooked meal on the table. It is in the act of preparing dinner that the slow cooker excels. You can prepare the foods at your convenience — even the night before — and layer them in the slow cooker, refrigerate the food overnight, set the slow cooker on low the next morning, and leave for work, trusting in complete faith that you will have a tasty, home-prepared meal, cooked to perfection, waiting for you when you return. All that's left for you to do is set the table, get a salad together if you want (using the aforementioned salad in a bag), and pour the drinks.

Slow cooked meals are convenient and nutritious — in that they use fresh, wholesome ingredients — and taste good. In many cases, you can easily adapt your favorite traditional-cooked dishes so you can make them in the slow cooker. In Chapter 5, we discuss various techniques you can use in making these adaptations. We also provide you with some of our favorite "before" and "after" (read "traditional" transformed to "slow cooker") recipes to help you see how it's done.

Snail crossing: The international slow food movement

While we are, perhaps, too familiar with fast food, a relatively new phenomena is *slow food,* a new twist on an old lifestyle: You eat what is produced locally and is part of the local fabric. In fact, in 1986 an organization dedicated to slow food was founded in Italy. With 60,000 members in 35 countries, the International Slow Food Movement (www.slowfood.com) seeks to preserve and promote local food traditions, while at the same time limiting the globalization and standardization of food and drink.

The symbol of the movement is appropriately the snail, a traditional emblem of slowness.

Although not denying the need for advancement, "slow foodees" want to savor the taste of each morsel as it was intended to look and taste. For example, we all know that with the right formula, your favorite brand of cola can be made almost anywhere in the world and taste the same no matter where you drink it. On the other hand, factory-made Parmesan cheese, sold in the cardboard shaker containers, tastes nothing like artisan-made Parmesan cheese from Italy — made from the milk of grass-grazing cows and aged following century-long traditions.

Here's Who's Slow Cooking

People never cease to envy people in the cooking profession. It's not that they're rich or better looking, or live in fancy houses and drive expensive cars. It's because they know how to cook *and* enjoy it. Because professional cooks work with food, most people naturally assume that their pantries and fridges are stocked with endless goodies and wonderful things to eat. We, the authors of this book, want to set the record straight on that score!

Usually we, as members of the culinary profession, *do* have plenty around to eat, but sometimes we too fall short — especially when life is getting the best of us and the last thing we want or have time to do is plan and prepare a delectable meal. Many a day, dinnertime rolls around, and regrettably, we haven't even thought about feeding our families. That's when we shake our heads and wish we had been better organized and had thought to put a meal in the slow cooker earlier in the day. Planning ahead is so much easier than racking your brain and wringing your hands when time is short and bellies are empty.

Many culinary professionals besides us also use slow cookers, as attested to by Julia Child in her recent cookbook, *Julia and Jacques Cooking at Home* (Alfred A. Knopf, Inc., 1999). In the section on cooking beans, Julia claims that her favorite way to cook beans is overnight in a slow cooker with water and seasonings until the beans are done the next morning. That has become our favorite method, too.

The U.S. love affair with the slow cooker

Estimates claim that over 40 million slow cookers are being used in the United States at least three times a week. With new sales estimated at 6 million a year, we have to believe that people in the United States find slow cookers to be a value and useful kitchen appliance. But who exactly is using them? You may be surprised.

✔ 73 percent of *Good Housekeeping* readers polled own slow cookers (1997).

✔ Largest age group is 34 to 54 years old and married with children under age 18.

✔ Most are college educated and work at least part-time.

✔ 82 percent of *Better Homes and Gardens* readers own slow cookers; 18 percent use them more now than two years ago (1998).

Slow cooking is for *everyone* on a tight schedule who has to eat but who doesn't want to rely on prepared convenience foods and take-out, except on occasion. Slow cookers are for working families, married couples, single individuals, students, the retired, those on fixed incomes, and even for those with live-in help who get a day off once in a while. They are for all of us who want to eat real food, made in the comfort and convenience of our home but without spending hours tending a simmering pot or a hot oven.

The Benefits of Owning a Slow Cooker

Slow cookers are convenient and portable — that's why they show up at potlucks and church suppers! Moreover, in the heat of summer, when you don't want to add to the heat or stress your air conditioner by cooking on the stove or turning on the oven, slow cookers provide a welcome alternative. On Thanksgiving, when your oven is full, there's always the slow cooker, ready and waiting. These are just a few of the benefits of owning a slow cooker. And there are more, as you find out in this section!

Slow cooked versus grilled

When food is seared and then grilled over very high heat, the natural juices caramelize, altering the taste. But food cooked with low heat produces tender, flavorful results. For generations, women in small towns throughout Europe have known this and have been using the town bread baker's cooling ovens to slow cook their family's meals. In fact, when Tom was living in Spain, he remembers going to the bakery in his wife's hometown midmorning with his mother-in-law to use the cooling ovens. For a small price, the baker rented oven space to anyone who wanted to slow cook a joint of meat or fish. The food was left in the oven unattended and picked up in the early afternoon for dinner. Although the practice of slow cooking food in a wood-burning oven was also common practice in the United States during the 1800s, it died out with the introduction of cast-iron stoves, with the concept revitalized in the 1970s with the electric slow cooker.

Slow cookers (see Figure 1-1) cook food at a low temperature for an extended period of time, with minimum evaporation. By doing so, tough cuts of meat tenderize in their own juices, the same as they would in a heavy, cast-iron Dutch oven set over low heat. What an electric slow cooker provides, however, is the convenience of being able to walk away and come back later in the day to a fully cooked meal that requires virtually no intervention. The introduction of the slow cooker in the United States in the early 1970s benefited a generation of women and their families.

Figure 1-1:
A slow
cooker.

The introduction and evolution of the Crock-Pot

Without a doubt, the transition from the 1960s to the 1970s was a time of radical social and lifestyle change. Fast food was on its way to becoming an American icon as Mom, to her family's dismay (especially at dinnertime!), went back to work, redefining the workplace, as well as the American family.

In 1971 a revolutionary new appliance was introduced to millions of people in the United States, allowing moms nationwide to transform raw ingredients into a home-cooked meal while they were away at work or play. The appliance was the Rival Crock-Pot. And guess what colors it came in? Those good old 1970s colors of copper, harvest gold, and avocado.

Although the slow cooker remains faithful to the original premise of cooking a one-pot meal from start to finish without mortal intervention, today's slow cooker is no longer harvest gold — unless you have one of the original ones. It has evolved over the past three decades to fit in with today's kitchen decor in colors, sizes, and shapes.

Slow cooker convenience and healthy cooking in the 21st century

The 1970s are not exactly remembered as a period of culinary growth. In fact, it was more like a wasteland, best known for fast food and convenience. In looking over some of the early slow cooker recipes, we're not surprised to see such a large dependence on canned and dehydrated soup mixes. Once again, during a period of economic crisis, people in the United States had turned to their old reliable choices to get dinner on the table quickly and inexpensively. This time, though, they were also relying upon a brand-new gadget, the slow cooker.

In some culinary circles, slow cooker cooking is frowned on for a variety of reasons: The food is overcooked, high in sodium and fat, bland, and too wet. But despite these criticisms, slow cooking has overcome the negatives, and 6 million are sold on average each year. In reality, the problem doesn't lie with the slow cooker, but with the recipes, which reflect how people want to eat.

Over the past 30 years since the first slow cooker was made, our knowledge of nutrition and our culinary horizons have boomed. We have a better understanding of what to include in our diet, as well as what food items to consume in moderation or even avoid altogether. In developing the recipes for this cookbook, we decided to rethink how to use the slow cooker. We knew that we had to follow certain basic parameters, such as cooking with sufficient liquid and filling the slow cooker up at least half full but no more than two-thirds. But we also wanted the food to reflect how most people are eating today.

We use as few prepared ingredients as possible, making concessions for the sake of convenience only rarely. Our recipes call for fresh vegetables and herbs as often as possible for flavor and color. To bring out the true flavors of the food, we cut back as much as possible on fat and instead use olive oil, a monosaturate, whenever appropriate. At times, you may be called upon to brown certain ingredients on the stovetop for added flavor, as well as for appearance. By incorporating these changes with traditional slow cooker cooking methods, we are impressed with the end results. But the best approval will come from you as you prepare and sample the recipes.

Our recipes

Once we knew what we could achieve in the slow cooker, we set out to assemble a well-balanced list of recipes. We wanted to include traditional slower cooker recipes like pot roast, chili, and soup as well as some all-time perennial classics like sweet 'n' sour meatballs and nacho cheese sauce.

We wanted to give our updated versions of some of the more popular casserole dishes, such as the vegetable casserole with French-fried onions, without having to rely upon sodium- and fat-rich canned soup. And we wanted to provide some "exotic" ethnic and regional dishes that have become mainstream over the years, such as jambalaya and Moroccan vegetable stew with couscous. These recipes, as well as the others, turned out to be perfect for the slow cooker.

The slow cooking method using just the right amount of liquid accentuates and draws out the flavors of the different ingredients. The time-saving convenience of being able to spend no more than 20 minutes in the kitchen reassures us that we can still make and eat real food that's good for us at home without having to spend hours slaving over a hot stove.

As with any recipe, let it be your guide. If you lack cooking confidence, follow the recipe to a tee; if not, adjust and modify the ingredients as you desire. In some instances, we provide variations within a given recipe. If we don't offer variations, let your taste buds and whatever you have on hand be your guide.

Here's and example of one of our rcipes. It may not be the most exotic or sophisticated of dishes, but it is comfort food with a capital C. Our Quick and Easy Turkey Vegetable Soup that follows is most definitely a good recipe to get you started cooking in the slow cooker. Its name says it all: It's quick, it's easy, and it sure does taste good. And best of all, it cooks up all by itself in the slow cooker.

Quick and Easy Turkey Vegetable Soup

For a well-balanced meal, serve this soup with a tossed green salad and fresh fruit.

Preparation time: *10 minutes*

Cooking time: *Low 6 to 7 hours*

Yield: *4 servings*

2 turkey drumsticks, skin and excess fat removed and discarded

2 large leeks, washed well to remove dirt and grit, white and light green parts only, sliced thin

3 carrots, peeled and cut into ¼-inch rounds

3 celery stalks, cut into ¼-inch slices

1 package (10 ounces) frozen corn kernels, thawed

1 package (10 ounces) frozen cut green beans, thawed

½ cup uncooked pearl barley

1 tablespoon chopped fresh parsley or dill weed

2 chicken bouillon cubes, dissolved in 4 cups hot tap water

Salt

Freshly ground black pepper

1 Combine all the ingredients in the slow cooker.

2 Cover and cook on low for 6 to 7 hours, or until the turkey and vegetables are tender.

3 Before serving, remove the turkey meat from the bones. Shred into small pieces and return to the soup. Season with salt and pepper to taste.

Vary It: *You can also make this hearty soup by using the roasted turkey carcass from Thanksgiving dinner or from the Master Roast Turkey Breast recipe in Chapter 13. Remove any visible fat or gristle. Rinse the carcass under cold water and crush by applying pressure to the rib cage with the heel of your hand. Add with the rest of the ingredients to the slow cooker.*

Per serving: *Calories 346 (From Fat 46); Fat 5g; (Saturated 1.5g); Cholesterol 40mg; Sodium 885mg; Carbohydrate 52g (Dietary Fiber 10g); Protein 18g.*

Chapter 2

From the Fire to the Pot

*N*o one really knows how, where, or by whom fire was first domesticated for cooking and heating. At best, anthropologists, archaeologists, and the like, have been able to put together bits and pieces to determine that prehistoric Mom most likely served her family shanks of raw woolly mammoth, while there are some indications from charred stones and fossilized charcoal that Dad by the tenth millennium B.C. was also barbecuing on occasion. Nevertheless, it appears that our forefathers were quite content to eat barbecue for another 3,000 years or so, because the first indication of using cookware — clay to be exact — doesn't seem to happen until the 13th millennium.

Cooking in metal pots or cauldrons is a relatively new concept when you consider that it took us tens of thousands of years to do so: Evidence shows us that the Celts, 500 years before our era, began to make the forerunner of Irish stew in metal cauldrons hung over an open fire. We were slaves to stirring these cauldrons until given the choice — in the second half of the 20th century — of cooking with indirect heat. This chapter discusses the differences between cooking with direct and indirect heat, as well as how the slow cooker came to be, its components and their functions, and some of the types and styles of slow cookers available.

Cooking with Direct and Indirect Heat

Although we've come a long way since grilled Brontosaurus Bertha burgers, all the early cooking practices mentioned in this chapter's introduction, and most of the ones we use today, still rely upon direct heat to cook food. Direct heat is nothing more than the transfer of energy from fire (or a gas or electric burner) to a cooking vessel or surface, and then directly to the food. It's a fast, efficient way to cook; however, it does require attention and supervision.

Leave a piece of meat unattended on a hot grill, and before you know it, it's charred. Simmering tomato sauce, if not stirred periodically, will get too hot on the bottom of the pot where energy is directly being transferred, ultimately sticking and then burning. A tray of chocolate chip cookies, placed in a preheated oven, will blacken before your eyes if you don't remove it on time because the pan heats from the hot, convection air of the oven, confirming the all too true, negative image of being chained to a stove.

Because food cooked by using direct heat needs to be stirred, flipped, or turned, the only way to make cooking maintenance-free was to somehow take the heat and indirectly apply it to the food so that the food cooked slowly and evenly with neither mechanical nor human intervention. If the solution were to be an appliance, it had to be simple and safe to use. It had to use low heat so that the food wouldn't burn without stirring, but it also had to cook hot enough so that harmful bacteria would be killed and not grow.

How the slow cooker saved our energy bills

Oil is the lifeblood of the United States and the rest of the industrial world. Without it, we can't travel, manufacture, ship and receive merchandise, heat our homes, or even watch television or read a book into the night. As unbelievable as this may all seem, the U.S. lived through its worst nightmare for a five-month period during the winter of 1973–74, when Arab oil-producing countries turned off the petroleum tap as punishment for its support of Israel during the Yom Kippur War. Oil shipments to the United States came to a grinding halt.

In order to extend depleting oil supplies, Americans were asked to consume less energy by carpooling, shortening work hours, lowering their thermostats, and turning off lights. Even after the embargo came to an end, we felt its effect for years through inflationary spirals due to the increased cost of living — and learned the hard way that we were not invincible. We also added a new word to our vocabulary: conservation. After two decades of what seemed to be limitless prosperity, we were compelled to cut back and be conservative.

The slow cooker, a relatively new product when the energy crisis struck, benefited from America's change of perspective. Using as little electricity as a 75-watt lightbulb and substantially less energy than a conventional oven, the slow cooker was propelled from simply a very popular appliance to a must-have item for almost everyone.

The solution also had to meet the sociological needs of the time. Because women joining the work force in masses in the late 1960s and early 1970s were out of the house most of the day, they needed an easy way to jump-start making dinner. Yes, frozen TV dinners and foods were readily available, but they were expensive and not nearly as tasty as home-cooked meals. Manufacturers and food companies, therefore, were faced with finding an acceptable alternative to traditional cooking. The ensuing product, introduced by Rival in 1971, was called the Crock-Pot, and an appropriate name it was.

How a Slow Cooker Works

The authentic, slow cooker is a simple, uncomplicated appliance with no moving parts. Even though you most likely know what one looks like, we describe it for you here anyway and provide an illustration (see Figure 2-1) so that you can get a better understanding of how it works. Here are the parts of every slow cooker:

Figure 2-1: An exploded diagram of a slow cooker.

✓ **Glass cover:** Most slow cookers have a heavy glass lid, but some are plastic. Always cover the slow cooker when cooking, to retain heat. The clear lid lets you look in, eliminating possible heat loss from having to remove the lid. The heavy weight of the lid creates a tight seal.

- ✔ **Highly glazed stoneware insert pot or crock:** In keeping with the original Rival Crock-Pot design, most *true* slow cookers have a removable, highly glazed, thick, round or oval ceramic stoneware pot or crock.

- ✔ **Wrap-around heating elements:** The low wattage, wrap-around, electric heating elements are encased between the outer and inner metal housing and never make direct contact with the stoneware crock.

- ✔ **Metal wrap-around housing:** The base of the slow cooker is made up of a double-walled metal housing that contains the heating elements. As the elements heat up, they warm the insulated air trapped between the two metal walls, ultimately heating the metal. Heat is then transferred to the cushion of air between the inner metal wall and the stoneware crock. The hot air gently heats and cooks the food slowly and evenly. Because the heating elements never make direct contact with the stoneware insert pot, there are no hot spots, eliminating the need for stirring.

- ✔ **Variable controls:** All slow cookers have dial controls on the front. They usually include off, low, high, and perhaps auto or keep warm.

Types of Slow Cookers

With the time and effort that a slow cooker saves you in the kitchen, it's no surprise that slow cookers are as well received in homes as they are. Their popularity over the past 30 years, however, has also given rise to a variety of similar products and derivations that warrant mention to avoid confusion and misunderstanding. In this section, we attempt to decipher the differences for you so that you fully understand what makes your slow cooker significantly different from these other appliances.

"True" slow cookers, Crock-Pots, and Crockery Cookers

Slow cookers, Crock-Pots, and Crockery Cookers are basically one and the same. *Slow cooker* is the generally accepted generic name most commonly associated with this appliance. Rival, the inventor of the slow cooker, calls its product the Crock-Pot, with registered rights to the name, while West Bend has trademarked its product as the Crockery Cooker.

To avoid confusion, you should understand what makes an appliance a *true* slow cooker.

- ✔ A *true* slow cooker has low and high settings. The settings are never given as temperatures.

✔ To be a *true* slow cooker, the appliance must be able to cook slow enough for all-day cooking unattended — and yet be able to reach certain temperatures at given periods to be bacteria-safe.

✔ Contrary to conventional cooking methods that require food to first be cooked at a high temperature and then at a lower temperature for the remaining cooking time, slow cookers start off at a low temperature and gradually become hotter and hotter during the slow cooker process. This gradual heating cooks the food slowly at a low temperature between 170° and 280°. The combination of heat, lengthy cooking, and steam created within the tightly covered pot works together to destroy bacteria and make slow cooking a safe process.

✔ Slow cookers have nonmetal cooking containers, usually made from stoneware, ceramic, or heat-resistant glass. The containers are never in direct contact with the heat source, eliminating the possibility of hot spots and the need for stirring, with the exception of foods like granola and party mix (Chapter 6).

False slow cookers

If the appliance has characteristics other than what we have given, then it is not a *true* slow cooker, but an appliance that cooks *slowly*. The following sections discuss why these appliances are not true slow cookers.

The recipes in this cookbook have been developed for *true* slow cookers, Crock-Pots, and Crockery Cookers.

Other slow cookers

Another appliance on the market is called a slow cooker by manufacturers, but it is not a true slow cooker. These appliances look like electric deep-dish skillets with lids. (Note: West Bend has such an appliance that goes by the name of Slow Cooker. Its *true* slow cookers are called Crockery Cookers.) Here are the features of these appliances:

✔ Instead of being a crockery cooking container, the cooking container is usually a removable *metal* container with a nonstick cooking surface.

✔ Instead of having wrap-around heating elements, the cooking container usually sits on a base in close proximity to the electric heating elements or coils that transfer heat to the cooking surface.

✔ Instead of having Low and High settings, these appliances are controlled by a variable temperature thermostat with a wide range of temperatures that allow you to do everything from keeping cooked food warm to deep-frying.

✔ Instead of a gradual heating process, the appliance heats rapidly — the same as a pan on a stove burner. The heat is centered in the bottom of the cooking container, and the food must be stirred frequently so that it doesn't stick and burn.

This appliance is great as a backup to using your range or cooktop. Beware, however! It is not a slow cooker. Other than its name, it doesn't share any of the characteristics of a slow cooker, and if you attempt to make any slow cookers recipes in it, they will most likely burn because they cook way too hot compared to the real thing.

Variable temperature multipurpose cookers

Like an electric pot with a variable thermostat, a multipurpose cooker fulfills a wide variety of cooking functions, including browning, sautéing, boiling, braising, simmering, and deep-frying. Some manufacturers claim that they can also be used as slow cookers, but they are not *true* slow cookers. They are more like the *other* slow cookers that we describe in the preceding section. Here are the characteristics of variable temperature, multipurpose cookers, often called "multi-cookers."

✔ The heating elements are imbedded into the base of the pot so that the appliance cooks with direct heat. Unlike slow cookers, these appliances require supervision and stirring while cooking because the bottom of the pot heats up.

✔ Variable temperature multipurpose cookers usually have a dial-controlled thermostat that allows you to choose from a wide variety of temperatures. For example, you can keep foods warm at 200° or deep-fry foods at 375°.

When used as a pot for cooking food slowly, this appliance, from our standpoint, is best suited for preparing *very wet* foods like soups and stews. This is because the cooking liquid evaporates quickly as a result of the direct heat method of cooking. Other types of food can't endure the traditional 7 to 8 hours of true slow cooking.

Gearing Up for Slow Cooking: The Right Model for You

If you don't already own a slow cooker, or if you're in the market to purchase a new one, choose the one that best suits your cooking needs. With a wide variety of options, today's basic models are made to appeal to many needs and tastes.

This is not your mother's slow cooker

The original slow cookers were designed to fit in with the décor of America's kitchens of the 1970s. The color selection was usually limited to white, harvest gold, avocado, and copper, and all were round. Not all the units had removable crocks, which were usually standard on larger units only.

The slow cooker of the 1980s and early 1990s also reflected how Americans were decorating their kitchens, with print designs on the metal housing depicting folksy country themes. The recipes also continued to rely upon prepared convenience ingredients.

As we enter the new millennium, however, the slow cooker has become even more mainstream, with a certain level of sophistication and flair in its appearance and recipes. There's a look for every kitchen and decor. Today's slow cookers are available in plain vanilla (white) and also come in stainless steel for a high-tech look. Some have colored cooking containers. You can also find slow cookers with decorative patterns featuring fruits, vegetables, and herbs.

Sales are also booming — as women, men, and even kids face the dilemma of getting dinner on the table with limited cooking skills, in the least amount of time, and with the least amount of energy! Fortunately for us, some very creative companies are developing great, user-friendly slow cookers!

We've come a long way from the early slow-cooker colors of the '70s. Slow cookers today are available in a wide variety of designer colors with matching stoneware pots and have heat-resistant legs and handles.

Shapes and sizes

The slow cooker of the 21st century is truly a pleasure to use. Manufacturers seem determined to outdo themselves in adding new features to make this appliance more user-friendly and convenient.

Slow cookers are now available in two shapes: round and oval. The traditional round shape is perfect for making soups, chilis, and stews. The introduction of the oval slow cooker is a boon to home cooks, who can now prepare larger pieces of food like whole chickens and roasts in the slow cooker without cutting them up. In fact, a large 6-quart oval slow cooker can easily accommodate two 3-pound chickens or one 5-pound turkey breast. Resembling a casserole dish, the oval insert is also great for making casserole-type, baked dishes because the pan is shallower than a round one.

For convenience, slow cookers come in a wide variety of sizes ranging from 1 quart for dips, to 3-, 3½-, 4-, 4½-, 5-, 5½-, 6-, 6½-, and 7-quart capacity. Because a slow cooker needs to be filled at least halfway and no more than three quarters full, this wide variety of sizes makes it easy to choose the right one for the dish you're making. The most popular size units, however, are the 4- and 6- quart versions, for which we have developed our recipes.

Latest innovations and improvements

Some of the newest slow cookers coming off the assembly line today have features — such as heat-resistant glass cooking containers, nonstick coating, digital settings, and transport innovations — that differentiate them from existing models. Although they don't affect the basic use and operation of the slow cooker, they in most cases make a simple-to-use appliance even more user-friendly.

Heat-resistant glass cooking containers

Some new slow cookers have cooking containers made by Corningware. This heat-resistant glass enables the user to brown over direct heat on the stove-top and then continue cooking in the same container in the slow cooker.

The traditional slow cooker still has a glazed, nonporous stoneware, ceramic cooking container. These traditional cooking containers provide even heat distribution and encase the food in low, even heat. They cannot, however, be used over direct heat on the stovetop for browning or reheating because they can crack.

Because the container is already hot, the slow cooker may cook too quickly when using conventional slow cooker recipes, including the ones in this book. Foods may begin to break down — so we suggest that if you have one of these models, you carefully monitor the recipe's progress and shorten the cooking time, if needed.

Nonstick coating

The first step in most of our recipes calls to lightly coat the slow cooker cooking container with vegetable oil cooking spray. By doing so, you will find cleanup easier. West Bend has gone one step further and has incorporated a nonstick coating on the stoneware, ceramic cooking containers of some of its newer slow cookers. If you have one of these models, you can skip coating the container with vegetable oil spray.

Divided container

Rival has introduced a 5-quart slow cooker with an inner pot that is divided into two separate cooking compartments. This divided cooking system enables you to make, for instance, a pork roast in the larger 3½- quart compartment and a side dish of applesauce in the 1½- quart compartment without mixing flavors.

Digital settings

Most slow cookers have off, low, high, and perhaps keep-warm settings. Rival has introduced a digital version. With the simple push of a button, you can choose the cooking time and temperature you desire. For example, if your recipe calls for 4 or 6 hours of cooking time, you press the button until 4 or 6 appears on the display. The slow cooker automatically cooks on high; if you had chosen 8 or 10 hours, it would cook on low. At the end of the cooking time, the slow cooker automatically shifts over to the keep-warm setting.

Easy-transport innovations

Because many slow cookers are pressed into service for potluck and community suppers, manufacturers have been coming up with new ideas on how to make transporting them easier. Hamilton Beach has developed two novel ideas. So that the lid doesn't shift in the car, resulting in a potential disaster, it has developed Lid Latch, which resembles crisscrossing rubber bands that anchor the lid to the base. Furthermore, so that your sweet potato casserole stays piping hot on the way to Grandma's on Thanksgiving Day, you can place your slow cooker in an insulated carrying case specially designed for certain Hamilton Beach models (see Appendix A for customer service phone numbers).

Part II
Making the Best and Safest Use of Your Slow Cooker

In this part...

With food safety a major concern today, we review some basic safe-cooking practices, including some that are specifically geared to the needs of your slow cooker. We also explain how to adapt your favorite conventional recipes to the slow cooker.

Chapter 3

Slow Cooker Basics from Start to Finish

In This Chapter

▶ Reading the owner's manual

▶ Mastering the basic slow cooking rules

*1*f you're the owner of a new slow cooker, congratulations! You're certainly in for a rare treat: delicious home-cooked meals, like Lemon and Thyme Pork Stew and Rosemary and Garlic Roasted Leg of Lamb, favorite side dishes like Macaroni and Cheese or Classic Vegetable Casserole with French-Fried Onions, and, for dessert, Apple Brown Betty or Creme Caramel. If you're a dyed-in-the-wool user, we congratulate you for having the wisdom to simplify your life by purchasing and using this time-saving kitchen device, and for your commitment and ongoing vision to use it even more after reading this book.

As with any appliance, you should have a good understanding of how it works. If you've been using a slow cooker for years, you should also pay attention because procedures and safe cooking practices have changed over time. So before you get started, sit back and take a few minutes to find out everything you need to know about slow cooking!

The owner's manual: An important message brought to you by the manufacturer

Take our advice. Read the owner's manual. By doing so, you can avoid failure and disappointment. The manufacturer has taken the time to put key information in writing so that you will have years of cooking and eating enjoyment! We also want you to read all the helpful tidbits we include in this book. In fact, in this chapter we collect the best of what we have discovered about the slow cooker from our years of using and demonstrating slow cookers, and are pleased to expand upon this information and share it with you.

First Things First: Wash Your Slow Cooker

As with any new small electrical appliance, you will want to wash each component, using the steps described in this section, to remove any manufacturing oils, dust, or grime before using the slow cooker for the first time. Also wash each part if the slow cooker has not been used for an extended period.

Never immerse the metal, wrap-around housing or the base in water. Also, always unplug the appliance before cleaning to avoid the risk of electrical shock.

1. **Use a clean, soapy cloth or sponge to wash the slow cooker for the first time and every time thereafter. Remove any soap film with a clean cloth or sponge. Dry well with a soft cloth.**

   The removable cooking container and cover may also be washed in the dishwasher. If your cover is plastic, place it on the top rack of the dishwasher to prevent the cover from warping.

2. **When you're sure that the cooking container is nice and clean, dry it and place it in the slow cooker base. You're ready to begin.**

Never clean any slow cooker components with harsh chemical or abrasive cleaners as these may damage the appliance.

Caring for Your Cooking Container

Most slow cookers have removable cooking containers. Although these removable containers make for easy cleanup, they require some care in handling. Some points to remember are discussed in this section.

Most slow cooker cooking containers are made of highly glazed porous stoneware. As is true with most clay cookware, stoneware is known for its heat-absorbing and -retaining qualities, allowing food to cook slowly and evenly without hot spots, eliminating the need for stirring.

Stoneware cannot withstand severe and sudden changes in temperature. To prevent damaging the cooking container as well as the glass cover, we recommend that you follow this advice at all times:

✔ Never heat the stoneware cooking container on a stove or cooktop.

✔ Check the owner's manual to see whether the container and cover are oven-, broiler-, and/or microwave-safe.

✔ Never place the cooking container in the freezer.

✔ Never place a hot cooking container and cover in the refrigerator.

✔ Never pour cold water or place cold food into a hot cooking container.

✔ Never plunge a hot cooking container and cover into water.

✔ Never run water over a hot cooking container or cover.

✔ Never use a cooking container or cover that's chipped, cracked, or severely scratched. Check the warranty section of the owner's manual and contact the manufacturer to purchase a replacement.

✔ Never preheat or heat the cooking container in the slow cooker without food.

As mentioned in Chapter 2, some specific types of slow cookers have heat-resistant, Corning glass, cooking containers. These containers can be used to brown over direct heat and then placed in the slow cooker.

Preparing to Slow Cook: Some Tips

After the slow cooker is clean and dry, you're ready to begin cooking. Prepare all the ingredients for the recipe you plan to make. You may find it more comfortable to fill the cooking container before putting it in the slow cooker. Just remember one thing: The average weight of a ceramic, stoneware cooking container is 6 pounds, before adding food! When filled, the container may weigh more than twice that. Here are some tips:

- ✔ Before filling the container with food, decide whether you can comfortably lift a 12-pound container and put it in the slow cooker. If doubtful, fill the container after you place it in the slow cooker.
- ✔ To avoid making a sloshing mess, add liquids (more than 2 cups) after the cooking container is in the slow cooker.
- ✔ To make cleanup easier, lightly spray the inside of the cooking container with vegetable oil cooking spray.

If your slow cooker cooking container has a nonstick surface, season it before using it the first time and periodically thereafter by rubbing 1 to 2 teaspoons of vegetable oil over the cooking surface.

If your slow cooker has a ceramic, stoneware cooking container, never place it on a stove or cooktop because it will break from direct contact with the heat. Brown ingredients in traditional cookware on the stove or cooktop before placing them in the slow cooker cooking container.

Getting a jump start the night before

To save time in the morning, you can prepare your ingredients the night before. Place everything in the slow cooker cooking container, as called for in the recipe. Cover with the glass or plastic cover and refrigerate immediately.

The next day, remove the cooking container from the fridge and place it in the slow cooker. Cook covered, as specified in the recipe. Do not preheat the slow cooker before inserting the cooking container. The overnight method works well with most recipes, with the following exceptions:

- ✔ Unless potatoes are layered on the bottom of the cooking container (such as underneath a pot roast), don't add them until you're ready to cook because they will discolor.
- ✔ Don't add uncooked rice or pasta until ready to cook because it may absorb some of the cooking liquid.
- ✔ If you're making soup or a recipe with a large amount of cooking liquid — that is, more than 2 cups — don't add the liquid until you're ready to cook.
- ✔ Fruit desserts are better if prepared just before cooking because cut fruit will discolor and sugar will cause fruit to release its juices.

Never, ever leave the slow cooker filled with uncooked food on the counter overnight or for an extended period of time. Doing so causes bacteria growth, which can be harmful to your health! The same rule applies to cooked food. *Only hot,* thoroughly cooked food can be safely kept in the slow cooker on the keep warm setting, and then only for approximately 2 to 3 hours. After that, the food should be refrigerated. See Chapter 4 for more details regarding food safety.

The browning issue

Slow cookers save you time by cooking food so that it requires little or no intervention. You simply place the ingredients in the cooking container. Stir them all together. Put the cover on and turn the control knob to low or high. About 8 hours later, dinner is done and ready to be served. Because slow cookers cook at a low temperature, they don't get hot enough to brown the food.

As you read some of our recipes, you may be surprised to see that we ask you to brown or sauté some ingredients like onions, garlic, and meat or poultry in a skillet on the stovetop burner with some oil before adding them to the slow cooker. The reason is quite simple: flavor. High heat alters the appearance and flavor of food. The natural sugar found in food causes it to brown, making it more appealing to look at. The meat loses that raw look, while at the same time becoming more complex in flavor than if it was just boiled.

Besides being advocates of slow cookers, we also like to advocate food that tastes as good as it looks. We feel that certain foods and recipes benefit tremendously when you take the extra time to brown them before placing them in the slow cooker. This may mean spending 15 to 20 minutes in the kitchen to do so. When you taste the results, you know that time will have been well spent. In some recipes where the difference between browning and not is negligible, we give you the option, so the call is always yours. Browning is discussed in greater detail in Chapter 9.

The high and low of it

With the rare exception, most slow cooker recipes, including the ones found in this book, are prepared on the low setting. When we cook in an oven, recipes are based on temperature. For example: *Bake in a preheated 350° oven for 30 minutes, or until golden brown.* Slow cookers don't have thermostats like ovens do, and slow cooker recipes never specify a temperature, because the cooking process is based on the electrical wattage of the appliance. After reading this information, you don't need to think about it again nor ponder it. We mention it simply so that you understand the reasons to choose between low or high.

Most slow cookers, when set on high, use a maximum of less than 300 watts of electricity. When used on low, the appliance draws about half the wattage it does on high. One hour on high is approximately 2 to 2½ hours on low. High, therefore, cooks almost twice as fast as low and should be used when you wish to have dinner ready faster than you normally would on low. Because the slow cooker is heating up hotter and faster, you may need to stir the food occasionally when cooking on high so that it doesn't stick to the sides of the cooking container.

Some recipes, such as the Old-Fashioned Beef Stew in Chapter 8, start off on the low setting the first 8 to 10 hours. Quick-cooking ingredients like peas are not added until the stew is almost done cooking. The setting is then increased to high, and the peas cook for 15 to 20 minutes, or until they test done.

The high setting is also a great way to thicken a loose sauce or gravy after the food is thoroughly cooked. Uncover the slow cooler and raise the setting to high. The liquid will begin to simmer. Let it cook down for 35 to 45 minutes, stirring periodically.

Now You're Cooking

After you load the cooking container with food and place it in the slow cooker, plug the appliance into a 120-volt AC-rated electrical outlet. Turn the control knob to either the low or high setting.

Never select the keep warm setting until after the food has been thoroughly cooked for the length of time specified in the recipe!

The electrical heating elements heat up slowly, warming the metal, wrap-around housing, which in turn indirectly warms the air trapped between the housing and the cooking container. The cooking container directly heats and cooks the food in the slow cooker at a low temperature, generally between 170° and 280°. The exact temperature depends on the type of food being cooked, the amount of cooking liquid, and the length of cooking time. Nevertheless, the direct heat from the cooking container, the lengthy cooking time, and the moist, steam-infused heat in the tightly covered slow cooker combine to destroy bacteria and make the slow cooker a safe process for cooking food.

Don't use the slow cooker if the cord and plug have been damaged in any way or if it is not working properly. Contact the manufacturer, who will advise you of the appropriate steps to take for repair and service.

Smoke in your eyes?

When using a new slow cooker the first few times, you may notice, as with any new small electrical appliance, some slight smoke and/or odor. Smoke and odor are the result of manufacturing oils being released upon initial heating. This is normal and will subside after a few uses.

Don't touch that lid!

As simple as it may appear, the cover that comes with your slow cooker is almost as important a component as the cooking container. As you probably know, heat rises. With the cover positioned on top of the slow cooker heater, heat is trapped and converts into hot steam, which in tandem with the slow cooker, cooks your food safely. Remove the cover or cook without it, and steam and heat go up into thin air.

Unless specified in the recipe, food must always be cooked covered, for the recommended time, before checking for doneness. The cover doesn't form a tight fit on the slow cooker. If it did, it could seal and form a vacuum. For best cooking results, center the lid over the cooking container.

Don't remove the cover while cooking because doing so results in major heat loss, ultimately affecting the cooking time. To understand this, think of cooking in your slow cooker as you would in your oven — if you leave the oven door open, all the heat will escape, and you'll never get the cooking results you hope for.

The cover heats up during cooking and can get very hot. After cooking, remove the cover with a pot holder or oven mitts. To avoid steam burns, tilt the cover toward you when removing it.

To stir or not to stir? That is the question

To whole idea behind using a slow cooker is to get you in and out of the kitchen as quickly as possible and off doing whatever else you need to do. With the even transfer of heat and no hot spots, slow cooker cooking eliminates the need for stirring during the initial cooking time. In fact, every time you remove the cover, valuable heat and steam are lost, prolonging the cooking time.

Even though you may have this terribly strong urge to uncover, peek, and stir, please don't, unless specified in the recipe, and even at that, be quick about it. If you find yourself longing to peek and unable to control the desire, we suggest you try some behavior modification therapy and leave the house altogether!

Is it done yet?

One of the hardest things for people to understand when reading a slow cooker recipe is how long it takes to cook something and the fact that most recipes have a 1- to 2-hour range when the food is supposed to be ready. For example, a pot roast normally cooks in about 2½ hours on the stovetop in a Dutch oven. Our slow cooker version requires 9 to 10 hours. Why the additional 7 to 8 hours, and how can you be certain that the food is ready to be served?

A slow cooker saves you time by eliminating the need for you to be in the kitchen overseeing the cooking process. The food cooks slowly, covered, between 170° and 280°, with plenty of moist steam. The temperature of the cooked food is about 200°. This combination of low heat and hot moisture cooks the food, inhibits bacteria growth, and eliminates the need for stirring. Varying factors, such as liquid and fat content, the temperature of the food, and the size of the pieces, also play a direct role in how quickly a recipe will cook.

Although all slow cookers provide the same end results — thoroughly cooked food — some are a bit faster than others, another reason why your food may be done on the low end of the estimated cooking time. The temperature of the food when you begin cooking or whether the cooking container was in the refrigerator beforehand can also influence exact cooking times. Another factor is how full the slow cooker is. Ideally, the slow cooker should be one-half to three-quarters full for efficient use and to conform to the suggested cooking times.

After It's Done: From Slow Cooker to Server

Today's slow cookers have attractive stoneware or heat-resistant glass cooking containers that are completely finished on the outside. You can serve directly from the slow cooker, or you can remove the cooking container and use it as serving dish at the table. The cooking container will be hot and heavy. Turn the appliance off. Carefully remove the cooking container using pot holders or oven mitts. Place on a heat-resistant trivet or hot pad and never directly on the serving surface or counter. If serving from the slow cooker, turn the control knob to the keep warm or off setting after you determine that the food is thoroughly cooked and is ready to be served.

Slow cooker dishes are also a mainstay at potluck or pitch-in suppers. The attractive outer housing and cooking container make them ideal for serving. To keep your food warm while in transit, some manufacturers sell insulated carrying cases. Contact the customer service number for your brand of slow cooker to see whether such cases are available for your slow cooker (see the appendix).

Storing food in the slow cooker

Once the food you are preparing is thoroughly cooked, you can turn the slow cooker to the keep-warm setting. Food can safely stay on keep warm at least 2 hours before the cooking container should be removed from the slow cooker and the food cooled to room temperature and then refrigerated.

Never store cooked food unrefrigerated. Thoroughly cooked food can be stored in the covered cooking container in the refrigerator. Food should be eaten or discarded within 3 to 4 days. Do not store food in ceramic, stoneware slow cooker containers in the freezer.

Reheating food in the slow cooker

Cold or room-temperature food can be reheated in the slow cooker cooking container, inserted in the housing, on either low or high. Once it is reheated, food can be kept warm on the keep warm setting.

Don't use the slow cooker for defrosting or thawing frozen foods because getting the foods heated up to the correct temperature takes too long, running the risk of food contamination.

Reheating food in the slow cooker takes almost as long as it does to cook it. We suggest that you reheat food in the cooking container if it fits in your microwave oven. If not, remove the food to a microwave-safe dish to reheat. Cooked food can be kept warm in the slow cooker. Food must be hot enough to prevent bacteria growth before using the keep warm setting.

Scrubbing those nooks and crannies

Always clean your slow cooker well after each use. Unplug it from the electrical outlet and allow all components to cool to room temperature before cleaning. We mention some cleaning tips earlier in the chapter. Here are some reminders and some further tips:

   ✔ To prevent personal injury or electric shock, do not immerse the slow cooker housing/base, its cord, or the plug in water or any other liquid.

✔ Use a soft cloth or sponge to wash the slow cooker cooking container and cover with warm water and dishwashing liquid. Rinse off and towel dry. The container and cover are usually dishwasher safe; check with the owner's manual to verify.

✔ Hard-to-clean spots can be removed by using a nonabrasive cleaning powder like Bon Ami on a clean, damp sponge or cloth.

✔ The metal housing, inside and out, should always be wiped down with soapy water. Never use any abrasive metal scouring pads or harsh cleansers on the metal housing, cooking container, or cover because these can damage the finish.

✔ Always make sure that the inside of the base is clean and that there are no food particles or old spills. If so, wipe out with a clean, damp cloth or sponge, and towel dry.

✔ Always make sure that the cooking container is clean inside and out and that no food particles are stuck to the bottom before placing it in the slow cooker base.

Chapter 4

Food Safety 101

• •

In This Chapter

▶ Fighting bacteria in the kitchen

▶ Following specific safety rules for slow cooking

• •

*B*ecause food safety is such a concern today, we want to offer some safe cooking practices and discuss how they relate to slow cooker cooking. Even the most careful of cooks is sure to learn something.

B Is for Bacteria

We're surrounded by bacteria. But don't lose sleep over it. Fortunately, our autoimmune defense system is able to fight off most bacteria that can make us feel bad. But sometimes a bug does come along, and — wham! — we can't fight it off. Most times you suspect intestinal flu, but food poisoning may be the real culprit. Because most foodborne illnesses go unreported, the Council for Agricultural Science and Technology estimated there were somewhere between 6.5 million and 33 million cases in 1994. Experts believe that home-based, foodborne illness may become a greater problem over time because today's families are less and less familiar with food safety than they were years ago. Perhaps our modern conveniences like preservatives and frost-free refrigerators provide a false sense of limitless safety. Most likely, the problem can also be attributed to a basic lack of knowledge that has grown over the course of time as many people move further away from traditional home-focused lifestyles and regular home-cooked meals.

Food poisoning is avoidable, especially when you're in control of your own kitchen. In this chapter, we give you some very basic, safe cooking practices we picked up from the good folks at the United States Food and Drug Administration. We then tie these in with using the slow cooker safely.

A little soap and water go a long way when used properly

Although most people know that they should wash their hands well before handling food, many people don't follow that safety guideline. Most germs and bacteria are passed from one person to another by hand contact. You shake hands with someone, or someone touches something you eat and — bingo — you wind up getting contaminated.

Wash your hands well for at least 20 seconds with warm water and soap before touching and preparing food and after using the bathroom, changing diapers, and handling pets. As logical as this may seem, not everyone takes the time to do so. Sure, people may wash their hands, but is it as thorough as it should be? Probably not. Take the test yourself. Set a kitchen timer for 20 seconds and begin washing your hands immediately. Doesn't it feel like the longest 20 seconds of your life?

Even though you wash your hands before preparing food, you must also wash them well after touching food and before moving on to another food. For example, if you handle raw chicken that has salmonella and then handle salad makings without washing your hands well, you most likely will contaminate the salad and ingest salmonella when you eat it, even though it will be killed off in the chicken when it is done cooking.

You may have the world's cleanest kitchen. But if you don't wash the cutting boards, knives, utensils, and countertops in hot soapy water after preparing each food item and before going on to the next one, you're only assisting in the transfer of bacteria from one food to the next. So take the extra time and clean up as you go along. Countertops, cutting boards, and all other surfaces that come in contact with food should be periodically cleaned with hot water and soap and then with a bleach solution or a commercial sanitizing agent.

Cloth towels and dishrags are great bacteria breeding grounds. They are usually moist and allow the active growth of certain bacteria. Either use paper towels to clean up kitchen surfaces, or wash dishrags and towels in plenty of hot water with detergent and bleach.

Separate: Don't cross-contaminate

Picture this: You're in the kitchen making chicken. You place the raw chicken on the cutting board and cut it up into pieces with a utility knife. You place the chicken in a roasting pan and cook it in a hot oven until it registers 180° on a meat or instant-read thermometer, indicating that it is cooked and safe to eat. While the chicken cooks, you rinse off the cutting board and knife with only hot water, dry them off with a kitchen towel, and use them to prepare a salad.

Washing fruits and vegetables

As nostalgic and folksy as it may seem to pick a piece of fruit from a tree in an orchard or a ripe tomato from the vine and take a bite, you maybe be getting more than you bargained for. Unfortunately, more times than not, our fruit and vegetable produce has been treated to pesticides to ward off unwelcome vermin, and it requires thorough washing with cool water and a small amount of liquid dishwashing soap, as shown in the accompanying figure.

Another culprit popping up lately is *E. coli* bacteria. If crops are watered with contaminated water, *E. coli* bacteria can be left on or in the fruit or vegetables. The bacteria can usually be eliminated with a thorough rinsing. It is also a good idea to re-rinse prewashed leafy vegetables such as salad makings and spinach because recent findings have reported elevated levels of the bacteria.

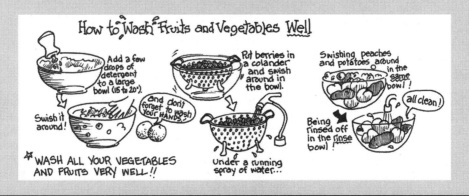

Unknowingly, you have transferred potentially dangerous bacteria from the raw chicken to the cutting board, knife, and kitchen towel only to be passed on to the lettuce and other salad makings, which will be eaten raw, bacteria and all. Now, if you take that kitchen towel and dry some dishes, they too will become contaminated. Unknowingly, you've taken your kitchen and turned it into a science experiment!

Always wash your cutting boards and utensils well with hot soapy water and towel them dry before using them to prepare other foods. A simple rinsing will never do This advice is especially true when cooking with raw poultry, meat, and seafood. You may even consider sanitizing weekly with a mild bleach solution or with a commercial sanitizing agent.

Unfortunately, cross-contamination can start even before you bring the food home. Here are some tips for safe shopping, transport, and storage of perishables:

✔ Shop for nonperishable foods and goods before perishable or frozen foods.

✔ Always keep raw meat, poultry, and seafood away from other foods in the grocery shopping cart and in grocery bags. Because meat, poultry, and seafood packages may leak, some stores have plastic bags in the area where these foods are kept. If not, take a few from the produce department. This way, if these foods do leak, at least the leak will be self-contained, and food juices will not contaminate the other food in your grocery cart.

✔ If it is hotter than 90° outside, or if it takes you longer than an hour to get home, you may want to pack your perishable food items in coolers for the trip home. Never run errands after grocery shopping with food in the car and always get perishable foods back into the refrigerator or freezer as quickly as possible.

✔ Never store raw meat, poultry, and seafood on the top shelves of your refrigerator because juices may accidentally drip onto other foods. Always store them on the lowest shelf.

Cooking is the key to killing bacteria

High heat kills off bacteria; lower levels of heat allow bacteria to thrive and grow. Bacteria growth in food is most active between 40° and 140°, which is referred to as the danger zone. At 40°, bacteria growth is slow, with some spoilage. As the temperature rises, so does potentially dangerous bacteria growth. Low cooking and holding temperatures between 140° and 165° prevent bacteria from growing even though some forms continue to live. As the temperature rises past 165°, killing bacteria takes less and less time. In fact, food safety experts agree that foods are properly cooked when they're heated for a long enough time and at a high enough temperature to kill harmful bacteria that cause foodborne illness.

Don't partially cook or brown foods to cook later. If you do, harmful bacteria will be present that will not have been destroyed. When in doubt, always refer to a cooking temperature chart like the one in Table 4-1. A meat thermometer or an instant-read thermometer should be inserted into the thickest part of the cooked food. To get an accurate reading, insert the thermometer so that it doesn't touch the bone or the cooking container. See Chapter 9 for an illustration of where to place the meat thermometer.

Table 4-1	Cooking Temperatures
Food	*Safe Cooking Temperature*
Eggs	
Whole	Cook until yolk and white are firm
Egg dishes	160°

Food	Safe Cooking Temperature
Ground meat and meat mixtures	
Turkey, chicken	165°
Veal, beef, lamb, pork	160°
Fresh beef	
Medium rare	145°
Medium	160°
Well done	170°
Fresh veal	
Medium rare	145°
Medium	160°
Well done	170°
Fresh lamb	
Medium rare	145°
Medium	160°
Well done	170°
Fresh pork	
Medium	160°
Well done	170°
Poultry	
Chicken, whole	180°
Turkey, whole	180°
Poultry breasts, roast	170°
Poultry thighs, wings	180°
Duck and goose	180°
Ham	
Fresh (raw)	160°
Precooked (ready to eat)	140°

(continued)

Table 4-1 *(continued)*	
Food	*Safe Cooking Temperature*
Seafood	
Fish	Cook until opaque and flaky
Shrimp, lobster, crab	Should turn red, and flesh should become pearly opaque
Clams, mussels, oysters	Cook until shells open; discard unopened shellfish

Giving bacteria the cold shoulder

Food safety experts advise refrigerating foods as quickly as possible because cold temperatures keep most harmful bacteria from growing and multiplying. Place perishable groceries in the refrigerator upon arriving at home. After cooking, prepared food and leftovers should be refrigerated within 2 hours. If they sit out longer than 2 hours or at a room temperature in excess of 90°, they should not be eaten. Discard them at once.

Divide up large quantities of foods in small shallow containers for quick cooling in the refrigerator. Cooling sauces, soups, and stews should be frequently stirred to cool down faster. To slow bacteria growth, your refrigerator should be set as low as 40°, where bacteria growth, if present, is slow. Your freezer should be set as low as 0°. At this temperature, any bacteria present will survive, but is inhibited from growing.

Although refrigerating and freezing food slow down the spoiling process, food cannot be kept indefinitely. Table 4-2 provides valuable information on how long to store food safely. But remember, the best advice we can give you is when in doubt, throw it out!

Table 4-2	Cold Storage Times	
Product	*Refrigerator (40°)*	*Freezer (0°)*
Eggs		
Fresh, in shell	3 weeks	Don't freeze
Raw yolks, white	2 to 4 days	1 year
Hard-cooked	1 week	Doesn't freeze well

Product	Refrigerator (40°)	Freezer (0°)
Liquid pasteurized eggs or egg substitutes		
Opened	3 days	Don't freeze
Unopened	10 days	1 year
Mayonnaise, commercial		
Refrigerate after opening	2 months	Don't freeze
Frozen casseroles		
Keep frozen until ready to serve		3 to 4 months
Soups and stews		
Vegetable or meat-added	3 to 4 days	2 to 3 months
Hamburger, ground and stew meats		
Hamburger and stew meats	1 to 2 days	3 to 4 months
Ground turkey, veal, pork, lamb, and mixtures of them	1 to 2 days	3 to 4 months
Fresh meat		
Steaks, beef	3 to 5 days	6 to 12 months
Chops, pork	3 to 5 days	4 to 6 months
Chops, lamb	3 to 5 days	6 to 9 months
Roasts, beef	3 to 5 days	6 to 12 months
Roasts, lamb	3 to 5 days	6 to 9 months
Roasts, pork and veal	3 to 5 days	4 to 6 months
Meat leftovers		
Cooked meat and meat dishes	3 to 4 days	2 to 3 months
Gravy and meat broth	1 to 2 days	2 to 3 months
Fresh poultry		
Chicken or turkey, whole	1 to 2 days	1 year
Chicken or turkey pieces	1 to 2 days	9 months

(continued)

Table 4-2 (continued)

Product	Refrigerator (40°)	Freezer (0°)
Cooked poultry, leftover		
Cooked poultry dishes	3 to 4 days	4 to 6 months
Pieces, plain	3 to 4 days	4 months
Pieces covered with broth or gravy	1 to 2 days	6 months

Always defrost frozen food in the refrigerator, never at room temperature. If you defrost by using a microwave, the food must be cooked immediately.

Marinating foods should be kept in the refrigerator and not on the counter. The marinating time should never exceed the recommended storage time for fresh meats, poultry, and seafood, as shown in Table 4-2. Even if marinades contain acidic ingredients like vinegar or lemon juice, they do not kill bacteria. In fact, bacteria from marinating foods will be passed on to the marinade. Therefore, if you wish to baste with the marinade, you must boil it before basting or cooking along with the meat — in the case of sauerbraten, for example. Discard all used marinades and do not store them for reuse.

Safe Cooking in Your Slow Cooker

By following the recommendations we outline for you earlier in this chapter, you should be able to minimize the risk of foodborne illness when handling food and cooking, including slow cooking. In addition, we offer a few additional tips and suggestions specific to slow cooker cooking.

Safe food handling before slow cooking

Cook only with fresh food that was handled and stored properly. By doing so, you minimize the potential for food contamination and bacteria growth. Perishables should be refrigerated no longer than the times specified in Table 4-2.

Keep perishable foods refrigerated until preparation time. Because the slow cooker may take several hours to reach a safe, bacteria-killing temperature, constant refrigeration assures that bacteria, which multiply rapidly at room temperature, don't get a head start during the first few hours of slow cooking.

If you cut up meats and vegetables beforehand, store them separately in the refrigerator and never use the same cutting board or knife in preparing these ingredients unless it is thoroughly washed with soap and hot water beforehand.

When short on time, you can do the prep work for most meals the night before and place the cooking container in the refrigerator overnight. The next day, remove the container from the refrigerator, place it in the slow cooker housing, and begin cooking at once. Do not bring the refrigerated container to room temperature first. For the most part, recipes with long cooking times (over 5 hours) will not need to cook longer because the food will reach room temperature as the slow cooker heats up. Recipes with cooking times of two hours or less may need to cook approximately 30 to 45 minutes longer.

Get food cooking quickly. This advice may sound contradictory for slow cooking, but it's not. The danger zone for food bacteria growth is from 40° to 140°, the range when bacteria growth is fastest. Ideally, you want to reach 140° to 165°, a range that prevents rapid bacteria growth before the bacteria are killed off at approximately 165° to 200°.

The heating rate of slow cookers, when used properly on the low setting, is 140° in approximately 3 to 4 hours. That same temperature is reached in approximately 2 hours on high. After the slow cooker reaches 140°, the food temperature will continue to increase to over 200° in about 6 to 8 hours on low and approximately 3 to 4 hours on high.

So that the slow cooker can effectively transfer heat from the walls of the slow cooker to the cooking container and then to the food, the cooker should be filled no less than half full and no more than two-thirds full. So that you don't delay the slow cooker from reaching 140° in under 4 hours, follow these procedures:

- ✔ Always safely defrost meat or poultry and other ingredients before putting them in the slow cooker.
- ✔ Cut food into chunks or bite-sized pieces to ensure thorough cooking.
- ✔ When cooking large pieces of meat like roasts, brown them first so that they heat up quickly in the slow cooker and don't remain in the bacterial danger zone too long.
- ✔ Don't use frozen vegetables, unless thawed beforehand.
- ✔ If possible, cook boneless cuts of meat only or boned roasts, because meat with bones requires longer cooking time.

Heat rises, so no peeking! Every time you remove the lid, the slow cooker takes about 20 minutes to recover temperature. Because it's essential to reach 140° when cooking most foods in under 4 hours, we highly recommend that you refrain from lifting the lid.

Safe food handling after slow cooking

While food is cooking and once it's done, it will stay safe as long as the slow cooker is operating. Properly cooked hot food can be kept in the slow cooker for up to 2 hours on the off position. If your slow cooker has a keep-warm setting, you can always turn it to that setting when you want to keep food hot for serving. At this setting, the food will not dry out as it would on low or high.

You can refrigerate cooked food in the slow cooker cooking container. Refer to Table 4-2 for specific information.

Reheating leftovers in the slow cooker is not recommended. However, you can bring cooked food to steaming on the stovetop or in a microwave oven and then put it in the slow cooker container in a preheated slow cooker to keep it hot for serving.

If you're not home during the entire slow cooker cooking process and you discover that the power was off while you were gone, you must throw away the food even if it looks done. You have no way of knowing how long the power was off or at what temperature the food was sitting, which may lead to a potential health hazard. If you are home, remove the food from the slow cooker cooking container and finish cooking by another cooking method if power is available. If you are home and certain that the food was completely cooked before the power went off, the food can remain safe for up to 2 hours unrefrigerated.

Cleanliness is next to godliness when slow cooking. Always wash the cooking container well with soap and hot water after each use, or if the slow cooker is not used periodically. Never use a cracked or chipped cooking container. Besides the fact that it could split during cooking, it may also be a refuge for bacteria.

Chapter 5

From the Stove to the Slow Cooker

In This Chapter

▶ Adapting your favorite recipes for the slow cooker

▶ Determining which recipes adapt well and which do not

▶ Trying out some of our favorite recipes and their slow cooker adaptations

*O*ld, favorite recipes often get upstaged by frozen entrees or take-out meals. Because of busy schedules and, worse yet, indecision about what to fix for dinner, people are gradually cooking less and less every year. But slow cookers can help you turn back the hands of time to the days of well-balanced, home-cooked meals. All you need to do is adapt a favorite recipe, perhaps one which you haven't made in years, to the slow cooking method. That way, dinner can be slowly simmering while you're away from home. You no longer have to spend hours in the kitchen in order to enjoy those classic dishes from the past. And what is more wonderful than coming home at the end of the day to the aroma of dinner?

Adapting Your Favorite Recipes for the Slow Cooker

The best and easiest way to adapt a traditional recipe for the slow cooker is to find a similar slow cooker recipe and use it as your guide. For example, if you want to make your Aunt Milly's blue ribbon-winning pot roast recipe, you can probably adapt it by using Our Favorite Pot Roast recipe from Chapter 9. Not only do you find out how to brown the meat beforehand for maximum flavor, but you discover how much liquid to use and how long to cook the pot roast in the slow cooker.

Because we're avid slow cooker users, we continually look for ways to convert our favorite recipes to the slow cooker without sacrificing taste and appearance. Some of our best examples are Stuffed Peppers and our Stuffed Cabbage Casserole found in Chapter 10. But then again, check almost any good slow cooker recipe, and you're certain to find it's a traditional recipe modified for slow cooker use.

Remember that slow cooker cooking differs from conventional cooking methods in terms of ingredients, the amount of liquids, and length of cooking. Please keep in mind the practical points described in the following sections.

Ingredients

With the exception of certain ingredients such as fast-cooking peas, cooked pasta, and rice, all the ingredients used in slow cooker recipes are usually added at the same time. Some ingredients must be handled differently than in conventional cooking. To obtain the best results possible, remember these tips when using the following ingredients:

- **Vegetables:** To ensure that vegetables of the same type cook evenly, cut them into uniform, equal-sized pieces. Root vegetables like potatoes, carrots, turnips, and so forth, in many instances, take as much time to cook — if not longer — than a roast or other large-sized piece of food. For best results, layer the cut-up root vegetables on the bottom of the cooking container and/or along the sides. Place the other ingredients on top of the root vegetables, along with the cooking liquid. Quick-cooking vegetables such as peas can be added 20 to 30 minutes before the recipe has finished cooking. All other vegetables should be added at the beginning.

- **Dairy products:** Milk and most dairy products, such as cream, sour cream, and yogurt, tend to curdle in the slow simmering slow cooker. If you must use them, add them during the last 30 to 60 minutes of cooking, or use canned evaporated or condensed milk, which is more stable. If you opt to use fresh dairy products at the end of the cooking cycle, combine them with approximately ½ cup of the cooking liquid in order to warm them slightly before adding to the slow cooker. Processed cheeses, such as American and Velveeta, perform better than naturally aged cheese such as cheddar, which can break down and separate.

- **Pasta and rice:** Uncooked pasta and rice can be disappointing in the slow cooker, because the long cooking time makes them cook up pasty and starchy. To get around this problem, cook pasta and rice on the stove and then add them to your recipe in the slow cooker a few minutes before serving, or add them uncooked 30 to 60 minutes before the end of the cooking time.

✔ **Seafood:** Fish and shellfish are fast-cooking foods that don't fare well in a slow cooker because they tend to overcook and fall apart. They are best added toward the end of the recipe, 30 to 60 minutes before the dish is done.

Liquids

Unless making spoon foods like soups, chowders, chili, or sauces, use approximately half the liquid called for in the traditional stovetop or oven version of the recipe. Because the slow cooker cooks covered with low heat, liquid doesn't boil away as quickly. Unless you're cooking rice, pasta, or beans, which are dehydrated and absorb large amounts of liquid, 1 cup of liquid is usually sufficient for most recipes.

Always add the liquid ingredients last for convenience and to avoid splashing. Pouring liquids over solid ingredients is easier and less messy than dropping solids into liquids.

When browning food on the stovetop before placing it in the slow cooker, you may want to deglaze the pan with some of the cooking liquid to pick up some of the caramelized juices for added flavor. Simply pour about ⅓ cup of liquid into the hot pan after removing the browned food. Bring to a boil, gently scraping the bottom of the pan to remove any food particles and caramelized juices. After a minute or two, pour this mixture into the slow cooker.

Liquidy sauces can be thickened with flour or cornstarch and added 15 to 30 minutes before the food is ready to be served. Flour should be mixed with some cool tap water to make a thin paste before adding. Add enough water to cornstarch until you have a liquidy mixture. Or you can also cook on high for the last 30 to 60 minutes, uncovered, until some of the excess liquid has evaporated.

Cooking times

When looking for recipes to convert, choose those that take at least 45 minutes to 1 hour to make. These recipes usually contain ingredients that hold up well to long cooking times. Tougher cuts of meat, such as chuck and bottom round, do exceptionally well in the slow cooker.

The times listed in Table 5-1 can be used as a general rule when converting cooking times.

Table 5-1	Converting Cooking Times	
Traditional Recipe Setting in Minutes	*Slow Cooker Low Setting in Hours*	*Slow Cooker High Setting in Hours*
45	6–10	3–4
50–60	8–10	4–5

Some of Our Favorite Recipes Adapted to the Slow Cooker

Although we know you'll enjoy the recipes we developed especially for this book, we also know that at times you will want to eat something of your own creation. As we discuss earlier in this chapter, traditional recipes can, for the most part, be adapted to the slow cooker. To show you how to do it, we chose five of our favorite all-time recipes and adapted them for the slow cooker. In making our selection, we looked for recipes that, although perhaps not exactly difficult to prepare, were somewhat labor intensive, requiring frequent stirring or basting, forcing us to stay close to the kitchen and limiting what we could be doing with our time.

We give you both versions of the recipe, the original version and then the slow cooker adaptation, as well as information on what we did to adapt it. Hopefully, you too will be inspired to experiment and convert some of your favorite traditional recipes for use in the slow cooker!

Traditional Bolognese Tomato and Meat Sauce

Bolognese sauce is a classic meat sauce from Bologna, Italy, that is traditionally served over *tagliatelle,* Italian egg noodles. The sauce, which is full of finally chopped vegetables and ground meat and made creamy with the addition of milk, simmers slowly to allow the flavors to blend and the tomato purée to thicken.

If you're trying to stick to a lowfat diet, you can substitute ground turkey for the ground beef. Check the package label, however, because some brands of ground turkey contain ground-up fat and skin.

Preparation time: *45 minutes*

Cooking time: *1 hour and 45 minutes*

Yield: *10 servings*

4 tablespoons extra-virgin olive oil	*¼ teaspoon freshly ground black pepper*
½ cup finely chopped onions	*¼ teaspoon freshly grated nutmeg*
⅔ cup finely chopped carrots	*1¼ cups milk*
⅔ cup finely chopped celery	*4 cups canned, plum tomatoes, finely strained, with their juice*
2 ounces prosciutto, finely minced	
1 pound very lean ground beef	*1 sprig fresh basil*
1½ teaspoons salt	*Hot cooked pasta*
	Parmesan cheese

1 In a large saucepan, heat the olive oil. Add the onions. Sauté over low heat, 5 to 8 minutes, until translucent. Stir frequently so the onions do not brown. Add the carrots, celery, and prosciutto. Cook for 5 minutes, stirring frequently.

2 Raise the heat to high and add the ground beef. Mix the meat and vegetables until well combined. Cook, stirring frequently, just until the meat loses its pink color. Break up any large pieces with a spoon. Add the salt, pepper, nutmeg, and milk. Stir to blend. Bring to a boil. Lower the heat and simmer the sauce until most of the milk has evaporated.

3 Add the tomatoes and basil. Bring to a boil. Lower the heat and let simmer for 1¾ hours, stirring periodically. Season to taste with salt and pepper.

4 Serve over pasta with grated Parmesan cheese.

Tip: *If you have a food processor, use it to chop the onions, carrots, and celery. Begin by placing the onion in the food processor container. Press pulse a couple of times until coarsely chopped. Add the carrots and celery (cut into 1-inch pieces) and pulse a couple of times until chopped.*

Per serving: *Calories 301 (From Fat 164); Fat 18g (Saturated 6g); Cholesterol 56mg; Sodium 1176mg; Carbohydrate 17g (Dietary Fiber 4g); Protein 18g.*

Slow Cooker Bolognese Tomato and Meat Sauce

This sauce comes out perfect in the slow cooker when some slight changes are made to the original recipe. Best of all, we eliminate the need to stir every 10 minutes or so!

To simplify the recipe for the slow cooker, we cook all the vegetables together, rather than sauté the onions first and then the carrots and celery. To save additional time, we add the milk directly to the slow cooker along with the remaining ingredients instead of slow-simmering it with the meat and vegetables. Because normal milk tends to curdle in the slow cooker, we use canned evaporated milk, which does not curdle. The results are very good, thanks to the fact that the slow simmering nature of the slow cooker tenderizes the meat as it cooks, developing the rich flavor we were looking for.

Because you can cook large quantities in the slow cooker without worrying about the sauce boiling over, this recipe increases the amount of vegetables, meat, and tomatoes in order to make a larger batch of sauce.

If you're cutting your fat grams, you can substitute ground turkey for the ground beef, but make sure it's low in fat by checking the package label.

Preparation time: *25 minutes*

Cooking time: *Low 8 to 9 hours*

Yield: *10 servings*

3 tablespoons extra-virgin olive oil	*½ teaspoon ground black pepper*
⅔ cup finely chopped onions	*½ teaspoon grated nutmeg*
¾ cup finely chopped carrots	*1 can (12 fluid ounces) evaporated milk*
¾ cup finely chopped celery	*2 cans (28 ounces each) tomato purée*
1½ pounds very lean ground beef	*1 sprig fresh basil*
3 ounces prosciutto, finely minced	*Pasta*
3 teaspoons salt	*Grated Parmesan cheese*

1 Lightly spray a 4- to 6-quart slow cooker with vegetable oil cooking spray.

2 Heat the olive oil in a large nonstick skillet over medium-high heat. Add the onions, carrots, and celery. Cook for 6 to 8 minutes, or until soft. Add the ground beef and cook until no longer pink, breaking up any large pieces with a spoon. Add to the slow cooker with the prosciutto, salt, pepper, nutmeg, evaporated milk, tomato purée, and basil.

3 Cover and cook on low for 8 to 9 hours.

4 Remove and discard the basil. Season to taste with salt and pepper. Serve over pasta with the Parmesan cheese.

Per serving: *Calories 334 (From Fat 180); Fat 20g (Saturated 7g); Cholesterol 64mg; Sodium 1273mg; Carbohydrate 19g (Dietary Fiber 4g); Protein 20g.*

Traditional Sweet Potato and Rosemary Soup

After raising nine kids and working for a major corporation for over 13 years, Glenna fulfilled her life-long dream by getting a degree in professional communications. When Tom and his family visited her in Milwaukee the weekend of her graduation, she prepared this wonderful creamy, sweet potato soup flavored with just a touch of rosemary and thyme. Tom says, "Upon tasting it, our first thoughts were naturally of Thanksgiving, even though it was the end of May. Our second thought was that this recipe could easily be adapted for the slow cooker."

As a result of those initial thoughts, we came up with the idea of preparing this soup in the slow cooker as we sleep on Thanksgiving Eve. We can purée it on Thanksgiving morning and serve it straight from the slow cooker as our guests arrive later in the day.

Preparation time: *35 minutes*

Cooking time: *30 minutes*

Yield: *6 servings*

⅓ cup finely chopped onions

1 clove garlic, minced

1 tablespoon olive oil

4 cups peeled and finely chopped sweet potatoes

⅔ cup finely chopped carrots

½ cup finely chopped celery

1 teaspoon chopped fresh rosemary, or ¼ teaspoon dried rosemary, crushed

½ teaspoon chopped fresh thyme, or ⅛ teaspoon dried thyme, crushed

4 cups chicken or vegetable broth

½ cup real dairy sour cream for garnishing (optional)

1 In a saucepan, cook the onions and garlic in the olive oil until tender. Add the potatoes, carrots, celery, rosemary, and thyme. Cook and stir for 5 minutes. Add the broth. Bring to a boil; reduce heat. Simmer, covered, for 30 minutes. Cool slightly.

2 Place a third of the vegetable mixture in a blender container. Cover and blend till smooth. Pour in bowl. Repeat with the remaining mixture. Return all the soup to the saucepan; heat through.

3 To serve, ladle the soup into bowls. If desired, spoon sour cream atop each serving.

Per serving: Calories 380 (From Fat 51); Fat 7g (Saturated 2.5g); Cholesterol 7mg; Sodium 411mg; Carbohydrate 73g (Dietary Fiber 8g); Protein 8g.

Slow Cooker Sweet Potato and Rosemary Soup

We made a few changes to the original recipe to adapt it to the slow cooker. Because root vegetables take a long time to cook and they must be very soft to purée well, we speed things up by shredding the raw sweet potatoes and carrot on the large-hole side of a handheld grater or in a food processor. We also sliced the carrots and celery very thin. If you happen to own an immersion or stick blender, by all means use it to purée the soup right in the slow cooker.

Preparation time: *15 minutes*

Cooking time: *Low 7 to 8 hours*

Yield: *6 servings*

⅓ cup finely chopped onions

1 clove garlic, minced

2 pounds sweet potatoes, peeled and coarsely shredded

1 carrot, coarsely shredded

1 celery stalk, sliced very thin

1 teaspoon chopped fresh rosemary, or ¼ teaspoon dried rosemary, crushed

½ teaspoon chopped fresh thyme, or ⅛ teaspoon dried thyme, crushed

1 teaspoon salt

⅛ teaspoon freshly ground black pepper

6 cups Master Chicken Broth (see Chapter 14) or low-sodium canned chicken broth

½ cup real dairy sour cream for garnishing (optional)

1 Lightly spray a 4-quart slow cooker with vegetable oil cooking spray. (**Note:** This recipe can be doubled and made in a 6-quart slow cooker.)

2 Place the onions, garlic, sweet potatoes, carrot, celery, rosemary, thyme, salt, black pepper, and chicken broth in the slow cooker. (See Figure 5-1 for illustrations of the herbs used in this recipe and other recipes in this book.) Stir to combine.

3 Cover and cook on low for 7 to 8 hours, or until the vegetables are very tender.

4 Place one-third of the vegetable mixture in a blender container. Cover and blend till smooth. Return to a bowl. Repeat with the remaining mixture. Return all soup to the slow cooker and heat on high for 15 minutes before serving.

5 To serve, ladle into bowls. If desired, spoon sour cream atop each serving.

Per serving: Calories 360 (From Fat 52); Fat 5g (Saturated 2g); Cholesterol 8mg; Sodium 411mg; Carbohydrate 73g (Dietary Fiber 8g); Protein 8g.

Figure 5-1:
Common
varieties of
herbs.

Annie's Traditional Chicken Provençal

This recipe is a favorite of Ann, Glenna's third daughter, who makes it all the time for her family. A wonderfully French inspired dish, this recipe includes some of the wonderful ingredients and flavors associated with the cooking of Provence in France: garlic, tomatoes, olives, and olive oil.

Preparation time: *25 minutes*

Cooking time: *1½ hours*

Yield: *4 servings*

1 whole head fresh garlic, broken into cloves, peeled, and slivered

3- to 4-pound chicken, quartered

4 large potatoes, peeled and quartered lengthwise

3 carrots, sliced diagonally

2 onions, quartered

20 cherry tomatoes

20 white button mushrooms

1 cup pitted ripe olives, drained

1 cup olive oil

Salt

Freshly ground black pepper

1 tablespoon dried thyme

1 Preheat oven to 350°.

2 Place the garlic slivers under the skin of the chicken and in holes that have been poked into the chicken with a knife.

3 Place the chicken in a roasting pan. Place the potatoes, carrots, onions, tomatoes, mushrooms, and olives around the chicken. Drizzle with the olive oil. Season with salt and black pepper to taste. Sprinkle with the thyme. Bake, uncovered, for 1½ hours, basting every 15 minutes.

Fat Buster: *To reduce the saturated fat content of the recipe, remove and discard the chicken skin before seasoning with salt and pepper.*

Vary It: *Substitute your family's favorite chicken parts, such as breast halves or legs, for a whole cut-up chicken.*

Per serving: *Calories 659 (From Fat 378); Fat 42g (Saturated 7g); Cholesterol 106mg; Sodium 561mg; Carbohydrate 32g (Dietary Fiber 6g); Protein 42g.*

Annie's Slow Cooker Chicken Provençal

Because Annie, Glenna's third daughter loves her slow cooker almost as much as she loves garlic, she made the following changes to the original recipe to adapt it to her slow cooker:

To save some time, she eliminated inserting the garlic slivers into the chicken, because slow simmering in the slow cooker causes the garlic to release its fragrant aroma and flavor anyway. The root vegetables take longer to cook than the chicken, so she cut them into even slices that she layers on the bottom of the slow cooker.

Because a slow cooker simmers slowly, food stays moist, eliminating the need for basting every 15 minutes as called for in the original recipe.

Serve the chicken with French bread to soak up the wonderful juices.

Preparation time: *15 minutes*

Cooking time: *Low 6 to 7 hours*

Yield: *4 servings*

4 medium potatoes, peeled and cut into ½-inch-thick slices	*2 medium onions, quartered*
3 carrots, cut diagonally into ¼-inch-thick slices	*20 cherry tomatoes*
	20 white button mushrooms
1 whole head fresh garlic, cloves peeled and sliced thin	*1 cup pitted ripe olives, drained*
Salt	*1 cup olive oil*
Freshly ground black pepper	*1 tablespoon dried thyme*
1 chicken (3½ to 4 pounds), cut into pieces	

1 Lightly spray a 6-quart slow cooker with vegetable oil cooking spray.

2 Layer the potatoes and carrots in the slow cooker. Scatter half the garlic slices over the vegetables. Season with salt and black pepper to taste.

3 Salt and pepper the chicken pieces. Place on top of the vegetables. Scatter the remaining garlic, the onions, tomatoes, mushrooms, and olives around the chicken.

4 Drizzle the olive oil over the chicken and vegetables. Sprinkle the thyme over the chicken.

5 Cover and cook on low for 6 to 7 hours, or until the chicken and vegetables test done.

Fat Buster: *To reduce the saturated fat content of the recipe, remove and discard the chicken skin before seasoning with salt and pepper.*

Per serving: *Calories 659 (From Fat 378); Fat 42g (Saturated 7g); Cholesterol 106mg; Sodium 561mg; Carbohydrate 32g (Dietary Fiber 6g); Protein 42g.*

☙ Tom's Mom's Traditional Stuffed Artichokes

This wonderful Mediterranean vegetable, the bud of a thistle plant, is a favorite at Tom's house. In fact, the original recipe is one that his mother, a great cook in her own right, has prepared for years.

Cooked large artichokes are eaten by pulling off the leaves and scraping the underside along your upper teeth. Smaller artichokes and the centers of large artichokes are usually tender enough to eat whole. They are wonderfully adaptable and can be eaten steamed and served with lemon juice and melted butter, stuffed with a savory bread crumb or egg mixture, or pickled in brine.

Preparation time: *25 minutes*

Cooking time: *20 to 30 minutes*

Yield: *4 servings*

4 large artichokes, approximately 8 to 10 ounces each	*2 tablespoons grated Parmesan cheese*
⅔ cup plain, dry bread crumbs	*Pinch freshly ground black pepper*
2 cloves garlic, peeled and minced	*6 tablespoons extra-virgin olive oil*
1 tablespoon minced Italian flat-leaf parsley	*2 cups water*
	1 teaspoon salt

1 Remove the stems from the artichokes with a sharp knife. Tear off and discard the top two to three layers of tough outer leaves. Trim the base so that the artichokes stand flat. Cut off ½ to 1 inch from the tops of the artichokes. Carefully open the center of the artichoke to expose the center leaves and choke. Pull out and remove any thorny leaves, which are usually tinged with purple. With a teaspoon, scoop out and discard any fuzzy matter from the center choke found in the middle. Set aside.

2 Prepare the filling by mixing together the bread crumbs, garlic, parsley, Parmesan cheese, black pepper, and 4 tablespoons of the olive oil.

3 Starting with the outer leaves, stuff a small amount of filling between the leaves, taking care not to break off the leaves. Sprinkle the tops with any remaining filling.

4 Pour the water into a 4-quart saucepan. Add the salt and stir to dissolve. Stand the artichokes upright in the pan. Drizzle with the remaining 2 tablespoons of olive oil. Bring to a boil, covered, over medium-high heat. Lower to a simmer and continue cooking, approximately 20 to 30 minutes, or until the leaves are tender.

Per serving: Calories 392 (From Fat 198); Fat 22g (Saturated 3.5g); Cholesterol 2mg; Sodium 1152mg; Carbohydrate 40g (Dietary Fiber 12g); Protein 16g.

🍅 Tom's Mom's Stuffed Artichokes for the Slow Cooker

Artichokes hold up great in a slow cooker because the tightly closed leaves need to slowly steam in order to cook up tender. (See Figure 5-2 on preparing an artichoke.) To eat the outer leaves, you scrape the inside of the leaf along your teeth, removing the delicious flesh. As you get closer to the more tender inner leaves, bite into them to see whether they're tender enough to eat whole.

The traditional version of the recipe was almost picture-perfect for the slow cooker. We simply reduced the amount of water and salt called for in the original version.

Preparation time: *25 minutes*

Cooking time: *Low 6 to 7 hours*

Yield: *4 servings*

4 large artichokes, 8 to 10 ounces each	*Pinch freshly ground black pepper*
⅔ cup plain, dry bread crumbs	*6 tablespoons extra-virgin olive oil*
2 cloves garlic, peeled and minced	*1½ cups water*
1 tablespoon minced Italian flat-leaf parsley	*¾ teaspoon salt*
2 tablespoons grated Parmesan cheese	

1 Lightly spray a 6-quart slow cooker with vegetable oil cooking spray.

2 Remove the stems from the artichokes with a sharp knife. Tear off and discard the top two to three layers of tough outer leaves. Trim the base so that the artichokes stand flat. Cut off ½ to 1 inch from the tops of the artichokes. Carefully open the center of the artichoke to expose the center leaves and choke. Pull out and remove any thorny leaves, which are usually tinged with purple. With a teaspoon, scoop out and discard any fuzzy matter from the center choke. Set aside.

3 Prepare the filling by mixing together the bread crumbs, garlic, parsley, Parmesan cheese, black pepper, and 4 tablespoons of the olive oil.

4 Starting with the outer leaves, stuff a small amount of filling between the leaves, taking care not to break off the leaves. Sprinkle the tops with any remaining filling.

5 Pour the water into the slow cooker. Add the salt and stir to dissolve. Stand the artichokes upright in the slow cooker. Drizzle with the remaining 2 tablespoons olive oil.

6 Cover and cook on low for 6 to 7 hours, or until the leaves test tender.

Tip: *Some 4-quart slow cookers are tall and cylindrical, making it difficult to insert and cook four artichokes. They should fit, however, if you have a shallower round or oval model.*

Per serving: *Calories 392 (From Fat 198); Fat 22g (Saturated 3.5g); Cholesterol 2mg; Sodium 1007mg; Carbohydrate 40g (Dietary Fiber 12g); Protein 16g.*

Figure 5-2:
How to prepare an artichoke.

Traditional White Bean Stew

Since the days of the Neolithic period, characterized by primitive agriculture, beans have been part of man's culinary heritage. An excellent source of protein, beans are extremely adaptable and can take on many different guises. We personally like them in any shape, form, or size, in soup, stews, or casseroles — and, while traveling in the Orient, have even eaten them when made into ice cream and pastries. Nevertheless, one of our favorite ways to prepare beans is simply to stew them in a fragrant combination of sautéed onions, garlic, and herbs with perhaps a small piece of cured pork.

Here are a couple tips to help ensure a perfect pot of beans. Keep in mind that beans can't be rushed, so either make this recipe the day before or put the beans on to cook overnight. And never salt beans until they're done cooking. Salt keeps the outer skin tough.

Preparation time: 20 minutes, plus 1 hour for soaking the beans

Cooking time: About 1 hour and 20 minutes

Yield: 8 servings

1 pound (about 2 cups) Great Northern or other small white beans, picked over, rinsed, and soaked in boiling water at least 1 hour before cooking

6 cups water

1 tablespoon olive oil

3 ounces lean pancetta or bacon, diced into ¼-inch pieces (optional)

1 large onion, chopped

5 large cloves garlic, peeled and sliced

2 teaspoons minced fresh thyme, or 1 teaspoon dried thyme, crumbled

¼ teaspoon freshly ground black pepper

2 teaspoons salt

2 tablespoons chopped Italian flat-leaf parsley

1 Drain the soaked beans and place in a large pot with the water.

2 Bring the beans to a boil and simmer gently, partially covered. Cook for 40 minutes. Check for doneness. If still hard, continue simmering until tender, but not mushy.

3 While the beans are cooking, heat the olive oil in a large skillet over medium-high heat. If desired, add the pancetta or bacon pieces and cook for 2 minutes. Add the onions, garlic, thyme, and black pepper and cook over low heat about 10 minutes, or until the garlic and onions are soft. Set aside.

4 When the beans are nearly tender, stir in the salt and onion mixture and return to simmering. Cook, partially covered, over low heat, stirring occasionally, for about 20 minutes, or until the beans are fully cooked and soft.

5 Remove from heat. Season to taste with salt and pepper before serving. Sprinkle with the parsley before serving.

Per serving: Calories 259 (From Fat 51); Fat 6g (Saturated 1.5g); Cholesterol 6mg; Sodium 710mg; Carbohydrate 38g (Dietary Fiber 9g); Protein 16g.

 Both the traditional and slow cooked versions of this stew are extremely versatile. Sometimes we mash the beans with the cooking liquid to make a low-fat version of refried beans. You can also add 2 cups of ditalini pasta, cooked al dente, for a bowl of that classic Italian pasta and bean soup, *pasta e fagioli.*

Slow Cooker White Bean Stew

The slow cooker and beans were made for each other because soaked beans need to simmer slowly as they absorb the cooking liquid.

To adapt the original recipe to the slow cooker, we made a few changes. To save time, we cook the onion and garlic first, along with the optional pancetta or bacon, which we then add to the other ingredients in the slow cooker. By adding this mixture early in the recipe, the beans absorb the rich flavor of the pancetta, onions, and garlic. We also eliminate the need for stirring near the end of the cooking time, as called for in the original recipe.

Here are a couple tips to help ensure a perfect pot of beans. Keep in mind that beans can't be rushed, so either make this recipe the day before or put the beans on to cook overnight. And never salt beans until they're done cooking. Salt keeps the outer skin tough.

Preparation time: *20 minutes, plus 1 hour for soaking the beans*

Cooking time: *Low 6 to 8 hours*

Yield: *8 servings*

1 tablespoon olive oil

3 ounces lean pancetta or slab bacon, diced into ¼-inch pieces (optional)

1½ cups chopped onions

5 large cloves garlic, peeled and sliced

2 teaspoons minced fresh thyme, or 1 teaspoon dried thyme, crushed

¼ teaspoon freshly ground black pepper

1 pound (about 2 cups) Great Northern or other small white beans, picked over, rinsed, and soaked in boiling water at least 1 hour before cooking

6 cups hot water

2 teaspoons salt

2 tablespoons chopped Italian flat-leaf parsley

1 Lightly spray a 4- or 6-quart slow cooker with vegetable oil cooking spray.

2 Heat the olive oil in a large nonstick skillet over medium-high heat. If desired, add the pancetta or bacon and cook for 2 minutes, stirring frequently. Add the onions, garlic, thyme, and black pepper. Cook for 6 to 8 minutes, or until the onions are soft.

3 Place the onion mixture in the slow cooker. Add the beans and the water.

4 Cover and cook on low for 6 to 8 hours, or until the beans are tender.

5 If the beans are soupy, ladle off some of the cooking liquid. Add the salt and cook on high for 15 minutes longer before serving.

6 Just before serving, sprinkle the chopped parsley (see Figure 5-3) over the beans.

Per serving: Calories 259 (From Fat 51); Fat 6g (Saturated 1.5g); Cholesterol 6mg; Sodium 710mg; Carbohydrate 38g (Dietary Fiber 9g); Protein 16g.

Chopping Parsley & Other Fresh Herbs

1.
Rinse and dry well

2.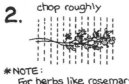
chop roughly

*NOTE:
For herbs like rosemary and thyme, remove and chop leaves. Discard thick stem.

3.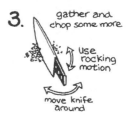
gather and chop some more.
Use rocking motion
move knife around

Figure 5-3: How to chop parsley.

Part III

Basic and Delicious Recipes for the Slow Cooker

The 5th Wave By Rich Tennant

Eat your dinner, young man! That's your father's special recipe for broccoli-bean casserole made in the slow cooker.

Not slow enough...

In this part...

*H*ere, we share with you some of our favorite slow cooker recipes. These cover the gamut from snacks and beverages, stews and soups, roasts and side dish casseroles, to desserts. All are quick and easy to get started, and delicious to eat!

Chapter 6

Snacks, Dips, and Beverages

In This Chapter

▶ Making treats for munching and dipping

▶ Preparing popular party fare

▶ Using the slow cooker as a punch bowl

*I*t should come as no surprise that snack food is as American as slow cookers. In fact, according to the Snack Food Association, Americans spend an average of $22 million a day on snack food. Slow cookers have been used in preparing snack foods since they were sold in the early 1970s, and they continue to be as popular as ever. What could be more convenient than preparing a tasty dip or snack mix and serving it straight from the slow cooker that it was made in?

You may want to invite a few friends over for snacks, appetizers, and steaming cups of cider or mugs of Irish coffee. Slow cookers demonstrate their convenience most noticeably in party and entertaining situations. Because the slow cooker cooks while you make other party-related preparations, you can think of it as a helper in getting the party together. Chatting with friends and family, we came up with some new versions of slow cooker party classics, such as sweet and sour meatballs and spicy cocktail franks, that are sure to satisfy your guests. You'll definitely want to invite your slow cooker to the next social function you host!

Slow Cooker Munchies and Dipping Sauces

Even though you may not be able to imagine that food items like granola and salsa were either unknown or far from mainstream 30 years ago, they've become standard fare in today's culture. This section includes our slow cooker versions of granola and salsa and such snack and party favorites as Chex party mix, chunky chili sauce, and nacho cheese sauce for you to adapt to your snack recipe repertoire.

You may be surprised that you can make things like granola and Chex party mix in your slow cooker, but when we adapted our favorite recipes, we found that our trusty slow cooker outperformed the conventional oven every time. With its slow, even cooking, we never had to worry that the cereals would overcook and burn if not supervised continuously. The same was true with nacho cheese sauce, which usually requires frequent stirring. What a pleasure to let it cook almost on autopilot while we were busy doing something else.

⟲ *Good Morning Granola*

Granola has a natural goodness, especially when it's homemade. Although store-bought granola is convenient, it can be very high in fat. We reduced the amount of oil as much as possible in our recipe and added powdered milk for calcium, and honey for sweetness. Making granola in a slow cooker is easy and better than in the oven because it cooks more evenly and doesn't burn. Try some today with milk and fresh fruit, or sprinkle some over plain yogurt for a delicious snack or dessert.

Preparation time: 10 minutes

Cooking time: High 2 hours, Low 4 to 6

Yield: About 24 half-cup servings

10 cups old-fashioned oats (do not use quick-cooking oats)	1 can (12 ounces) frozen, unsweetened apple juice concentrate, thawed
1 cup sliced almonds	¼ cup vegetable oil
1 cup nonfat powdered milk	½ cup honey
2 cups dried cranberries or raisins	½ teaspoon salt

1 Lightly spray a 6-quart slow cooker with vegetable oil cooking spray.

2 Combine the oats, almonds, powdered milk, and dried cranberries in the slow cooker.

3 Combine the apple juice concentrate, oil, honey, and salt in a bowl and pour over the oat mixture. Stir to combine.

4 Cook, uncovered, on high for 2 hours, stirring every 30 minutes. Reduce to low and continue cooking, uncovered, for 4 to 6 hours, or until dry and crisp. Stir frequently while the granola is on low to prevent overbrowning.

5 Let cool to room temperature and store in an airtight container.

Per serving: Calories 305 (From Fat 70); Fat 8g (Saturated 1g); Cholesterol 0mg; Sodium 70mg; Carbohydrate 50g (Dietary Fiber 5g); Protein 8g.

☽ Slow Cooker Party Mix

This classic Chex cereal party mix from the '50s is as popular today as it was back then. Even though you can buy it already made in the snack section of most supermarkets, we think the homemade version still tastes better!

Preparation time: *15 minutes*

Cooking time: *High 1 hour, Low 30 minutes*

Yield: *About 24 half-cup servings*

½ cup (1 stick) butter or margarine, melted

1¼ teaspoons seasoned salt

4 teaspoons Worcestershire sauce

3 cups Corn Chex cereal

3 cups Rice Chex cereal

3 cups Wheat Chex cereal

¾ cup salted mixed nuts

1 Lightly spray a 6-quart slow cooker with vegetable oil cooking spray.

2 Combine the melted butter, seasoned salt, and Worcestershire sauce in the slow cooker. Add the cereal and mixed nuts. Stir to combine.

3 Cook, uncovered, on high for 1 hour, stirring every 30 minutes. Reduce to low and continue cooking, uncovered, 30 minutes, or until dry and crisp.

4 Let cool to room temperature and store in an airtight container.

Vary It: Make Curry Party Mix by adding 2 teaspoons curry powder along with the melted butter. Add 1 cup golden raisins with the cereal.

Per serving: *Calories 138 (From Fat 70); Fat 7.5g (Saturated 3.5g); Cholesterol 13mg; Sodium 376mg; Carbohydrate 16g (Dietary Fiber 1.5g); Protein 2g.*

☽ *Chunky Chili Sauce*

We don't know what's better, the smell of this sauce as it cooks or eating it afterward! Perfect for dipping chips or nachos, mixing in with ground meat for meat loaf, or even slathering on barbecued meat and poultry, this sauce is so tasty that you'll be coming back for more. Don't be put off by the long list of ingredients — we're sure that you likely have much of it on hand. If you have a food processor, by all means use it to save time chopping the fruit and vegetables. You can store the chili sauce in sealed containers up to 30 days in the refrigerator, or 2 months in the freezer.

Preparation time: *25 minutes*

Cooking time: *Low 8 to 9 hours*

Yield: *40 fourth-cup servings*

2 cans (28 ounces each) crushed tomatoes

1 can (5 ounces) tomato paste

2 cups chopped and peeled Granny Smith apples (about 2 medium apples)

2 cups chopped Spanish or Vidalia onions (1 large onion)

1½ cups packed light brown sugar

1½ cups (12 ounces) cider vinegar

1 large green bell pepper, cored, seeded, and chopped

1 large red bell pepper, cored, seeded, and chopped

1 cup chopped celery

2 tablespoons ground chili powder

2 teaspoons mustard seed

2 teaspoons ground cinnamon

1 teaspoon ground cloves

1 teaspoon ground ginger

½ teaspoon cayenne pepper

1 tablespoon salt

1 Lightly spray a 4- or 6-quart slow cooker with vegetable oil cooking spray.

2 Combine all the ingredients in the slow cooker.

3 Cover and cook on low for 8 to 9 hours, or until the sauce is thick and the vegetables are tender.

Tip: *If you have a food processor, use it to chop the apples and vegetables. Before placing the ingredients in the food processor, slice the apples, quarter the onion, and cut the pepper into eighths and the celery into 1-inch pieces. Chop the apples and onions separately in the food processor by pressing the pulse switch twice. Chop the peppers and celery together by pressing the pulse switch twice.*

Per serving: *Calories 43 (From Fat 3); Fat 0g (Saturated 0g); Cholesterol 0mg; Sodium 287; Carbohydrate 11g (Dietary Fiber 1g); Protein 1g.*

☺ Holy Guacamole Tomato Salsa

More salsa is sold in this country than ketchup, which is amazing when you consider that a little over 20 years ago virtually no one even knew what it was! Our homemade version outshines any store-bought salsa. Its bright, fresh flavors make it great for dipping or to use in preparing any of your other favorite south-of-the-border recipes. This salsa can be stored in sealed containers up to 30 days in the refrigerator, or 2 months in the freezer. Garnish with avocado, for a traditional guacamole touch!

Preparation time: *25 minutes*

Cooking time: *Low 8 hours*

Yield: *40 fourth-cup servings*

2 cans (28 ounces each) crushed tomatoes	*⅔ cup packed light brown sugar*
2 cans (14.5 ounces each) diced tomatoes	*½ cup cider vinegar*
6 stalks celery, diced	*½ cup freshly squeezed lime juice*
4 large onions, finely chopped	*2 tablespoons salt*
4 cloves garlic, minced	
2 tablespoons minced pickled jalapeño pepper	

1 Lightly spray a 4- or 6-quart slow cooker with vegetable oil cooking spray.

2 Combine all the ingredients in the slow cooker.

3 Cover and cook on low for 8 hours.

Tip: *If you have a food processor, use it to chop the vegetables. Before placing the vegetables in the food processor, cut the celery into 1-inch pieces and quarter the onions. To chop the celery, press the pulse switch twice, or until chopped. Then chop the onions and garlic together by pulsing twice.*

Per serving: *Calories 30 (From Fat 0); Fat 0g (Saturated 0g); Cholesterol 0mg; Sodium 511mg; Carbohydrate 7g (Dietary Fiber 1g); Protein 1g.*

☽ Nacho Cheese Sauce

Cheesy with as much zip as you want, our nacho cheese sauce is the perfect accompaniment to a big bag of your favorite tortilla chips at your next party. Spoon some of the nacho cheese sauce over tortilla chips on a plate. Top with sliced scallions, sliced black olives, and pickled jalapeño slices. Add hot pepper sauce to taste for another way to spice up the nacho cheese sauce.

Preparation time: *15 minutes*

Cooking time: *Low 3 to 4 hours*

Yield: *24 third-cup servings*

1 package (2 pounds) Velveeta Pasteurized Prepared Cheese Product, cut into 1-inch cubes

2 cups (8 ounces) shredded sharp cheddar cheese

4 cups Holy Guacamole Tomato Salsa (see recipe earlier in this chapter) or your favorite store brand

2 cans (6 ounces each) chopped green chiles, undrained

1 Lightly spray a 4- or 6-quart slow cooker with vegetable oil cooking spray.

2 Combine all the ingredients in the slow cooker.

3 Cover and cook on low for 3 to 4 hours. Stir after the first 1½ hours. Stir again before serving.

Per serving: *Calories 182 (From Fat 113); Fat 13g (Saturated 8g); Cholesterol 41 mg; Sodium 696mg; Carbohydrate 5g (Dietary Fiber 0g); Protein 11g.*

A New Twist on Some Classic Party Favorites

Savory appetizer and finger foods are a 20th-century phenomenon. Preceded by bland and simple canapés in the late 1800s, the art of making and serving tasty appetizers to guests grew in popularity from the 1920s throughout the century, with each decade making its own unique contribution. One of our favorites, cocktail-sized meatballs, was the hit of the 1950s, cocktail hot dogs emerged in the 1960s, Buffalo wings became popular in the 1970s, and anything and everything Tex-Mex was in vogue in the 1980s. The 1990s were a time of reflection and moderation, but that didn't stop homemakers from serving appetizers. In fact, we saw many updated and "lighter" versions of favorites from years gone by. Over the years we've tweaked and changed our favorite recipes and are pleased to share them with you.

Sweet 'n' Sour Meatballs

This is our version of that classic, all-time favorite, slow cooker party recipe. People just can't seem to get enough of these tasty little meatballs. If short on time, you can also use frozen meatballs rather than make your own. Because they are precooked, just let them defrost about 30 minutes at room temperature before adding to the slow cooker. Figure on about 2 to 2½ pounds of frozen meatballs.

Preparation time: *20 minutes*

Cooking time: *Low 2 to 3 hours*

Yield: *25 servings*

2 pounds lean ground beef

2 large eggs, slightly beaten

¼ cup dry bread crumbs

1 teaspoon salt

¼ teaspoon freshly ground black pepper

2 jars (12 ounces each) apple or grape jelly

2 bottles (12 ounces each) chili sauce, or 3 cups Chunky Chili Sauce (see the recipe earlier in this chapter)

¼ cup minced onions

1 Mix thoroughly the ground beef, eggs, bread crumbs, salt, and black pepper. Shape into 100 small ½-inch meatballs. Arrange in two shallow baking pans. Broil 4 inches from heat until browned, turning once. Pour off the fat.

2 Lightly spray a 4-quart slow cooker with vegetable oil cooking spray. Combine the jelly, chili sauce, and minced onions in the slow cooker. Add the browned meatballs and stir well.

3 Cover and cook on low for 2 to 3 hours. Serve from the slow cooker.

Per serving: *Calories 187 (From Fat 60); Fat 7g (Saturated 2.5g); Cholesterol 42mg; Sodium 321mg; Carbohydrate 24g (Dietary Fiber 1g); Protein 8g.*

Spicy Lil' Piggies

At times it wouldn't seem like a party without cocktail franks. We especially like them spicy in a tomato barbecue sauce. Serve these straight from the slow cooker on the buffet table at your next party. This recipe can be doubled and made in a 6-quart slow cooker.

Preparation time: *15 minutes*

Cooking time: *High 2 to 3 hours*

Yield: *About 40 appetizer servings*

2 cans (5 ounces each) tomato paste

4 cups water

¼ cup minced onion

¼ cup Worcestershire sauce

¼ cup packed light brown sugar

2 tablespoons white vinegar

2 tablespoons molasses

2 teaspoons dry mustard

1 teaspoon salt

2 pounds cocktail franks, separated if attached

1 Lightly spray a 4-quart slow cooker with vegetable oil cooking spray.

2 Combine all the ingredients except the franks in the slow cooker.

3 Cover and cook on high for 1 to 2 hours, or until hot. Add the franks and cook for 1 hour longer.

Shortcut: *Eliminate Step 2 and substitute 5 cups of Chunky Chili Sauce (see the recipe earlier in this chapter) for the sauce ingredients. Proceed with Step 3.*

Per serving: *Calories 77 (From Fat 29); Fat 3g (Saturated 1g); Cholesterol 12mg; Sodium 273mg; Carbohydrate 9g (Dietary Fiber 0g); Protein 3g.*

Asian Chicken Wings

Our Asian Chicken Wings, smothered with the tasty mixture of honey, soy, and spices, are finger-licking good at almost any party or get-together. They also make a great entrée when served with white rice and stir-fried Asian vegetables. Check to see whether your supermarket carries those extra-large chicken wings that are already separated at the joint. They are perfect for appetizers because the part that was originally attached to the chicken is exceptionally meaty, resembling a tiny chicken leg. The flat part of the wing is much meatier, too.

Preparation time: *20 minutes*

Cooking time: *Low 4 to 5 hours*

Yield: *32 appetizer servings, or 4 entrée portions*

Salt and pepper

3 pounds (about 16 large) chicken wings, separated at the joint to make wing drums and flats (see Figure 6-1)

1½ cups barbecue sauce, or Chunky Chili Sauce (see the recipe earlier in this chapter)

¼ cup honey

¼ cup soy sauce

4 scallions, white and green parts, sliced thin

2 cloves garlic, minced

2 tablespoons finely chopped fresh gingerroot

3 tablespoons toasted sesame seeds

1 Salt and pepper the chicken wings. Place on a broiler pan. Broil 4 to 5 inches from heat about 5 to 8 minutes on each side, or until browned.

2 Lightly spray a 4- or 6-quart slow cooker with vegetable oil cooking spray.

3 Combine the barbecue sauce, honey, soy sauce, scallions, garlic, ginger, and sesame seeds in the slow cooker. Add the browned wings and stir to combine.

4 Cover and cook on low for 4 to 5 hours, or until the chicken is tender and tests done.

Per serving: *Calories 162 (From Fat 70); Fat 9g (Saturated 1g); Cholesterol 10mg; Sodium 516mg; Carbohydrate 8g (Dietary Fiber 0g); Protein 12g.*

Separating Chicken Wings for Drums and Flats

Separate the wing at the joint. The fatter part looks like a mini drumstick.

the mini drumstick or drum

(flat)

For the flat part (or wing flap), trim off some excess skin and remove the little piece of bone that is attached to it.

the flat

Figure 6-1: Separating chicken wings from the joint.

Drinks That Warm Down to Your Toes

Because many people are cocooning and entertaining more at home nowadays, we have turned the slow cooker into a heated punch bowl of sorts and have come up with some delicious hot toddies to warm you, your family, and friends on even the coldest of days. These punches and hot beverages are sure to be the hit of your next get-together.

Ruby Red Cider

This hot punch is as ruby red as its name says it is. Besides looking pretty and tasting great, it fills your home with the spicy aroma of cinnamon and citrus. You can double this recipe and make it in a 6-quart slow cooker.

Preparation time: *10 minutes*

Cooking time: *High 1 to 2 hours*

Yield: *About twelve 6-ounce servings*

½ gallon (64 ounces) cranberry juice

2 large oranges

4 pieces cinnamon stick, 3 inches long

4 pieces of fresh gingerroot, 1 inch long, peeled and crushed

¼ to ½ cup sugar

1 Pour the cranberry juice into a 4-quart slow cooker.

2 Using a sharp paring knife, remove four 3-inch-long strips of peel from the oranges. Juice the oranges and strain out the pulp. Add the peel and juice to the slow cooker along with the cinnamon sticks and ginger. Stir to combine.

3 Cover and cook on high for 1 to 2 hours, or until hot. Add sugar to taste and stir until dissolved. Turn to low and serve in mugs.

Vary It: *You can also use cranapple or raspberry-cranberry juice in this recipe.*

Per serving: *Calories 117 (From Fat 0); Fat 0g (Saturated 0g); Cholesterol 0mg; Sodium 3mg; Carbohydrate 30g (Dietary Fiber 0g); Protein 0g.*

Mulled Wine

To *mull* means to flavor a hot beverage with sugar and spices. One of our personal favorites, mulled wine, has been enjoyed throughout the world for centuries — especially in cold weather climates. Make sure that you use a full-bodied red wine so that it holds up well when heated with the citrus fruit and spices. This recipe can be doubled and made in a 6-quart slow cooker.

Preparation time: *10 minutes*

Cooking time: *High 1 to 2 hours*

Yield: *12 servings*

2 bottles (750 ml each) dry red wine

2 lemons, sliced thin

2 oranges, sliced thin

½ teaspoon grated nutmeg or ground cardamom

1 teaspoon whole cloves

4 pieces cinnamon stick, 3 inches long

½ to ⅔ cup sugar

1 Combine the wine, lemon and orange slices, nutmeg, cloves, and cinnamon sticks in a 4-quart slow cooker.

2 Cover and heat on high for 1 to 2 hours, or until hot. Add sugar to taste and stir until dissolved. Turn to low and serve in mugs.

Per serving: Calories 134 (From Fat 0); Fat 0g (Saturated 0g); Cholesterol 0mg; Sodium 7mg; Carbohydrate 14g (Dietary Fiber 10g); Protein 0g.

Spiced Cider

Cider has always been an important American beverage. Made from pressed apples picked in the autumn months, cider is a harbinger of cooler days ahead. Although it's delicious served cold, we also enjoy it warm mulled and provide you (on the following page) with our secret combination of mulling spices to make at home. Packaged in a decorative jar, the Mulled Spice Mix makes a great gift to give along with a gallon of locally pressed cider. This recipe can be doubled and made in a 6-quart slow cooker.

Preparation time: *10 minutes*

Cooking time: *High 1 to 2 hours*

Yield: *8 servings*

½ gallon (64 ounces) unfiltered apple cider

¼ cup Mulled Spice Mix (see following recipe)

½ cup golden raisins (optional)

1 Pour the cider into a 4-quart slow cooker.

2 Add the Mulled Spice Mix (see recipe on the following page) and stir to combine.

3 Cover and cook on high for 1 to 2 hours, or until hot. Turn to low. **Warning:** To prevent pieces of Mulled Spice Mix from getting into your drink, strain before serving or take care not to stir up when serving. Add the raisins, if desired, ten minutes before serving.

Per serving: Calories 122 (From Fat 27); Fat 3g (Saturated 0g); Cholesterol 0mg; Sodium 1mg; Carbohydrate 10g (Dietary Fiber 0g); Protein 0g.

Mulled Spice Mix

You can purchase mulled spice mix at most specialty or gourmet food stores during the holidays and winter months. It's so simple to prepare, however, you can also make it at home, as shown in Figure 6-2.

Rather than buy chopped dried orange rinds, make your own. When peeling oranges to eat, use a sharp paring knife and cut off the thin top layer of the orange peel. Place the rinds on a cookie sheet and let them dry at room temperature until brittle. When you've accumulated a sufficient quantity, chop them in a food processor by using the pulse switch.

Preparation time: *5 minutes*

Yield: *Approximately 1½ cups*

¾ *cup crushed cinnamon sticks*   ⅓ *cup whole allspice*

¾ *cup chopped dried orange rinds*   ¼ *cup whole cloves*

Combine all the ingredients in a clean glass jar. Cover and seal well.

Figure 6-2:
Making
mulled spice
mix.

Irish Coffee for a Crowd

Glenna and I have fond memories and recollections of our annual Irish coffee — a San Francisco creation — at the Buenavista after an after-dinner walk through Fisherman's Wharf. We especially like to make our slow cooker Irish coffee when celebrating an important occasion like a birthday or anniversary. It is indeed a special finale to a special day. This recipe can be doubled and made in a 6-quart slow cooker.

Preparation time: *15 minutes*

Cooking time: *High 1 to 2 hours*

Yield: *Ten 8-ounce servings*

8 cups (32 ounces) hot fresh brewed coffee

½ cup sugar

2 cups (16 ounces) Irish whiskey

½ pint heavy cream, whipped to soft peaks

1 Combine the hot coffee and sugar in a 4-quart slow cooker. Add the whiskey and stir to combine.

2 Cover and heat on high for 1 to 2 hours before serving. Turn to low and serve in mugs with a dollop of whipped cream on top.

Per serving: Calories 239 (From Fat 70); Fat 9g (Saturated 5.5g); Cholesterol 33mg; Sodium 11mg; Carbohydrate 11g (Dietary Fiber 0g); Protein 0g.

Mexican Coffee — Café de Olla

Traditional Mexican coffee is called *café de olla*. It is usually prepared in an earthenware pot with cinnamon sticks and cloves and then sweetened with *piloncillo*, unrefined Mexican sugar. Our slow cooker recipe, made in the stoneware crock, is a close approximation.

Preparation time: *5 minutes*

Cooking time: *High 1 to 2 hours*

Yield: *12 servings*

12 cups hot, strong brewed coffee	2 cinnamon sticks, 3 inches long
½ cup packed dark brown sugar	½ teaspoon whole cloves

1 Combine the hot coffee, brown sugar, cinnamon sticks, and cloves in a 4-quart slow cooker.

2 Cover and heat on high for 1 to 2 hours before serving. Turn to low and serve in mugs.

Per serving: *Calories 39 (From Fat 0); Fat 0g (Saturated 0g); Cholesterol 0mg; Sodium 8mg; Carbohydrate 10g (Dietary Fiber 0g); Protein 0g.*

Spirited Tea

Although cookbooks often contain recipes for spirited hot toddies, ones made with tea are not that common — so here's one for you tea lovers! Feel free to use whatever kind of tea you prefer, as long as it is brewed strong for maximum flavor. This recipe can be doubled and made in a 6-quart slow cooker.

Preparation time: *15 minutes*

Cooking time: *High 1 to 2 hours*

Yield: *8 servings*

4 cups hot, strong fresh brewed tea

1 cup packed light brown sugar

1 bottle (375 ml) brandy

1 bottle (375 ml) dark rum

½ cup freshly squeezed lemon juice

2 cinnamon sticks, 3 inches long

Lemon slices for garnishing

1 Combine the hot tea and brown sugar in a 4-quart slow cooker. Add the brandy, rum, lemon juice, and cinnamon sticks. Stir together.

2 Cover and heat on high for 1 to 2 hours before serving. Turn to low and serve in mugs with lemon slices.

Per serving: Calories 290 (From Fat 0); Fat 0g (Saturated 0g); Cholesterol 0mg; Sodium 12mg; Carbohydrate 19g (Dietary Fiber 0g); Protein 0g.

Chapter 7

Spoonfuls of Goodness: Soups, Chowders, and Chili

• •

In This Chapter

▶ Defining soups, chowders, and varieties of chili

▶ Enjoying soups, chowders, and chili from your slow cooker

▶ Using Mother's secrets for the ultimate soup experience

• •

Recipes in This Chapter

↻ Cuban Black Bean Soup

▶ Beef Barley Mushroom Soup

▶ Split Pea Soup with Ham

↻ Minestrone Soup

▶ Borscht

▶ Fisherman's Chowder

▶ Corn and Lima Bean Chowder

↻ Chunky Vegetable Chili

▶ Tailgate Chili for a Crowd

▶ White Bean and Chicken Chili

*E*veryone likes soup. In fact, there's nothing to dislike. Soups taste good and can even make us better when we we're not feeling well. Because they come in an endless variety, they're never boring. Some are thick like chowders, while others are creamy. Some are bland, and others, like chili, can be spicy. But the one thing they all have in common is that they come out great when made in a slow cooker, because slow simmering extracts all the goodness found in each and every ingredient.

What's in a Name?

Order soup from a menu, and you have a preconceived notion of what you will be served. Generically, soup is any combination of meat, poultry, fish, or vegetables, cooked together with liquid. Naturally it is "soupy" and is always eaten with a spoon. Soups are filling and nurturing and are a part of every culture.

Soups like chowder and chili have also created a popular following. When it comes to clam chowder, there are two very distinct types: New England clam chowder, which is white and made with milk, and the Manhattan version, which is red and made from tomatoes. Both sides claim theirs is the true chowder and the other an impostor! Chowder doesn't necessarily have to be made with seafood. As you can see with our Corn and Lima Bean Chowder, it can also be made with ingredients such as vegetables.

Chili, on the other hand, has developed a cultlike following over the years. Chili cookoffs are a culinary pastime in many American communities nationwide, with local cooks plying their culinary skills to see who makes the meanest chili in town!

Making the Very Best Soups

Close your eyes and think of the soup. What associations come to mind? Mom? Grandma? Or perhaps the Campbell's Soup kids? Soups, chowders, and chili are bowls full of goodness that evoke strong emotions of well being and, yes, love. They also are relatively simple to prepare. In the following list, we share with you some of the soup secrets we picked up along the way, with 60 years of collective cooking practice between the two of us.

✔ Soups are flexible, forgiving dishes as long as you don't overdo cooking them. You want to cook them sufficiently so that the ingredients are tender but not overcooked to the stage that they begin to lose flavor and become insipid.

✔ Flavors should be balanced so that one flavor doesn't overwhelm another.

✔ Always use the freshest ingredients available in order to extract maximum flavor during cooking.

✔ Always use a sufficient amount of seasoning so that the soup is flavorful, without one spice or herb overpowering the other. With the exception of cooking dried beans, season with salt from the beginning in order to enhance flavor.

Salt dried beans *after* they have cooked and are tender. When dried beans are cooked with salt, the outer skins remain tough and never seem to soften.

✔ If time allows it, sauté any onion and vegetables in a bit of oil in a skillet. Doing so provides the dish with a mellow base to get things off to a good start.

✔ Because you eat these dishes with a spoon, cut the ingredients into bite-sized uniform pieces. By cutting them into the same size, you also reduce the chance that one ingredient will overpower another.

Soups, chowders, and chili don't like to be rushed, so that's why making them in a slow cooker is ideal. If you don't have time in the morning for all the chopping and dicing, do so the night before and assemble the soup before heading out the next day. Imagine the wonderful aroma that will welcome you when you return eight hours later!

Soups

There should be no doubt in anyone's mind that the United States is a melting pot, especially when you peek into its soup kettle. Recipes for soups from the Caribbean, Central and Eastern Europe, the Mediterranean, and Asia, are as mainstream today as macaroni and cheese. America's love of soup is so strong and we have accepted and adapted so many different types that eventually the cultural boundaries dividing these soups have been erased. We share with you an eclectic but popular selection of soup recipes ranging from Cuban black bean soup to Russian borscht, especially adapted to be made even easier in the slow cooker.

Cooking dried beans in a slow cooker

Did you know that you can cook dried beans in your slow cooker for use in your recipes? The overall cooking time is about 15 hours, so plan accordingly.

1. Pick over dried beans to remove any foreign particles.

2. Rinse well under cold water. Place in a 4- to 6-quart slow cooker.

3. For every pound of dried beans (approximately 2 cups), add 6 cups of room temperature water. Do not cook less than 1 pound of beans, nor more than 2 pounds at a time.

   One cup of dried beans, such as kidney, navy, and black, yields approximately 2 cups cooked beans.

Do not add salt, because it toughens the skin of the bean. Beans can be salted after cooking, when they're tender.

4. For added subtle flavor, include a bay leaf and an onion stuck with a few cloves with the beans.

5. If you like your bean soup thick, add a diced potato to the soup. When the soup is done cooking, smash it along the side of the pot with back of large spoon.

6. Cover and cook on low for 13 to 15 hours, or overnight, until tender.

7. Season cooked beans with salt to taste.

8. Store cooled beans in the cooking liquid in the refrigerator for up to 4 days.

⟋ *Cuban Black Bean Soup*

Black beans or turtle beans are a Cuban staple served — if not at every meal — at least at every other meal. This wonderfully thick bean soup makes the perfect one-pot meal.

Preparation time: *20 minutes*

Cooking time: *Low 7 to 8 hours*

Yield: *8 servings*

2 tablespoons olive oil	½ teaspoon freshly ground black pepper
1 large onion, chopped	2 cans (14.5 ounces each) diced tomatoes
2 cloves garlic, minced	4 cans (15.5 ounces each) black beans, drained and rinsed under cold water
1 medium green bell pepper, cored, seeded, and diced	2 chicken or vegetable bouillon cubes, crumbled
2 carrots, chopped	2 bay leaves
2 celery stalks, chopped	6 cups water
1 tablespoon ground cumin	2 tablespoons balsamic vinegar
2 teaspoons dried thyme	
½ teaspoon cayenne pepper	

1 Spray a 6-quart slow cooker with vegetable oil cooking spray.

2 Heat the olive oil in a large nonstick skillet over medium heat. Add the onion, garlic, and green pepper and cook until soft, 7 to 8 minutes. Add the carrots, celery, cumin, thyme, cayenne, and black pepper and cook for 5 minutes.

3 Place the cooked vegetable mixture in the slow cooker. Add the diced tomatoes, black beans, bouillon cubes, bay leaves, and water. Stir to combine.

4 Cover and cook on low for 7 to 8 hours, or until the vegetables are tender.

5 Stir in the vinegar before serving.

Per serving: Calories 204 (From Fat 34); Fat 4g (Saturated 0.5g); Cholesterol 0mg; Sodium 1529mg; Carbohydrate 39g (Dietary Fiber 12g); Protein 10g.

Beef Barley Mushroom Soup

It's unfortunate that barley is not as popular as it should be. Known to mankind since the Stone Age, this hardy grain has been used over the course of time as a form of currency, ground into flour to make bread, turned into porridge, and slowly simmered in soups and stews. Today most home cooks use barley, an excellent source of soluble fiber, only in soup.

This happens to be one of our favorite dishes to prepare on those crazy days leading up to the holidays in December. We simply place all the ingredients in the slow cooker before heading out in the early morning to beat the mall crowds. Then we return home in the evening tired and hungry and ready to be refortified by a bowl of this rich and satisfying soup.

Preparation time: *10 minutes*

Cooking time: *Low 5 to 7 hours*

Yield: *6 servings*

1 large onion, minced	*3 tablespoons minced Italian flat-leaf parsley*
½ pound very lean beef stew meat, cut into ½-inch cubes	*1 cup pearl barley*
3 carrots, diced	*1 teaspoon salt*
3 celery stalks, diced	*¼ teaspoon freshly ground black pepper*
½ pound small white mushrooms, stems trimmed, quartered	*6 cups Master Chicken Broth (Chapter 14), or 1 can (48 ounces) low-sodium canned chicken broth*
¼ pound shiitake mushrooms, stems trimmed, quartered	*2 cups water*
1 bay leaf	

1 Lightly spray a 4- to 6-quart slow cooker with vegetable oil cooking spray.

2 Place the meat, onion, carrots, celery, white and shiitake mushrooms, bay leaf, parsley, barley, salt, and pepper in the slow cooker. Pour the broth and water over all and stir to combine.

3 Cover and cook on low for 5 to 7 hours, or until the meat, vegetables, and barley are tender. Add salt to taste.

Per serving: *Calories 281 (From Fat 70); Fat 8g (Saturated 2.5g); Cholesterol 24mg; Sodium 969mg; Carbohydrate 38g (Dietary Fiber 8g); Protein 17g.*

Split Pea Soup with Ham

We always make this soup whenever we've had ham for a celebration or holiday dinner because ham makes the difference between good split pea soup and the best. Don't add too much, or you will overpower the mellow flavor of the peas. Add just enough to impart some smoky flavor. If you were lucky and the ham had a bone, add that, too, as long as it fits in the slow cooker. You'll be amazed how much more flavor you'll get. Just be sure to remove any visible fat from the bone before doing so.

Cooking the vegetables first adds depth to the flavor of this soup. However, if preparation time is an issue, eliminate Step 2 and proceed with Step 3, adding the vegetables raw.

Preparation time: *20 minutes*

Cooking time: *Low 8 to 9 hours*

Yield: *6 servings*

2 tablespoons olive oil

2 large onions, chopped

2 cloves garlic, minced

2 carrots, diced

2 celery stalks, diced

1 medium potato, peeled and diced

1 bag (16 ounces) green split peas, rinsed under cold water

1 cup diced smoked or boiled ham

1½ teaspoons dried marjoram

1 tablespoon salt

¼ teaspoon freshly ground black pepper

9 cups water

1 Spray a 6-quart slow cooker with vegetable oil cooking spray.

2 Heat the olive oil in a large nonstick skillet over medium heat. Add the onions and garlic and cook until soft, 7 to 8 minutes. Add the carrots, celery, and potato and cook for 5 minutes.

3 Place the cooked vegetable mixture in the slow cooker. Add the split peas, ham, marjoram, salt, pepper, and water. Stir to combine.

4 Cover and cook on low for 8 to 9 hours. Stir after 5 hours, if possible, or 1 hour before serving.

Tip: If you have a food processor, use it to mince the garlic and chop the vegetables. Begin by placing the garlic in the food processor container along with the carrots, cut into 1-inch pieces. Press the pulse switch two times; add the onion, quartered, and pulse two times. Add the celery and pulse two times. By the time you're done, the garlic should be minced and the vegetables coarsely chopped. If not, hit the pulse switch two more times.

Per serving: Calories 398 (From Fat 69); Fat 8g (Saturated 1.5g); Cholesterol 14mg; Sodium 1558mg; Carbohydrate 59g (Dietary Fiber 22g); Protein 26g.

⌕ Minestrone Soup

Minestrone is as Italian as pizza. Made with a wide variety of vegetables — our version includes eight different kinds — this Italian classic is also fragrant with herbs and grated cheese. Cooking the vegetables first adds depth to the flavor of this soup. However, if preparation time is an issue, eliminate Step 2 and proceed with Step 3, adding all the vegetables raw.

Preparation time: *20 minutes*

Cooking time: *Low 8 hours*

Yield: *6 servings*

3 tablespoons olive oil

1 medium onion, chopped

3 cloves garlic, minced

1 tablespoon dried Italian seasoning

1 can (14.5 ounces) basil-, oregano-, and garlic-flavored diced tomatoes

1 cup finely diced carrots

1 cup finely diced celery

1 cup finely diced zucchini

1 cup string beans, cut into ½-inch pieces

2 cups shredded cabbage

1 cup peeled and finely diced potatoes

1 tablespoon salt

½ teaspoon freshly ground black pepper

8 cups water

1 can (19 ounces) red kidney beans, drained and rinsed under cold water

1½ cups ditalini (small, tube-shaped pasta)

⅓ cup freshly grated Parmesan or Pecorino Romano cheese

1 Spray a 6-quart slow cooker with vegetable oil cooking spray.

2 Heat the olive oil in a large nonstick skillet over medium heat. Add the onion and garlic and cook until soft, 7 to 8 minutes. Add the Italian seasoning, tomatoes, carrots, celery, and zucchini and cook for 5 minutes.

3 Place the cooked vegetable mixture in the slow cooker. Add the string beans, cabbage, potatoes, salt, pepper, and water. Stir to combine.

4 Cover and cook on low for 8 hours. Add the kidney beans and pasta 20 minutes before serving. Cook until the pasta is tender. (Figure 7-1 shows different types of pasta.)

5 Stir in the cheese and serve immediately.

Per serving: *Calories 297 (From Fat 27); Fat 10g (Saturated 2g); Cholesterol 4mg; Sodium 1770mg; Carbohydrate 42g (Dietary Fiber 9g); Protein 12g.*

Figure 7-1:
Types of
pasta.

Borscht

"I remember the first time I had borscht. I was in my mid-twenties and had been invited to dine at the then-renowned Russian Tea Room in New York City. It was the beginning of the holidays, and the atmosphere was charged. The borscht was served from a silver tureen, which only made it look redder than it really was. Served with a dollop of sour cream and a sprinkling of snipped dill, the soup had flavors that were earthy and yet at the same time exotic and memorable. Nowadays, I make it whenever my spirits need some uplifting since this wonderfully red soup brightens up even the gloomiest of days and moods!" — Tom

Preparation time: *15 minutes*

Cooking time: *Low 8 to 10 hours*

Yield: *6 servings*

2 pounds beets, peeled and cut into ½-inch cubes

1 large onion, coarsely chopped

2 carrots, coarsely chopped

1 celery stalk, coarsely chopped

1 large potato, peeled and diced

2 cloves garlic, minced

2 tablespoons snipped fresh dill, plus extra for garnish

½ teaspoon caraway seeds

1 teaspoon salt

¼ teaspoon freshly ground black pepper

6 cups Master Chicken Broth or canned, low-sodium broth

Sour cream (optional)

1 Lightly spray a 4- to 6-quart slow cooker with vegetable oil cooking spray.

2 Place the remaining ingredients in the slow cooker and stir to combine.

3 Cover and cook on low for 8 to 10 hours, or until the vegetables are tender. Add salt to taste.

4 If desired, serve with dollops of sour cream and fresh dill.

Per serving: *Calories 145 (From Fat 12); Fat 1.5g (Saturated 0g); Cholesterol 1mg; Sodium 1046mg; Carbohydrate 28g (Dietary Fiber 6g); Protein 7g.*

Forms of barley

Most of the barley eaten in the United States has been milled to remove the bran. Less-refined forms are available at health food stores. Here are the most common types of barley you'll find at the store:

✔ **Hulled barley:** This form of barley is worth seeking out because of its high nutrient and fiber content. Because only the outer hull is removed, the bran is left intact. It contains more iron and trace minerals than pearled barley, and four times the thiamin.

✔ **Pearl barley:** To produce these pearly white granules, the barley grains are scoured six times during milling to completely remove their double outer husk and bran layer. This process also removes nutrients and some firmness. Pearl barley cooks faster than hulled barley and has a delicate, nutty flavor, making it very popular for cooking.

✔ **Pot or Scotch barley:** Usually found in health food stores, this less-refined version of pearl barley is milled only three times, retaining part of the bran.

Chowders

Chowders remind us of vacation. Unlike chicken soup, they are regional and vary depending on geography and the local population. When we go to places on the coast, we seek out fish and seafood chowders that reflect the nautical heritage of the area. In rural farming communities, we expect bowls filled with chunky, garden-fresh vegetables simmered in a thick soup base. With this in mind, we share with you two of our favorite chowder recipes.

Fisherman's Chowder

This is the sort of chowder we imagine that fishermen have slowly simmering in the galley on their trawlers as they bring in their nets with the day's catch. It lends itself to the addition of many types of seafood. Try substituting 16 ounces of peeled, cleaned shrimp along with a dozen little neck clams for the monkfish.

Preparation time: *20 minutes*

Cooking time: *Low 7 to 8 hours*

Yield: *6 servings*

2 tablespoons olive oil

1 medium onion, chopped

2 cloves garlic, chopped

1 medium green bell pepper, cored, seeded, and diced

2 celery stalks, chopped

2 large potatoes, peeled and diced

2 cans (14.5 ounces each) basil-, oregano-, and garlic-flavored diced tomatoes

2 cups clam-flavored tomato juice

1 cup dry white wine or vegetable broth

¼ teaspoon cayenne pepper

1 teaspoon salt

¼ teaspoon freshly ground black pepper

1 pound of monkfish or other firm-fleshed whitefish, cut into 1-inch pieces

3 tablespoons minced Italian flat-leaf parsley

1 Spray a 4- to 6-quart slow cooker with vegetable oil cooking spray.

2 Heat the olive oil in a medium nonstick skillet over medium heat. Add the onion, garlic, green pepper, and celery and cook until soft, 7 to 8 minutes.

3 Place the cooked vegetable mixture in the slow cooker. Add the potatoes, canned tomatoes, tomato juice, wine, cayenne pepper, salt, and black pepper. Stir to combine.

4 Cover and cook on low for 7 to 8 hours, or until the potatoes are tender. Add the fish and parsley and cook for 15 to 20 minutes, or until the fish flakes when cut with a fork.

Per serving: Calories 264 (From Fat 54); Fat 6g (Saturated 1g); Cholesterol 19mg; Sodium 1390mg; Carbohydrate 31g (Dietary Fiber 3g); Protein 15g.

Corn and Lima Bean Chowder

Lima beans are one of those foods that evoke strong emotions: Either you like them or you hate them — there's really no middle ground. We both happen to like them. Having grown up on a farm in Ashtabula, Ohio, Glenna remembers sitting on the back porch on hot August afternoons shelling lima beans with her mother. Tom, on the other hand, thinks of lima beans as a tender version of his favorite fava bean. Regardless how you see it, we decided to turn these pale green oval beans into an end-of-the-summer chowder by pairing them up with farm-fresh corn and vibrant red bell peppers.

Preparation time: *20 minutes*

Cooking time: *Low 7 to 8 hours*

Yield: *6 servings*

2 tablespoons vegetable oil

1 large onion, chopped

1 large leek, white and light green parts only, washed well to remove all the grit, sliced thin

1 large red bell pepper, cored, seeded, and diced

1 cup fresh lima beans or 1 package (10 ounces) frozen lima beans, thawed

6 ears fresh corn, kernels sliced from the cob, or 3 cups frozen corn kernels, thawed

2 large potatoes, peeled and diced

4 cups Master Chicken Broth (Chapter 14) or canned low-sodium chicken broth

1 can (12 ounces) evaporated milk

1 teaspoon salt

¼ teaspoon freshly ground black pepper

4 fresh basil leaves, cut into very thin strips

1 Spray a 4- to 6-quart slow cooker with vegetable oil cooking spray.

2 Heat the vegetable oil in a large nonstick skillet over medium heat. Add the onion, leek, and red pepper and cook until soft, 7 to 8 minutes.

3 Place the cooked vegetable mixture in the slow cooker. Add the lima beans, corn, potatoes, chicken broth, evaporated milk, salt, and black pepper. Stir to combine.

4 Cover and cook on low for 7 to 8 hours, or until the vegetables are tender. Stir in the basil strips before serving.

Per serving: Calories 317 (From Fat 91); Fat 10g (Saturated 3g); Cholesterol 17mg; Sodium 813mg; Carbohydrate 47g (Dietary Fiber 6g); Protein 13g.

Chili

Not unlike clam chowder's outspoken "white versus red" aficionados, chili enthusiasts are equally passionate about what they consider to be authentic chili. Originating in what is today Texas, the original chili con carne most likely consisted of meat cooked with chili peppers. Although no one is certain, it is believed that beans were added sometime around the 1920s and tomatoes ten years later. This regionally popular dish became mainstream during the Depression and WWII, when home cooks were looking for cheap and easy ways to turn a small amount of meat into a meal.

With guarded recipes and secret ingredients, many Americans are passionate about their chili. The slow cooker is perfect for making chili, which benefits from a slow simmer. We provide you with three very different recipes: a chunky vegetable chili that can easily become vegetarian by substituting vegetable broth for chicken broth, a more traditional meat and bean chili to feed a small army, and — finally — an unusual but very delicious white chicken chili.

☞ *Chunky Vegetable Chili*

This chili, which is like a bowl of very thick vegetable soup, combines some of our favorite beans along with a rich, spicy tomato broth for added zest and flavor. You can be creative when you make this dish by adding other vegetables that may be in season or in your refrigerator.

Preparation time: *20 minutes*

Cooking time: *Low 7 to 8 hours*

Yield: *6 servings*

2 tablespoons olive oil

1 large onion, chopped

4 cloves garlic, minced

1 large green bell pepper, cored, seeded, and chopped

1 large red bell pepper, cored, seeded, and chopped

2 carrots, chopped

2 celery stalks, chopped

1 tablespoon ground chili powder

2 teaspoons ground cumin

1 teaspoon paprika

2 teaspoons dried oregano

1 teaspoon salt

1 can (15.5 ounces) black beans, drained and rinsed under cold water

1 can (15.5 ounces) red kidney beans, drained and rinsed under cold water

1 can (15.5 ounces) chickpeas, drained and rinsed under cold water

1 can (14.5 ounces) diced tomatoes

2 cups spicy tomato juice or Bloody Mary mix

1 bunch cilantro, leaves only, chopped

Shredded cheddar cheese (optional)

1 Spray a 6-quart slow cooker with vegetable oil cooking spray.

2 Heat the olive oil in a large nonstick skillet over medium heat. Add the onion, garlic, and peppers and cook until soft, 7 to 8 minutes. Add the carrots, celery, chili powder, cumin, paprika, oregano, and salt. Cook for 5 minutes.

3 Place the cooked vegetables in the slow cooker. Add the black beans, kidney beans, chickpeas, tomatoes, and tomato juice. Stir to combine.

4 Cover and cook on low for 7 to 8 hours, or until the vegetables are tender. Stir in the cilantro before serving. If desired, garnish with the cheddar cheese.

Per serving: Calories 276 (From Fat 58); Fat 6g (Saturated 1g); Cholesterol 0mg; Sodium 1645mg; Carbohydrate 47g (Dietary Fiber 15g); Protein 13g.

Tailgate Chili for a Crowd

This recipe is meant to feed a crowd of hungry people, providing at least 10 hearty servings. It's the perfect dish to prepare for a tailgate party before the game or at halftime. Because it freezes well, you could also make a batch of this chili and freeze it in dinner-size portions to be eaten on rainy days when time is short. You can spice it up or not, depending on the type of salsa you prefer.

Preparation time: *20 minutes*

Cooking time: *8 hours*

Yield: *10 servings*

2 pounds lean ground beef or ground turkey

2 jars (16 ounces each) your favorite brand of chunky salsa

2 cans (14.5 ounces each) diced tomatoes, undrained

2 cans (15 ounces each) red kidney beans, drained and rinsed under cold water

1 bag (16 ounces) frozen corn kernels, thawed

2 tablespoons ground chili powder

2 teaspoons ground cumin

2 teaspoons garlic salt

2 teaspoons dried oregano

Shredded cheddar cheese (optional)

1 Lightly spray a 6-quart slow cooker with vegetable oil cooking spray.

2 Brown the ground beef in a large nonstick skillet until no longer pink, stirring to break up any large pieces. Drain off any fat. Place the beef in the slow cooker.

3 Add the salsa, tomatoes, kidney beans, corn, chili powder, cumin, garlic salt, and oregano. Stir to combine.

4 Cover and cook on low for 8 hours. If desired, garnish with the cheddar cheese.

Per serving: *Calories 371 (From Fat 149); Fat 17g (Saturated 6.5g); Cholesterol 63mg; Sodium 1171mg; Carbohydrate 32g (Dietary Fiber 9g); Protein 25g.*

White Bean and Chicken Chili

This hearty stewlike chili is different from the typical chili in that it doesn't have any ground chili powder or tomato, and is made with chicken. Nevertheless, the flavors are bold, making for a different yet delicious chili.

Preparation time: *25 minutes*

Cooking time: *7 to 8 hours*

Yield: *6 servings*

3 tablespoons olive oil

2 boneless chicken breasts

1 medium onion, chopped

4 cloves garlic, minced

1 medium-size jalapeño pepper, seeded and chopped

2 teaspoons dried oregano

1 teaspoon ground cumin

2 cans (15 ounces each) white kidney beans, drained and rinsed under cold water

3 cups Master Chicken Broth (see Chapter 14) or canned low-sodium chicken broth

½ cup minced cilantro leaves (optional)

2 cups shredded sharp cheddar cheese (optional)

1 Lightly spray a 4- to 6-quart slow cooker with vegetable oil cooking spray.

2 Heat 2 tablespoons of the olive oil in a large nonstick skillet over medium-high heat. Add the chicken breasts and cook until no longer pink on the outside, about 5 to 6 minutes. Remove and place in the slow cooker. Add the remaining oil and cook the onion, garlic, jalapeño pepper, oregano, and cumin for 7 to 8 minutes, or until soft. Place in the slow cooker.

3 Add the white kidney beans and broth. Stir to combine.

4 Cover and cook on low for 7 to 8 hours, or until the chicken is very tender and shreds easily.

5 Remove the chicken from the slow cooker and shred with a fork. Return to the slow cooker and stir to combine. Add salt to taste. To thicken the chili, mash some of the beans against the side of the pot with the back of a large mixing spoon. If desired, garnish with the cilantro and cheese.

Per serving: *Calories 409 (From Fat 199); Fat 22g (Saturated 9.5g); Cholesterol 80mg; Sodium 1075mg; Carbohydrate 26g (Dietary Fiber 8g); Protein 34g.*

Chapter 8

Slow Simmering Stews

● ●

In This Chapter

▶ Preparing stew meats

▶ Discovering tips to great stew making

▶ Stirring up some savory one-pot meals

● ●

Stewed meat and vegetables appear in the cooking pot of every culture around the world. In fact, after meat roasted over an open fire, stew was probably the next dish to be discovered by primitive humans as they began to expand their culinary horizons, and there's no wonder why. When properly prepared, a well-made stew is rich in flavor and texture, its ingredients bound together in a glossy sauce. Although stew is relatively simple to prepare, you still need to follow some basic steps to achieve the best results possible.

Preparing Your Stew Meat

Stews are usually made with a combination of meat or poultry and vegetables, which should be cut into uniform cubes or pieces — about ½ to 3 inches — so that they cook evenly. For the most part, we prefer not to buy prepackaged meat labeled as "stew meat." You have no idea what's in those packaged meats, which may include bits and pieces from different cuts, not to mention lots of hidden gristle and fat.

We suggest that you buy a piece of steak or a small roast and trim and cut it yourself into cubes. The best beef stew is made from more flavorful, less tender cuts like chuck, rump, brisket, and shoulder. The great thing about using slow cookers for stews is that they tenderize these less tender cuts of meat during the long, slow cooking process!

Browning and Layering

Many slow cooker recipes simply say to add all the ingredients to the slow cooker without the benefit of browning the meat or poultry. We prefer the more traditional approach of browning on the stovetop in a skillet — a step that enhances the finished stew with deep color and flavor.

To brown the meat properly, the pan must be large enough to hold the meat or poultry without crowding. If need be, brown in small batches. The oil must also be hot enough to sear the cubed pieces so that they do not release their natural juices. The meat or poultry should achieve a brown crust without burning and blackening and should be cooked evenly on all sides. For more information on browning, see Chapter 9.

Most recipes call for meat and other ingredients to be browned, usually with oil or fat, so that the outside turns deep brown and the inside stays moist. The caramelization of the pan juices also adds intense flavor to the finished dish, especially when the pan is deglazed with liquid. If preparation time is an issue, however, you can eliminate browning the beef and onion in these recipes.

Root vegetables like potatoes, carrots, beets, and turnips take longer to cook than other ingredients and need the benefit of being in the warmest part of the slow cooker. We suggest placing them on the bottom or along the sides. Another good tip is to cut them into equal sizes so that each piece takes the same amount of time to cook.

Creating a Flavorful Sauce

After browning the meat or poultry and combining it with the vegetables, you need to add cooking liquid for flavor and braising. The options are pretty broad and include broth or stock, tomato purée or sauce, or wine or beer. You can even add water, although the sauce will have less flavor. Before adding all the cooking liquid to the slow cooker, pour about a cup of it into the hot pan where you browned the meat or poultry. Bring it to a simmer and carefully scrape up any of the browned bits and caramelized juices left in the pan. After a few minutes, pour this liquid into the slow cooker for added flavor and body.

Season the stew liberally with dried herbs and salt and pepper and let it cook slowly so that each ingredient can release its flavor, ultimately creating one flavorful sauce. When cooking with fresh herbs, add them during the last 30 to 60 minutes because they will lose their flavor and fragrance if added much earlier.

After cooking the stew, you can thicken the sauce by letting it reduce, uncovered, or by adding a small amount of flour a few minutes before serving. Some stews, like our Chicken Cacciatore, are served without the benefit of thickening so that there is plenty of liquidy sauce to sop up with white rice or crusty bread.

Old-Fashioned Beef Stew

If you make only one dish in a slow cooker, let it be a good old-fashioned American stew full of fork-tender cubes of meat and chunks of fresh vegetables held together in a rich, flavorful gravy. Even though this recipe calls for potatoes, we sometimes like to substitute a pound of wide egg noodles instead, cooked *al dente*.

Preparation time: *30 minutes*

Cooking time: *Low 8 to 10 hours*

Yield: *6 servings*

Salt and pepper

3 pounds of your favorite cut of beef for stew, like chuck, cut into 1½-inch cubes

3 tablespoons olive or canola oil

1 large onion, cut in half and sliced thin

3 cups beef broth

3 carrots, peeled and sliced into ¼-inch rounds

3 large potatoes, peeled and cut into 1-inch cubes

1 bay leaf

½ teaspoon whole black peppercorns

1 cup canned tomato sauce

1 teaspoon dried thyme

2 cups frozen peas

1 tablespoon minced fresh parsley

1 Lightly spray a 6-quart slow cooker with vegetable oil cooking spray.

2 Salt and pepper the beef. Heat the olive oil in a large nonstick skillet over medium-high heat. Brown the meat in batches. Remove to a large plate and continue browning the remaining meat. Add the onion and cook until soft. Remove the onion from the pan. Pour 1 cup of the beef broth into the pan, bring to a simmer, and scrape off any browned particles. Remove from heat and set aside.

3 Layer the carrots, potatoes, and cooked onions in the slow cooker. Top with the browned beef, bay leaf, and black peppercorns. In a large mixing bowl, combine the liquid from the skillet, the remaining 2 cups broth, the tomato sauce, and thyme. Pour over the meat and vegetables.

4 Cover and cook on low for 8 to 10 hours, or until the beef and vegetables are fork-tender.

5 Stir in the peas 15 to 20 minutes before serving and cook on high. Add salt to taste. Stir in the parsley before serving.

Per serving: Calories 604 (From Fat 210); Fat 23g (Saturated 6.5g); Cholesterol 111mg; Sodium 902mg; Carbohydrate 36g (Dietary Fiber 7g); Protein 60g.

Chunky South-of-the-Border Beef Stew

With just a hint of heat, this south-of-the-border stew goes great with icy bottles of beer or frosty glasses of unsweetened iced tea. Serve with warm flour tortillas and chunks of avocado and tomato seasoned with sliced red onion, lime juice, and extra-virgin olive oil.

Preparation time: *25 minutes*

Cooking time: *Low 8 to 10 hours*

Yield: *6 servings*

Salt and pepper

2 pounds boneless beef bottom or top round steak or chuck steak, cut into ½-inch cubes

2 tablespoons olive oil

2 tablespoons chili powder

1 teaspoon ground cumin

1 teaspoon paprika

¼ teaspoon cayenne pepper

1½ cups beef broth or beer

2 carrots, peeled and coarsely chopped

2 stalks celery, coarsely chopped

1 can (14.5 ounces) stewed tomatoes

1 can (19 ounces) chickpeas or pinto beans, drained and rinsed under cold water

1 can (6 ounces) tomato paste

1 teaspoon dried oregano

¾ teaspoon salt

¼ teaspoon freshly ground black pepper

1 cup frozen corn kernels

1 Lightly spray a 4- to 6-quart slow cooker with vegetable oil cooking spray.

2 Salt and pepper the beef. Heat 1½ tablespoons of the olive oil in a large nonstick skillet over medium-high heat. Brown the meat in batches. Place the browned meat in the slow cooker.

3 Heat the remaining ½ tablespoon olive oil over low heat. Add the chili powder, cumin, paprika, and cayenne. Heat 1 minute until fragrant. Add the broth, bring to a simmer, and scrape off any browned particles. Add to the slow cooker along with the carrots, celery, tomatoes, chickpeas, tomato paste, oregano, salt, and pepper.

4 Cover and cook on low for 8 to 10 hours, or until the meat and vegetables are tender.

5 Add the corn before serving and cook on high for 15 minutes.

Tip: If you have a food processor, use it to chop the vegetables. Place the carrots, cut into 1-inch pieces, in the food processor container. Press the pulse switch a couple times; add the onion, quartered, and pulse a couple times. Add the celery and again pulse a couple times. By the time you're done, the vegetables should be coarsely chopped. If not, hit pulse a couple more times.

Per serving: *Calories 416 (From Fat 116); Fat 13g (Saturated 4g); Cholesterol 74mg; Sodium 1232mg; Carbohydrate 33g (Dietary Fiber 9g); Protein 42g.*

Asian Beef and Vegetables

This fragrant Asian-inspired stew is a nice alternative to take-out. Made with ingredients readily available at any supermarket, this dish goes together in a matter of minutes.

Preparation time: *25 minutes*

Cooking time: *Low 8 to 10 hours*

Yield: *4 servings*

1 tablespoon vegetable oil

2 pounds fillet of beef, sliced thin and then into thin strips

2 cups beef broth

1 bunch scallions, trimmed, white and green parts cut into 1-inch pieces

2 cloves garlic, minced (see Figure 8-1)

1 tablespoon grated gingerroot

1 can (8 ounces) water chestnuts, drained and rinsed under cold water

1 can (8 ounces) bamboo shoots, drained and rinsed under cold water

¼ cup soy sauce

¼ cup all-purpose flour

¼ cup water

2 cups (8 ounces) broccoli florets

2 cups hot cooked white rice

1 Lightly spray a 4- to 6-quart slow cooker with vegetable oil cooking spray.

2 Heat the vegetable oil in a large nonstick skillet over medium-high heat. Brown the beef in batches. Place the browned beef in the slow cooker. Add 1 cup broth to the skillet, bring to a simmer, and scrape off any browned particles. Pour over the meat.

3 Add the remaining 1 cup broth, the scallions, garlic, gingerroot, water chestnuts, bamboo shoots, and soy sauce to the slow cooker.

4 Cover and cook on low for 8 to 10 hours, or until the beef is tender.

5 Before serving, whisk the flour and water together and stir into the slow cooker. Add the broccoli florets and cook on high for 15 minutes. Serve with white rice.

Tip: *Beef is easier to slice into thin slices and strips if cut while partially frozen with a sharp chef's or all-purpose knife.*

Vary It: *For Asian Chicken with Vegetables, substitute the same amount of thin sliced chicken breast strips for the beef, and chicken broth for beef broth.*

Per serving: Calories 480 (From Fat 119); Fat 13g (Saturated 5g); Cholesterol 109mg; Sodium 1469mg; Carbohydrate 29g (Dietary Fiber 5g); Protein 61g.

Coq au Vin

During the romantic Camelot years of the administration of President John F. Kennedy, French cooking became popular among homemakers preparing dinner parties. Glenna remembers *coq au vin,* or chicken in wine, as a very reliable standby. Even though we took a few liberties with the preparation of this classic French dish as we adapted it to the slow cooker, the results aren't any less spectacular.

Preparation time: *25 minutes*

Cooking time: *Low 6 to 7 hours*

Yield: *4 servings*

2 tablespoons olive oil

2 pounds boneless chicken thighs, skin removed and trimmed of all visible fat

1½ cups chicken broth

4 strips uncooked bacon, chopped

4 small onions, quartered

2 cloves garlic, crushed

½ cup dry red or white wine

1 bay leaf

2 teaspoons herbes de Provence or Italian seasoning

½ teaspoon salt

¼ teaspoon freshly ground pepper

⅓ cup all-purpose flour

¼ cup water

10-ounce package white mushrooms, washed and sliced thin (see Figure 8-2)

2 tablespoons minced Italian flat-leaf parsley

1 Lightly spray a 4- to 6-quart slow cooker with vegetable oil cooking spray.

2 Heat the olive oil in a large nonstick skillet over medium-high heat. Brown the chicken in batches. Place the browned chicken in the slow cooker. Add 1 cup of broth to the skillet, bring to a simmer, and scrape off any browned particles. Pour over the chicken.

3 Add the remaining ½ cup chicken broth, the bacon, onions, garlic, wine, bay leaf, herbes de Provence, salt, and pepper to the slow cooker.

4 Cover and cook on low for 6 to 7 hours, or until the chicken and vegetables are tender.

5 Before serving, whisk the flour and water together and stir into the slow cooker. Add the mushrooms and cook on high for 15 minutes. Sprinkle with parsley before serving.

Tip: *Boneless chicken thighs are available in most supermarkets in the meat case. You can also purchase them frozen in bulk at most warehouse clubs, making a very affordable cut of chicken even less expensive. If using the frozen version, thaw overnight in the refrigerator before using.*

Per serving: *Calories 480 (From Fat 185); Fat 21g (Saturated 4.5g); Cholesterol 194mg; Sodium 791mg; Carbohydrate 17g (Dietary Fiber 2g); Protein 52g.*

Mincing Garlic

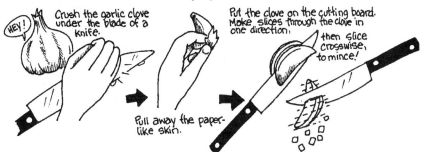

Figure 8-1: How to mince garlic.

How to Trim and Slice Mushrooms

Figure 8-2: Slicing mushrooms.

Wine for cooking

Purchasing wine to drink can be, at best, intimidating for the uninitiated. The same applies to wine that you buy for cooking. A good rule to follow is, if you wouldn't want to drink it, don't cook with it! If you're uncertain about what wine to purchase, go to a local, reputable liquor store and ask for some advice.

Also, please never use cooking wine that is marketed as such and sold in grocery stores. These wines are loaded with sodium and are of such poor quality that they can mask the fresh flavor of your ingredients.

Chicken Cacciatore

Cacciatore refers to hearty, stewlike dishes usually prepared with onions, tomatoes, mushrooms, wine, and peppers, ingredients that an Italian hunter might have in his pack. Cacciatore, in fact, is Italian for "hunter's style."

Chicken is an exciting addition to this popular Italian-American one-pot meal that we like to serve over cooked white rice. We recommend making this dish using chicken on the bone. Slow simmering in the slow cooker brings out maximum flavor.

Preparation time: *25 minutes*

Cooking time: *Low 8 to 9 hours*

Yield: *4 servings*

2 tablespoons olive oil

1 chicken (3 to 3½ pounds), cut into serving pieces

1 large onion, coarsely chopped

2 cloves garlic, sliced very thin

½ cup dry white wine

1 small pickled cherry or jalapeño pepper, seeded and coarsely chopped (optional)

10-ounce package white mushrooms, washed and sliced thin

2 cups canned crushed tomatoes

1 teaspoon salt

¼ teaspoon ground black pepper

1 tablespoon minced parsley

1 Lightly spray a 6-quart slow cooker with vegetable oil cooking spray.

2 Heat the olive oil in a large nonstick skillet over medium-high heat. Brown the chicken, onion, and garlic. Place the browned chicken in the slow cooker. Add the wine to the skillet, bring to a simmer, and scrape off any browned particles. Pour over the chicken in the slow cooker.

3 Add the cherry pepper, mushrooms, wine, tomatoes, salt, and pepper to the slow cooker.

4 Cover and cook on low for 8 to 9 hours, or until the chicken is tender. Sprinkle with parsley before serving.

Fat Buster: *To reduce the fat content, remove and discard the chicken skin before browning.*

Vary It: *Although cacciatore is usually made with chicken, it can also be made with cut-up rabbit or with thin-sliced pork chops on the bone. Just brown as indicated in Step 2 of the recipe and proceed as indicated.*

Per serving: *Calories 504 (From Fat 261); Fat 29g (Saturated 6g); Cholesterol 113mg; Sodium 1192mg; Carbohydrate 13g (Dietary Fiber 3g); Protein 40g.*

Provençal Chicken and Potato Stew

This dish is a great hearty chicken stew to savor on a cold winter's night, especially with crusty French bread and a bottle of burgundy. We particularly like this recipe when time is short because the chicken doesn't have to be browned beforehand.

Preparation time: *15 minutes*

Cooking time: *Low 8 to 10 hours*

Yield: *4 servings*

1 chicken (3 to 3½ pounds), cut into serving pieces

4 medium russet potatoes, peeled and cut into 1-inch cubes

3 large onions, thinly sliced

2 cloves garlic, sliced

1 green bell pepper, cored, seeded, and coarsely chopped

1 can (14½ ounces) plum tomatoes, coarsely chopped

½ cup red wine or chicken broth

2 teaspoons herbes de Provence or Italian seasoning

1 teaspoon salt

¼ teaspoon freshly ground black pepper

1 tablespoon minced Italian flat-leaf parsley

1 Lightly spray a 6-quart slow cooker with vegetable oil cooking spray.

2 Place the chicken, skin side down, in the slow cooker. Arrange the potatoes around the chicken.

3 In a medium bowl, combine the onions, garlic, green pepper, tomatoes, wine, herbes de Provence, salt, and pepper. Pour the mixture over the chicken.

4 Cover and cook on low for 8 to 10 hours, or until the chicken and potatoes are tender. Sprinkle with the parsley before serving.

Fat Buster: *To reduce the fat content, remove and discard the chicken skin before browning.*

Vary It: *Substitute your favorite chicken parts, such as legs or breast meat on the bone, for the whole, cut-up chicken.*

Per serving: *Calories 500 (From Fat 135); Fat 15g (Saturated 4g); Cholesterol 112mg; Sodium 969mg; Carbohydrate 42g (Dietary Fiber 3g); Protein 44g.*

Curried Chicken with Basmati Rice

This Indian-inspired recipe is seasoned with curry powder, paprika, and yogurt. Besides being good for you, plain yogurt is used throughout the world in preparing meat and poultry. Yogurt keeps food moist, tenderizes, and adds delicious flavor. For authentic results, serve this dish with fragrant basmati rice, grown in the foothills of the Himalayas for thousands of years and readily available today at most supermarkets.

Preparation time: *20 minutes*

Cooking time: *Low 8 to 10 hours*

Yield: *4 servings*

1 large onion, thinly sliced	*1½ teaspoons curry powder*
2 whole chicken breasts on bone, split (about 2 pounds)	*½ teaspoon paprika*
2 tablespoons olive oil	*1½ teaspoons salt*
1 cup beer	*Pinch freshly ground black pepper*
1 cup plain yogurt	*1 cup uncooked basmati rice*

1 Lightly spray a 4- to 6-quart slow cooker with vegetable oil cooking spray. Place the onion on the bottom of the slow cooker.

2 Remove and discard skin and all visible fat from the chicken. Cut each breast half into 3 or 4 pieces.

3 Heat the olive oil in a large nonstick skillet over medium-high heat. Brown the chicken pieces in batches. Place the browned chicken in the slow cooker. Add ½ cup of the beer to the skillet, bring to a simmer, and scrape off any browned particles. Pour over the chicken.

4 Combine the remaining ½ cup beer, the yogurt, curry powder, paprika, salt, and pepper in a large mixing bowl. Pour over the chicken.

5 Cover and cook on low for 8 to 10 hours, or until the chicken is tender.

6 Serve the chicken with the basmati rice, prepared according to the package instructions.

Per serving: *Calories 584 (From Fat 221); Fat 25g (Saturated 6g); Cholesterol 113mg; Sodium 1027mg; Carbohydrate 44g (Dietary Fiber 3g); Protein 42g.*

Lemon and Thyme Pork Stew

This dish of braised pork and vegetables with a hint of lemon makes for a delicious supper after a hard day's work, but it is also different enough to serve guests for a special occasion. With its bright colors and flavor, this dish needs only a tossed green salad and some crisp, crusty bread as accompaniments.

Preparation time: *25 minutes*

Cooking time: *Low 8 to 10 hours*

Yield: *4 servings*

1 tablespoon olive oil

2 pounds boneless pork loin, trimmed of all visible fat, cut into 1-inch cubes

3 cups chicken broth

2 large potatoes, peeled and cubed

4 parsnips, peeled and cut into 1-inch pieces

1 large red onion, coarsely chopped

2 stalks celery, coarsely chopped

2 teaspoons dried thyme

1 teaspoon freshly grated lemon rind

1 tablespoon freshly squeezed lemon juice

¾ teaspoon salt

¼ teaspoon freshly ground black pepper

¼ cup water

¼ cup flour

1 package (10 ounces) frozen French-style green beans

1 Lightly spray a 4- to 6-quart slow cooker with vegetable oil cooking spray.

2 Heat the olive oil in a large nonstick skillet over medium-high heat. Brown the pork in batches. Place the browned pork in the slow cooker. Add 1 cup of the broth to the skillet, bring to a simmer, and scrape off any browned particles. Pour over the meat in the slow cooker.

3 Add the remaining 2 cups broth, the potatoes, parsnips, onion, celery, thyme, lemon rind, lemon juice, salt, and pepper to the slow cooker.

4 Cover and cook on low for 8 to 10 hours, or until the meat and vegetables are tender.

5 Before serving, whisk the flour and water together and stir into the slow cooker. Add the green beans and cook on high for 15 minutes.

Tip: If you have a food processor, use it to chop the vegetables. Place the onion, quartered, in the food processor container and pulse a couple times. Add the celery and pulse again a couple times. By the time you're done, the vegetables should be coarsely chopped. If not, hit pulse a couple more times.

Per serving: *Calories 175 (From Fat 135); Fat 19g (Saturated 5.5g); Cholesterol 125g; Sodium 960mg; Carbohydrate 42g (Dietary Fiber 6g); Protein 58g.*

Italian Sausage Stew

When Tom was growing up on Long Island, New York, his father had an Italian-American deli renowned for its homemade sausage. Periodically his mother combined some sausage and vegetables — such as potatoes, peppers, and tomatoes — drizzled them with olive oil and a sprinkling of oregano, and roasted them in the oven for dinner, not unlike the recipe that follows.

Preparation time: *20 minutes*

Cooking time: *Low 8 to 10 hours*

Yield: *6 servings*

3 Idaho potatoes, peeled and cubed	*2 cups chicken broth*
1 tablespoon olive oil	*1 can (6 ounces) tomato paste*
2 pounds Italian sausage links, sweet, hot, or a combination	*2 teaspoons dried oregano*
	¾ teaspoon salt
2 cloves garlic, minced	*¼ teaspoon freshly ground black pepper*
1 medium onion, chopped	*2 green bell peppers, cored, seeded, and diced*
1 can (19 ounces) Italian stewed tomatoes	

1 Lightly spray a 4- to 6-quart slow cooker with vegetable oil cooking spray.

2 Place the potatoes on the bottom of the slow cooker.

3 Heat the olive oil in a large nonstick skillet over medium-high heat. Brown the sausage links. Cut each link into 1-inch pieces and place in the slow cooker along with the garlic and onion.

4 Combine the stewed tomatoes, broth, tomato paste, oregano, salt, and pepper in a large mixing bowl. Pour over the sausage.

5 Cover and cook on low for 8 to 10 hours, or until the potatoes are tender.

6 Before serving, add the green pepper and cook on high for 30 minutes.

Fat Buster: *To reduce fat content, use only sausage purchased from a reputable butcher or grocery store. Most supermarket brands are higher in fat content and contain fillers. You can also substitute lowfat chicken or turkey sausage for the Italian pork sausage.*

Per serving: *Calories 500 (From Fat 135); Fat 15g (Saturated 4g); Cholesterol 112mg; Sodium 969mg; Carbohydrate 42g (Dietary Fiber 3g); Protein 44g.*

Moroccan Vegetable Stew with Couscous

Some of the most exciting Mediterranean cooking is found in the southern Mediterranean basin of northern Africa. In the savory, exotic cooking of Morocco, fragrant stews and light, fluffy couscous are standard fare.

Preparation time: *25 minutes*

Cooking time: *Low 8 to 9 hours*

Yield: *6 servings*

2 tablespoons olive oil

2 leeks, washed well, white and light green parts only, sliced into thin rounds (see Figure 8-3)

1½ teaspoons ground cumin

1 teaspoon paprika

¼ teaspoon ground cinnamon

1 can (28 ounces) plum tomatoes

1 can (14½ ounces) chicken broth, or 1¾ cups homemade

3 medium carrots, cut into ½-inch pieces

3 small zucchini, cut into ½-inch pieces

2 large potatoes, peeled and cut into ¾-inch cubes

2 stalks celery, cut into ½-inch pieces

1 can (19 ounces) chickpeas, drained

1 teaspoon salt

Pinch freshly ground black pepper

1 package (10 ounces) frozen lima beans

1 package (10 ounces) couscous

1 Lightly spray a 4- to 6-quart slow cooker with vegetable oil cooking spray.

2 Heat the olive oil in a medium nonstick skillet over medium-high heat. Add the leeks and sauté over low heat for 3 to 4 minutes, or until soft. Add the cumin, paprika, and cinnamon and sauté for an additional minute. Place the sautéed leeks in the slow cooker.

3 Drain the tomatoes, reserving the liquid. Cut up the tomatoes. Mix the tomatoes, reserved liquid, chicken broth, carrots, zucchini, potatoes, celery, chickpeas, salt, and pepper in the slow cooker.

4 Cover and cook on low for 8 to 9 hours, or until the vegetables are tender.

5 Before serving, add the lima beans and cook on high for 15 minutes.

6 Serve the stew with cooked couscous, prepared according to package directions.

Per serving: *Calories 449 (From Fat 55); Fat 6g (Saturated 1g); Cholesterol 0mg; Sodium 1135mg; Carbohydrate 82g (Dietary Fiber 11g); Protein 17g.*

Cleaning & Trimming Leeks

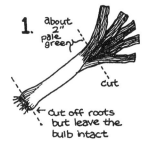

1. about 2" pale green — cut
← cut off roots but leave the bulb intact

2. slit in half
still intact

3. rinse under running cold water
I'm gonna wash that grit right outta my leeks...

Figure 8-3:
How to trim and wash leeks.

Chapter 9

The Big Cuts: Roasts

Roasting is a popular cooking method used to prepare large joints of meat, whole poultry, and even vegetables. When food is roasted, the natural juices are sealed inside, tenderizing and flavoring the food by the protective crust created when the food is either browned on the stovetop or in the oven at an initial high temperature. Once you have seared the outside of the food, sealing in the natural juices, you then lower the cooking temperature so that the food continues cooking slowly to achieve juicy, tender results. It's no wonder why a fragrant leg of lamb or crown of pork becomes the centerpiece of a holiday celebration. Besides being virtually foolproof to prepare, the resulting entrée never ceases to impress.

Using the Slow Cooker as a Roasting Pan

Neither of us can forget the first roast we made in the slow cooker. Though our experiences were at different times and in different places, the outcomes were much the same: We followed the recipe to a tee from start to finish. It smelled heavenly when we came home from running errands, but when we lifted the cover, the meat didn't resemble any roast that we've ever made before. After letting it sit 15 minutes for the juices to settle, we sliced away with ease. The meat was tender and juicy, but the flavor was lacking and the meat didn't look appetizing. It looked almost like airline food or, worse yet, hospital food — totally nondescript. What had gone wrong?

Nothing actually. In order for a good roast to develop complexity of flavors, the food has to be initially browned over high heat to sear in all that good flavor, not to mention help develop a dark, rich exterior. On the other hand, the meat couldn't possibly be any juicier or tender, and we didn't have to be at home or heat up the kitchen on a hot summer's day by turning the oven on.

After weighing the pros and cons, we set out to develop a method combining traditional roasting with the ease and convenience of a slow cooker. Our first attempt was a boneless leg of lamb. We decided to go boneless because we know that joints of meat on the bone take longer to cook and require more attention to cook evenly. After preparing the lamb with a fragrant garlic and herb paste, we browned it on the stovetop in a hot, large skillet. The aroma was intoxicating as the meat sizzled and browned before our eyes.

With step one completed, we had seared and browned the lamb to perfection. All that remained was to continue cooking it at a low temperature so that it would tenderize and cook to perfection in its own juices. Well, let us tell you, even our very own doubting Thomas (Tom, in case you hadn't guessed) was pleasantly surprised! We had proven our hypothesis to be correct — initial stovetop browning followed by slow roasting in the slow cooker makes for a perfect roast! But the best was yet to come!

As we continued cooking and testing, we were curious to see whether all cuts of meat fared equally as well. What we found was not surprising. The more expensive cuts like beef tenderloin, for example, that are usually cooked with dry, hot heat were completely acceptable, while less expensive cuts that require longer cooking in a moist environment were superb. Now we were truly impressed. Not only could we get excellent results roasting in the slow cooker, but we could also save some money along the way.

As we planned this chapter, we decided to naturally include our first home run — that incredible boneless leg of lamb, as well as other popular roasts that everyone seems to enjoy not only on Sunday but almost every day of the week.

Searing and Browning Food for Best Results

In order for your roast to cook picture perfect in the slow cooker , sear the food evenly on all sides over high heat to seal in the meat's juices so that it eventually cooks up tender and juicy with deep brown color on the outside.

Roasts sear naturally when cooked in a hot oven. Because slow cookers heat up slowly we recommend searing in a large nonstick skillet or chicken fryer on the top of the stove. The pan should be large enough to accommodate the size of the roast.

Searing is browning over a high heat.

Salt and pepper the roast generously before browning, unless otherwise indicated in your recipe. Brown on all sides over medium-high heat. Remember, you do not want to burn the food; you want to sear the exterior and at the same time give it a deep brown color. After browning, remove the food from the pan and place it in the slow cooker. Proceed as indicated in the recipe.

Always deglaze the pan with a cooking liquid like wine or broth to remove any caramelized juices or to loosen and scrape off any cooked-on food particles. These add to the depth and flavor of the gravy. Simply pour a small amount of liquid into the bottom of the pan to cover, bring to a simmer, and cook a minute or two, stirring.

Testing to See Whether the Roast Is Done

An instant-read thermometer, available at most housewares stores, is the fastest and easiest way to determine whether the roast is cooked to a safe temperature. The thermometer is a probe with a dial thermometer on the top. Insert it halfway down into the thickest part of the meat or poultry, as shown in Figure 9-1. In a couple seconds, the thermometer dial will register with the actual interior temperature.

Where to put a Dial (or Oven-proof) Meat Thermometer

Boneless Roast	Poultry	Meat with bone
Insert to core	Insert inside of the thigh	Insert into the thickest part of the meat

* For an accurate reading, do NOT touch the bone, fat, or bottom of the pan with the thermometer

Figure 9-1: Inserting a meat thermometer.

When testing a roast for doneness, remember that roasts continue to cook for 5 to 15 minutes after they're removed from the slow cooker.

Table 9-1	Thermometer Settings for Doneness		
	Rare	*Medium*	*Well Done*
Beef	135° to 140°	160°	170° to 180°
Pork	140°	160°	175°
Lamb	140°	160°	175°
Chicken			175°
Turkey, breast			170°

Warning: To avoid the risk of salmonella in poultry and *E.coli* in ground beef, they should be cooked until well done.

Favorite Roast Recipes

What could be simpler than a roast for dinner? All you have to do is season it, sear it over high heat, and let it cook up unattended while you are off doing something else. It looks good and tastes great, and hopefully you even have some leftovers for a sandwich or another meal. We provide you with some of our favorite recipes that are well suited to the slow cooker. Some of these cuts of meat benefit from the slow, moist cooking of a slow cooker, coming out meltingly tender. But we'll let you be the judge of that as you cut into your first slice.

Rosemary and Garlic Roasted Leg of Lamb

The Greeks know how to prepare lamb better than anyone in the world. We looked to the Greek isles for inspiration in preparing this leg of lamb — fragrant with garlic, lemon, herbs, and olive oil — and we believe we found it. The rubbed-on herb and garlic paste infuses into the meat as it is browned. Slow roasting in the slow cooker ensures juicy, tender results.

Preparation time: 25 minutes

Cooking time: Low 4 to 5 hours

Yield: 8 servings

4 large all-purpose potatoes, peeled and cut into ¼-inch-thick slices

1 teaspoon salt

½ teaspoon coarsely ground black pepper

6 cloves garlic, peeled and crushed

Grated zest of 1 lemon

4 sprigs fresh rosemary, needles chopped, or 1 teaspoon dried rosemary

1 trimmed, boneless leg of lamb (3 to 4 pounds), tied (see Figure 9-2)

2 tablespoons olive oil

½ cup dry white wine

1 Lightly spray a 4- to 6-quart slow cooker with vegetable oil cooking spray.

2 Layer the potatoes in the bottom of the slow cooker.

3 In a small bowl, mash the salt, pepper, garlic, lemon zest, and rosemary together with a fork to form a paste. Rub all over the lamb. Heat the olive oil in a large skillet over medium-high heat and brown the lamb evenly on all sides. Put the browned roast in the slow cooker on top of the potatoes.

4 Pour the wine in the skillet and bring to a boil, scraping to remove any pieces from the bottom. Pour over the meat.

5 Cover and cook on low for 4 to 5 hours, or until the meat tests done when sliced. The lamb should be a light pink color.

Per serving: Calories 514 (From Fat 297); Fat 33g (Saturated 13g); Cholesterol 117mg; Sodium 463mg; Carbohydrate 18g (Dietary Fiber 2g); Protein 33g.

How to Tie a Leg of Lamb

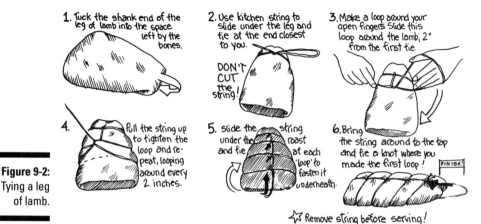

1. Tuck the shank end of the leg of lamb into the space left by the bones.

2. Use kitchen string to slide under the leg and tie at the end closest to you. DON'T CUT the string!

3. Make a loop around your open fingers. Slide this loop around the lamb, 2" from the first tie.

4. Pull the string up to tighten the loop and repeat, looping around every 2 inches.

5. Slide the string under the roast and tie at each 'loop' to fasten it underneath.

6. Bring the string around to the top and tie a knot where you made the first loop! FINISH!

☆ Remove string before serving!

Figure 9-2:
Tying a leg of lamb.

Roasted Lamb Shanks with White Beans and Herbs

If you've never eaten lamb shanks, you're in for a real treat. The lamb shank is the last joint of the leg. When prepared properly, the meat is so tender it literally falls off the bone, especially if made our way in the slow cooker. Beans and lamb make for a wonderful pairing when cooked together, as the beans absorb the hearty flavor of the lamb and herbs.

Preparation time: *35 minutes*

Cooking time: *Low 5 to 6 hours*

Yield: *4 servings*

3 lamb shanks, approximately 1¼ pounds each, trimmed of excess fat

Salt and pepper

2 tablespoons olive oil

1 medium onion, sliced thin

3 cloves garlic, peeled and crushed

1 carrot, scraped and coarsely chopped

1 vine-ripened tomato, or 2 canned plum tomatoes, seeded and coarsely chopped

2 teaspoons Italian seasoning

½ cup dry red wine

3 cans (15 ounces each) white kidney beans, drained and rinsed under cold water

1 Lightly spray a 6-quart slow cooker with vegetable oil cooking spray.

2 Salt and pepper the lamb shanks. Heat the olive oil in a large nonstick skillet over medium-high heat. Brown the lamb shanks, one at a time, until evenly browned on all sides. Place the shanks in the slow cooker.

3 Add the onion, garlic, carrot, and tomato to the skillet and cook for 6 to 8 minutes, or until soft. Add the Italian seasoning and red wine and bring to a simmer. Add the drained kidney beans and cook until heated through. Season with salt and freshly ground black pepper to taste. Spoon on top of the lamb shanks

4 Cover and cook on low for 5 to 6 hours, or until the lamb is fork-tender.

Per serving: Calories 661 (From Fat 243); Fat 27g (Saturated 9g); Cholesterol 150mg; Sodium 1244 mg; Carbohydrate 56g (Dietary Fiber 10g); Protein 59g.

Company's Coming Roast Beef with Browned New Potatoes

Roast beef has to be one of America's most popular Sunday dinner entrées. It's simple to prepare and doesn't require a lot of attention. Although roast beef is traditionally made in an oven, you can also get fine results when using the slow cooker. In fact, slow cooking gives you a great opportunity to get out of the house to take in a new museum exhibition or movie while dinner cooks on its own.

The combination of olive oil, garlic, herbs, and spices forms a great crust on the outside of the meat as it is browned. Either prepare the roast beef with the roasted potatoes called for in the recipe, or whip up a batch of mashed potatoes to serve with the pan drippings.

Preparation time: *25 minutes*

Cooking time: *Low 8 to 9 hours*

Yield: *8 servings*

1 large Spanish onion, cut into ¼-inch slices	*1 tablespoon dried thyme*
¼ cup water or beef broth	*1 teaspoon dry mustard*
1 boneless rib-eye roast (about 3 to 4 pounds), well trimmed and tied at 2-inch intervals	*1 teaspoon salt*
	½ teaspoon freshly ground black pepper
4 tablespoons olive oil	*1½ pounds very small new or red potatoes, peeled*
1 tablespoon minced garlic	

1 Lightly spray a 4- to 6-quart slow cooker with vegetable oil cooking spray.

2 Layer the onion slices on the bottom of the slow cooker. Add the water.

3 Pat the meat dry with a paper towel. Combine 2 tablespoons of the olive oil, the garlic, thyme, mustard, salt, and pepper in a small bowl. Rub all over the meat.

4 Heat a large nonstick skillet over high heat and brown the meat evenly on all sides. Place the meat in the slow cooker.

5 Heat the remaining 2 tablespoons olive oil in the skillet. Add the potatoes and cook on high heat for 5 to 8 minutes, or until golden brown. Place in the slow cooker.

6 Cover and cook on low for 8 to 9 hours, or until the meat and potatoes are fork-tender.

7 Remove the meat and let it rest, covered, 15 minutes before slicing.

Per serving: *Calories 543 (From Fat 203); Fat 23g (Saturated 7.5g); Cholesterol 127mg; Sodium 583mg; Carbohydrate 20g (Dietary Fiber 2g); Protein 61g.*

Cranberry Brisket

Brisket is a cut of meat that needs slow, moist cooking, making it perfect for the slow cooker. Thinly sliced brisket makes great party food, especially the recipe that follows. The meat can be prepared the day before and either served at room temperature or reheated. The cranberry sauce glaze makes the meat even more festive and delicious. Brisket is usually sold without the bone, cut into two parts. We recommend using the first cut, referred to as the "flat cut." It has less fat than the thicker point cut and therefore requires minimum trimming before cooking.

Preparation time: *25 minutes*

Cooking time: *Low 6 to 8 hours*

Yield: *8 servings*

3 tablespoons olive oil

2 large onions, coarsely chopped

4 cloves garlic, peeled and minced

2 carrots, scraped and coarsely chopped

2 stalks celery, coarsely chopped

1 can (16 ounces) whole berry cranberry sauce

Salt and pepper

1 trimmed fresh first-cut beef brisket, about 4 pounds

1 Lightly spray a 4- to 6-quart slow cooker with vegetable oil cooking spray.

2 Heat 2 tablespoons of the olive oil in a large nonstick skillet over medium heat. Add the onions, garlic, carrots, and celery and cook for 7 to 8 minutes, or until soft. Remove from heat and stir in the cranberry sauce. Spoon into the slow cooker.

3 Salt and pepper the brisket. Heat the remaining 1 tablespoon olive oil in the skillet over medium-high heat. Brown the brisket evenly on all sides. Place in the slow cooker on top of the cranberry mixture along with any pan drippings.

4 Cover and cook on low for 6 to 8 hours, or until the brisket is fork-tender.

5 To serve, slice the brisket into thin diagonal slices against the grain (see Figure 9-3, which shows pot roast being sliced across the grain), with plenty of sauce on the side.

Per serving: Calories 503 (From Fat 196); Fat 22g (Saturated 6.5g); Cholesterol 112mg; Sodium 352mg; Carbohydrate 27g (Dietary Fiber 2g); Protein 48g.

Cutting Pot Roast Across the Grain

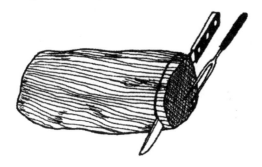

Figure 9-3:
Slicing meat across the grain.

Corned Beef and Cabbage

What would St. Paddy's Day be like without the annual wearing of the green and eating corned beef and cabbage for dinner? Readily available in most supermarkets, corned beef is beef brisket that has been cured in a seasoned brine. As with all brisket, corned beef needs to be cooked slowly so that it comes out tender. Save any leftover corned beef for great sandwiches or combine it with potatoes and onions for hash.

Preparation time: 20 minutes

Cooking time: Low 6 to 7 hours

Yield: 8 servings

4 large all-purpose potatoes, peeled and cut into ½-inch-thick slices

2 carrots, scraped and sliced thin

3- to 4-pound thin-cut corned beef brisket

1 head of green cabbage (2 pounds), cut into 8 wedges

1 tablespoon whole black peppercorns

1 bay leaf

1½ cups water

1 Lightly spray a 6-quart slow cooker with vegetable oil cooking spray.

2 Layer the potato slices on the bottom of the slow cooker along with the carrots. Place the corned beef on top of the vegetables. Position the cabbage alongside the meat. Add the peppercorns, bay leaf, and water.

3 Cover and cook on low for 6 to 7 hours, or until the meat and vegetables are fork-tender.

4 Remove the meat and let it sit, covered, 15 minutes before slicing against the grain.

Per serving: Calories 522 (From Fat 270); Fat 30g (Saturated 9.5g); Cholesterol 107mg; Sodium 274mg; Carbohydrate 28g (Dietary Fiber 5g); Protein 34 g.

Sauerbraten

This classic German dish requires that the meat sit in a sweet and sour marinade for 2 to 3 days before browning, so plan accordingly. The meat is then slow simmered for several hours until it is fork-tender.

We recommend serving sauerbraten as the Germans do — with lots of potato dumplings, boiled potatoes, or egg noodles, along with plenty of pickled red cabbage.

Preparation time: *3 days for marinating, plus 25 minutes*

Cooking time: *Low 10 to 12 hours*

Yield: *6 servings*

1 cup boiling water	2 stalks celery, coarsely chopped
½ cup red wine vinegar	2 large onions, coarsely chopped
½ cup dry red wine	1 clove garlic, peeled and crushed
¼ cup brown sugar, packed	2 bay leaves
1 teaspoon ground cloves	4-pound chuck or rump roast
1 teaspoon salt	2 tablespoons vegetable oil
½ teaspoon black peppercorns	¾ cup finely crushed gingersnaps
2 large carrots, coarsely chopped	

1 Make a marinade by combining the water, vinegar, red wine, brown sugar, cloves, salt, peppercorns, carrots, celery, onions, garlic, and bay leaves in a large glass or ceramic bowl. Place the meat in the marinade, cover, and refrigerate for 3 to 5 days, turning at least once a day.

2 Remove the meat from the marinade. Pat dry. Lightly spray the slow cooker with vegetable oil cooking spray. Pour the marinade and vegetables into the slow cooker.

3 Heat the oil in a large nonstick skillet over medium-high heat. Brown the meat evenly on all sides. Add to the slow cooker.

4 Cover and cook on low for 10 to 12 hours, or until fork-tender.

5 Remove the meat to a large platter and cover with foil. Pour the cooking liquid into a food processor or blender and process until smooth. Salt to taste. Pour back into the slow cooker. Add the gingersnaps and cook on high for 30 minutes.

6 Slice the meat across the grain into thick slices and return to the slow cooker with the gravy for serving.

Per serving: *Calories 572 (From Fat 203); Fat 19g (Saturated 5g); Cholesterol 160mg; Sodium 681mg; Carbohydrate 24g (Dietary Fiber 3g); Protein 71g.*

Our Favorite Pot Roast

There are as many variations of pot roast as there are cooks! The recipe that follows, which uses ingredients that are on hand in most home refrigerators and pantries, should be used as a guide to modify and adjust as you desire.

Rather than thicken the ensuing gravy with flour, we like to purée the cooking liquid, which is chock-full of vegetables. The puréed vegetables will thicken and add great body and taste to the liquid as it is puréed into gravy.

Preparation time: *30 minutes*

Cooking time: *Low 9 to 10 hours*

Yield: *6 to 8 servings*

2 tablespoons olive oil	*1 cup red wine or beef broth*
3- to 4-pound boneless, trimmed chuck or rump roast	*1 teaspoon dried thyme*
salt and pepper	*1 cup canned crushed tomatoes*
2 large onions, chopped	*2 tablespoons minced Italian flat-leaf parsley*
2 carrots, scraped and chopped	*1 teaspoon salt*
1 stalk celery, sliced thin	*¼ teaspoon freshly ground black pepper*

1 Lightly spray a 4- to 6-quart slow cooker with vegetable oil cooking spray.

2 Salt and pepper the meat.

3 Heat the olive oil in a large nonstick skillet over medium-high heat. Brown the meat evenly on all sides. Add to the slow cooker.

4 Add the onions, carrots, and celery to the skillet and cook for 7 to 8 minutes over medium heat until the onion is soft. Add the wine and cook for 2 minutes. Stir in the tomatoes, thyme, parsley, salt, and pepper. Bring to a simmer and cook for 2 minutes. Pour over the meat.

5 Cover and cook on low for 9 to 10 hours, or until fork-tender.

6 Remove the meat and let it sit, covered, for 15 minutes before slicing.

7 To thicken the cooking liquid for gravy, purée in a food processor or blender until smooth. Salt to taste.

Per serving (based on 6 servings): *Calories 597 (From Fat 215); Fat 24g (Saturated 7.5g); Cholesterol 181mg; Sodium 696mg; Carbohydrate 10g (Dietary Fiber 2g); Protein 75g.*

Roast Pork with Apples, Sweet Potatoes, and Plantains

If you've never cooked a pork tenderloin, you're in for a delicious surprise. Located between the loin and the spareribs, this very tender, lean cut of pork cooks up beautifully. We pair it with some great flavors and textures, including tart apples and sweet plantains. Plantains, shown in Figure 9-4, are a very large, firm variety of banana that has become increasingly more available in supermarkets over the years. The plantain increases in flavor, going from a squashlike consistency and flavor when green, to sweeter and softer as the fruit ripens and the skin turns from yellow to black.

Preparation time: *25 minutes*

Cooking time: *Low 8 to 9 hours*

Yield: *6 servings*

2 Granny Smith apples, cored and cut into ½-inch-thick slices

2 large sweet potatoes, peeled and cut into 1-inch-thick slices

2 ripe plantains (heavily spotted yellow to brown), peeled and cut into 1-inch-thick slices

1 large red onion, cut in half and sliced thin

2 tablespoons brown sugar

3 tablespoons olive oil

Salt and pepper

3-pound pork loin, tied

1 teaspoon ground cumin

1 teaspoon dried thyme

1½ cups chicken broth

1 Lightly spray a 6-quart slow cooker with vegetable oil cooking spray.

2 Add the apple slices, sweet potatoes, plantains, onion, brown sugar, and 2 tablespoons of the olive oil. Toss to combine. Spread evenly over the bottom of the slow cooker.

3 Salt and pepper the pork. Sprinkle with the cumin and thyme. Heat the remaining 1 tablespoon olive oil in a large nonstick skillet over medium-high heat. Brown the pork loin evenly on all sides. Place in the slow cooker. Pour the chicken broth over the meat.

4 Cover and cook on low for 8 to 9 hours, or until the meat, vegetables, and fruit are fork-tender.

Per serving: *Calories 692 (From Fat 329); Fat 37g (Saturated 11g); Cholesterol 125mg; Sodium 316mg; Carbohydrate 47g (Dietary Fiber 5g); Protein 44g.*

Figure 9-4:
Plantains are members of the banana family.

Lemon Chicken

Even though this chicken doesn't brown as it would if it were roasted, it's so fragrant and moist that it has become one of our favorite dinnertime meals! If you're using a large 6-quart slow cooker, you can fit two 3-pound chickens in it, but remember to adjust the other ingredients accordingly. If you cook two chickens, you can feed a large crowd or have plenty of leftovers for making chicken sandwiches or chicken salad.

Preparation time: *15 minutes*

Cooking time: *Low 7 to 8 hours*

Yield: *4 servings*

3- to 4-pound whole chicken

2 tablespoons poultry seasoning with salt

1 lemon, halved

4 cloves garlic, peeled and crushed

2 tablespoons olive oil

Freshly ground black pepper

1 tablespoon minced Italian flat-leaf parsley

1 Lightly spray a 4- to 6-quart slow cooker with vegetable oil cooking spray.

2 Rinse the chicken and pat dry with paper towels. Remove and discard any excess skin or fat. Rub the cavity with some of the poultry seasoning. Place the lemon halves and garlic cloves in the cavity. Rub the skin with the remaining poultry seasoning. Place the chicken in the slow cooker. Drizzle with the olive oil. Sprinkle liberally with the pepper and parsley.

3 Cover and cook on low for 7 to 8 hours, or until the chicken tests done.

Per serving: Calories 428 (From Fat 183); Fat 20g (Saturated 4.5g); Cholesterol 165mg; Sodium 432mg; Carbohydrate 5g (Dietary Fiber 1g); Protein 55g.

Pulled Pork Barbecue

If you've ever traveled to the South, you know that one of the great dishes enjoyed throughout the Carolinas is pork barbecue. Although barbecue for most of us evokes memories of grilled burgers or hot dogs, in the Carolinas, barbecue is pork butt that is slowly cooked with a "mop" or top-secret barbecue sauce over a smoldering fire until the meat is so tender that it virtually falls apart and can be pulled apart with a fork.

The shredded meat is then served with barbecue sauce and drippings over soft sandwich rolls. Coleslaw and pickles make crunchy sides to this dish.

Preparation time: *25 minutes*

Cooking time: *Low 8 to 10 hours*

Yield: *6 servings*

2 tablespoons olive oil

3- to 4-pound boneless pork butt or shoulder roast, trimmed of all visible fat, tied, and pierced all over several times with a knife

1 large onion, sliced thin

2 cloves garlic, minced

2 cups of your favorite bottled barbecue sauce

½ cup water

Hot pepper sauce (optional)

1 Lightly spray a 4- to 6-quart slow cooker with vegetable oil cooking spray.

2 Heat the olive oil in a large nonstick skillet over medium-high heat. Add the pork and brown evenly on all sides. Place in the slow cooker.

3 Add the onion and garlic to the skillet and cook for 7 to 8 minutes, or until soft. Add the barbecue sauce, water and, if desired, the hot pepper sauce. Bring to a simmer. Pour over the meat.

4 Cover and cook on low for 8 to 10 hours, or until fork-tender.

5 Remove the meat from the slow cooker and shred with a fork. Return the meat to the slow cooker and stir to combine with the sauce. Spoon meat onto sandwich buns.

Per serving: Calories 476 (From Fat 180); Fat 20g (Saturated 5.5g); Cholesterol 161mg; Sodium 863mg; Carbohydrate 13g (Dietary Fiber 1g); Protein 58g.

Chapter 10

Casseroles

*A*lthough many people like to sit down to a big three-course dinner with a seemingly endless variety of side dishes, it's probably best to save large dinners for weekends or special occasions when you have ample time to enjoy them. On the other nights, a dish of meat and vegetables bound together with a savory sauce will suffice, satisfying even the heartiest of appetites. Nothing is easier than whipping up a casserole to cook in the slow cooker for hours while you're at work or play.

The American Casserole: A 20th-Century Invention

Although dishes of scalloped meat, potatoes, and vegetables had been popular since the late 1800s, the casserole as we know it today came into play during World War I, when people were encouraged to use every scrap of food they had on hand. Early dishes prepared *en casserole,* a term coined around the turn of the century, usually included leftover or browned and cooked meat, poultry, or fish that was then mixed with vegetables, rice, crumbs, or macaroni, and bound together with a cooking liquid or sauce.

Each generation following World War I has come to rely upon the casserole as an expedient and thrifty way to get dinner on the table. During the Depression of the 1930s and the food-rationing of the World War II years of the 1940s, casseroles allowed Americans to take the few ingredients they had on hand and turn them into satisfying meals. As Americans began to prosper and began to entertain more and more at home in the 1950s and '60s, the casserole provided Mrs. Home Cook with quick and easy ways to prepare sophisticated dinners, such as shrimp creole and stroganoff, for family and friends.

As many women entered the work force in the 1970s and '80s, the slow cooker helped bolster the popularity of the humble casserole. Home cooks no longer had to scramble at dinner time to get a meal on the table. Instead, they needed only to combine some ground beef, canned veggies, and a can of condensed soup in the slow cooker before they left for work in the morning. During the 8 to 9 hours that Mom and Dad were at work and the kids were in school, the ingredients were cooking so dinner was ready when the family got home. Besides looking for convenience, consumers, faced with the ups and downs of an uncertain economy, were also trying to save money by using less expensive ingredients, like tougher cuts of meat, that would ultimately cook up tender and succulent in the slow cooker.

Even during periods of economic growth and prosperity, as we experienced during the 1990s, slow cooker casseroles continue to be a quick and easy alternative to take-out and fast food. As a sign of the times and our concern for healthy cooking, many of today's slow cooker casseroles rely less on high fat ingredients and more on whole grains, vegetables, and dried legumes. Today's slow cooker casseroles, elevated by new popular tastes and combinations of ingredients, appear not only on the household tables of the health conscious and time starved, but make their mark socially as well. When you think of it, where would potluck suppers, the backbone of many community fund-raisers, be without the slow cooker casserole?

New Favorites from Old Classics

Even in today's foodie culture and environment, where we can watch cooking and food-related shows on cable TV 24 hours a day, the casserole continues to thrive — though relying more on fresh ingredients than processed — providing a sense of comfort and relief when time is short.

Because we had a lot of recipes to choose from in writing this chapter, we decided to provide what we hope to be an interesting balance between updated all-time favorites and some new creations. Some of our classic favorites include Swiss steak and macaroni and cheese. We've seen Tex-Mex expand into cowboy and "on the range" cooking over the past few years, so we created a hearty beef and beans casserole that will satisfy even the hungriest of cowpokes. And because we don't always have time to make family favorites like stuffed cabbage rolls, we streamlined the recipe to get the same flavor, albeit in different packing, so to speak. With a bit of something for everyone, we're certain you won't be disappointed, nor hungry!

Stuffed Cabbage Casserole

This recipe of Eastern European origin is a godsend for anyone who enjoys eating stuffed cabbage but who doesn't have all day to prepare it. Known to Russians as *golubka*, Czechs and Hungarians as *halupki,* and Poles and Jews from around the world as *holishkes,* this recipe is perfect for those who don't have a grandmother to make the traditional version for them. Though it contains all the same flavors and ingredients, instead of rolling the meat mixture in cabbage leaves, everything gets layered in the slow cooker.

Preparation time: *25 minutes*

Cooking time: *Low 4 to 5 hours*

Yield: *6 servings*

2 tablespoons olive oil	*2 tablespoons minced Italian flat-leaf parsley*
1 large onion, chopped	*1 can (28 ounces) tomato sauce*
2 cloves garlic, minced	*2 cups water*
1 pound (½ medium head) green cabbage, shredded (see Figure 10-1)	*1 teaspoon salt*
1 pound lean ground beef	*¼ teaspoon freshly ground black pepper*
1 cup uncooked, long-grain converted rice	*½ cup grated Pecorino Romano cheese*

1 Lightly spray a 4- to 6-quart slow cooker with vegetable oil cooking spray.

2 Heat the olive oil in a large nonstick skillet over medium-high heat. Add the onion, garlic, and cabbage and cook for 7 to 8 minutes, or until soft. Remove to a large mixing bowl. Add the ground beef to the skillet and cook until no longer pink. Add to the cabbage along with the rice and parsley. Stir to combine.

3 Combine the tomato sauce, water, salt, and black pepper in a mixing bowl. Set 2 cups of the tomato sauce mixture aside for the top.

4 Cover the bottom of the slow cooker with half the tomato sauce. Cover with one-third of the cabbage and meat mixture. Cover with the remaining sauce and a third of the grated cheese. Repeat the layering, ending with the reserved 2 cups of tomato sauce and the last third of the grated cheese.

5 Cover and cook on low for 4 hours, or until the rice tests done and the casserole is hot through the center.

Per serving: Calories 419 (From Fat 193); Fat 20g (Saturated 7.5g); Cholesterol 59mg; Sodium 1397mg; Carbohydrate 37g (Dietary Fiber 3g); Protein 22g.

Shredding Cabbage

First, cut the cabbage into halves, then into quarters. Start with one quarter.

Put the round side down on the cutting board and hold it by the pointed side of the wedge.

Use a big, sharp knife and cut thin slices along the angle of the wedge.

Figure 10-1: Shredding cabbage.

Swiss Steak

It's anyone's guess why this English dish of smothered meat and vegetables is called Swiss steak, popular since the early 1900s. The slow cooking of the meat after browning makes the meat extremely tender.

Preparation time: *25 minutes*

Cooking time: *Low 5 to 7 hours*

Yield: *4 servings*

¼ cup all-purpose flour

1¼ teaspoons salt

½ teaspoon freshly ground black pepper

1½ pounds round or flank steak, cut into 4 to 6 pieces to fit in slow cooker

3 tablespoons olive oil

1 can (14½ ounces) basil-, oregano-, and garlic-flavored diced tomatoes

½ cup water

1 tablespoon Worcestershire sauce

½ teaspoon dried thyme

8 small new potatoes, quartered

1 large onion, thinly sliced

1 Lightly spray a 4- to 6-quart slow cooker with vegetable oil cooking spray.

2 Combine the flour, ½ teaspoon of the salt, and ¼ teaspoon of the pepper in a shallow dish. Place the meat in the flour mixture and press to coat. Turn and coat the other side.

3 Heat the olive oil in a large nonstick skillet over medium-high heat. Add the steak in batches and brown evenly on both sides, about 5 to 6 minutes per side.

4 While the steak browns, combine the tomatoes, water, Worcestershire sauce, thyme, and remaining ¾ teaspoon of salt in a mixing bowl.

5 Layer the potatoes, browned steak, and onion in the slow cooker. Pour the tomato mixture over the meat and vegetables. Sprinkle with the remaining ¼ teaspoon pepper.

6 Cover and cook on low for 5 to 7 hours, or until the meat and vegetables are tender.

Per serving: *Calories 528 (From Fat 229); Fat 26g (Saturated 7.5g); Cholesterol 72mg; Sodium 1136mg; Carbohydrate 31g (Dietary Fiber 3g); Protein 42g.*

Canned soup and casseroles

A milestone in the evolution of the casserole came in 1916, when Campbell Soup Company — which had invented and introduced canned soup in 1897 (sold for ten cents a can) — published *Helps for the Hostess,* a collection of recipes using condensed soup. For the first time, housewives could use canned soup, instead of long-simmering sauces, when making casseroles. Canned soup made cooking more convenient and appealing to housewives, who were looking for shortcuts in the kitchen and ways to cut

expenses. Casseroles were given another canned-soup boost in 1934, when Campbell Soup Company introduced cream of mushroom soup, resulting in an almost limitless array of dish possibilities. Not surprisingly, more than 80 years later, cooking with canned soup still remains popular — with over 440 million cans of Campbell's Soup used every year in an endless variety of easy-to-prepare recipes, many of which can be prepared in slow cookers.

Baked Beans and Beef

Chock-full of beans and beef in a sweet-and-spicy tomato sauce, this recipe is the perfect trail dish to feed all the hungry cowpokes in your family!

Preparation time: *20 minutes*

Cooking time: *Low 5 to 6 hours*

Yield: *10 servings*

1 pound lean ground beef

1 large onion, chopped

2 cans (28 ounces each) baked beans, any variety

1 can (15 ounces) kidney beans, drained and rinsed under cold water

1 can (15 ounces) black beans, drained and rinsed under cold water

1 can (14½ ounces) diced tomatoes

½ cup ketchup

½ cup brown sugar

2 tablespoons molasses or maple syrup

2 tablespoons dry mustard

Pinch of cayenne pepper

1 Lightly spray a 6-quart slow cooker with vegetable oil cooking spray.

2 Brown the ground beef and onion in a large nonstick skillet over medium-high heat. Drain and discard any accumulated fat. Place the ground beef mixture in the slow cooker.

3 Add the baked beans, kidney beans, black beans, tomatoes, ketchup, brown sugar, molasses, dry mustard, and cayenne. Stir together.

4 Cover and cook on low for 5 to 6 hours.

Per serving: Calories 372 (From Fat 79); Fat 9g (Saturated 3g); Cholesterol 31g; Sodium 1305mg; Carbohydrate 61g (Dietary Fiber 12g); Protein 21g.

Stuffed Peppers

Although this dish isn't really a casserole in the true sense, stuffed peppers — a classic, slow cooker recipe — are a self-contained meal: mini pepper casseroles stuffed with a savory meat and rice filling. Quick and easy to prepare, this recipe will be a welcome addition to your repertoire of meals. If you're using a 4-quart slow cooker, be sure that it's oval so that the peppers fit in one layer.

Preparation time: *20 minutes*

Cooking time: *Low 4 to 5 hours*

Yield: *6 servings*

6 large bell peppers, tops cut off, cored, and seeded

1 pound lean ground beef

1½ cups cooked, long-grain converted rice

2 large eggs, lightly beaten

½ cup grated Pecorino Romano cheese

2 tablespoons minced parsley

½ teaspoon salt

½ teaspoon black pepper

1 can (28 ounces) tomato sauce

½ teaspoon garlic powder

1 Lightly spray a 4- to 6-quart slow cooker with vegetable oil cooking spray.

2 Cut a very small hole in the bottom of each pepper. Doing so allows moisture and steam to enter the peppers, promoting more even cooking. Combine the ground beef, rice, eggs, cheese, parsley, salt, and ¼ teaspoon of the black pepper in a large mixing bowl. Spoon the meat mixture into the peppers, dividing evenly; do not pack down.

3 Stand the stuffed peppers upright in the slow cooker.

4 Combine the tomato sauce, garlic powder, and the remaining ¼ teaspoon black pepper in a large mixing bowl or mixing cup. Spoon the sauce over the peppers.

5 Cover and cook on low for 4 to 5 hours, or until the peppers are fork tender.

Per serving: Calories 352 (From Fat 158); Fat 18g (Saturated 5g); Cholesterol 130mg; Sodium 1222mg; Carbohydrate 26g (Dietary Fiber 3g); Protein 23g.

Noodles Stroganoff Casserole

Casseroles like noodles stroganoff were popular dishes for entertaining during the baby boomer days of the 1950s and early '60s. They were simple to assemble beforehand and then just pop into the oven before company arrived. With a foreign sounding name, they also added a bit of sophistication and flair to entertaining at home. This stroganoff-like casserole from Glenna's recipe file box has fed many a hungry mouth! It's simple to make because it uses already prepared Alfredo sauce, available in the refrigerated section of most supermarkets.

If you're watching your red meat intake, you may substitute ground turkey (or 5 cups diced, cooked chicken) for the ground beef.

Preparation time: *20 minutes*

Cooking time: *Low 2½ to 3½ hours*

Yield: *6 servings*

1½ pounds lean ground beef

1 large onion, chopped

1 clove garlic, minced

½ teaspoon dried marjoram

½ teaspoon dried thyme

1 can (4 ounces) sliced mushrooms, drained and rinsed under cold water

1 can (8 ounces) tomato sauce

1 container (10 ounces) Alfredo sauce

½ pound medium egg noodles, cooked al dente and drained

½ cup shredded Monterey Jack cheese

1 Lightly spray a 4- to 6-quart slow cooker with vegetable oil cooking spray.

2 Brown the ground beef, onion, and garlic in a large nonstick skillet over medium-high heat. Drain and discard any accumulated fat. Place the meat mixture in the slow cooker.

3 Add the marjoram, thyme, mushrooms, tomato sauce, Alfredo sauce, noodles, and cheese. Stir together.

4 Cover and cook on low for 2½ to 3½ hours.

Per serving: *Calories 540 (From Fat 259); Fat 29g (Saturated 13g); Cholesterol 136mg; Sodium 630mg; Carbohydrate 37g (Dietary Fiber 3g); Protein 33g.*

Macaroni and Cheese

Everyone likes good ole mac 'n' cheese. With as many recipes for it as there are fish in the sea, this is one of our quick and easy favorites for the slow cooker — made even simpler with the use of condensed cheddar cheese soup. If you want to make the recipe in a 6-quart slow cooker, double the ingredients.

Preparation time: *25 minutes*

Cooking time: *High 2½ hours*

Yield: *4 servings*

2 cans (10¾ ounces each) condensed cheddar cheese soup

1 soup can milk (10 fluid ounces)

2 teaspoons prepared mustard

¼ teaspoon freshly ground black pepper

4 cups cooked elbow macaroni, cooked al dente (3 cups uncooked)

1 clove garlic, minced

¼ cup bread crumbs

1 Lightly spray a 4-quart slow cooker with vegetable oil cooking spray.

2 Mix together the soup, milk, mustard, and pepper in the slow cooker. Add the macaroni, toss, and stir together.

3 Cover and cook on high for 2½ hours, or until hot in the center.

4 Lightly spray a large nonstick skillet with cooking spray. Add the garlic and bread crumbs. Lightly toast the bread crumbs over medium heat. Sprinkle over the macaroni and cheese before serving.

Vary It: *Add 1 package (10 ounces) frozen chopped broccoli, thawed and excess water squeezed out, along with the macaroni.*

Per serving: *Calories 331 (From Fat 105); Fat 12g (Saturated 4g); Cholesterol 19mg; Sodium 1325mg; Carbohydrate 55g (Dietary Fiber 3g); Protein 12g.*

Jambalaya

If you've ever been to Louisiana, then you are sure to have eaten jambalaya, a wonderful one-pot dish that combines a variety of the most popular ingredients used in Creole cooking. Some quintessentially Creole ingredients found in jambalaya include green peppers and onions, smoked ham, shrimp, and spicy tomato sauce.

Preparation time: *25 minutes*

Cooking time: *Low 3½ hours*

Yield: *4 servings*

2 tablespoons olive oil

1 large onion, chopped

3 cloves garlic, minced

2 stalks celery, sliced

1 green bell pepper, cored, seeded, and chopped

2 cups diced Black Forest ham or other smoky-flavored ham

1 can (28 ounces) crushed tomatoes

1 tablespoon minced Italian flat-leaf parsley

1 teaspoon dried thyme

2 teaspoons salt

¼ teaspoon freshly ground black pepper

Hot pepper sauce

1 cup uncooked, long-grain converted rice

1 pound large shrimp, shelled and deveined

1 Lightly spray a 4- to 6-quart slow cooker with vegetable oil cooking spray.

2 Heat the olive oil in a large nonstick skillet over medium-high heat. Add the onion, garlic, celery, and green pepper. Cook for 6 to 8 minutes, or until the onion is soft. Place in the slow cooker.

3 Add the ham, tomatoes, parsley, thyme, salt, black pepper, hot pepper sauce to taste, and rice. Stir to combine.

4 Cover and cook on low for 3 hours. Add the shrimp. Stir together and cook for 20 minutes longer, or until the shrimp are pink. Add salt to taste.

Shortcut: *If you're short on time, eliminate Step 2. Simply mix together all the ingredients, except the shrimp, in the slow cooker. Proceed with Step 4.*

Per serving: *Calories 552 (From Fat 142); Fat 16g (Saturated 5g); Cholesterol 22mg; Sodium 291mg; Carbohydrate 56g (Dietary Fiber 3g); Protein 44g.*

Tortilla Stack

An enchilada is Mexico's version of a casserole. Meat, poultry, or cheese fillings are rolled up in corn tortillas and then baked, covered with sauce. We simplify things a bit with our tortilla stack, which layers ingredients between soft corn tortillas, covered with shredded cheese. This is a great way to use leftover chicken or ground beef.

Preparation time: *15 minutes*

Cooking time: *High 2 to 3 hours*

Yield: *4 servings*

1 can (15 ounces) red kidney beans, drained and rinsed under cold water

1 cup frozen corn kernels, thawed

1 jar (12 ounces) salsa or 1½ cups Chunky Chili Sauce (Chapter 6) or Holy Guacamole Tomato Salsa (Chapter 6)

5 corn tortillas (6 inches each)

1 cup shredded cooked chicken, leftover chili, or cooked ground beef

1 cup (4 ounces) shredded sharp cheddar cheese

4 scallions, white and green parts, thinly sliced

2 tablespoons pickled jalapeño slices or canned, roasted mild chili peppers

1 Lightly spray the bottom of a 4- or 6-quart slow cooker with vegetable oil cooking spray.

2 Lightly mash the beans in a mixing bowl. Add the corn and salsa; stir to combine.

3 Place a tortilla on the bottom of the slow cooker. Top with one fourth of the bean mixture, one fourth of the chicken, one fourth of the cheese, one fourth of the sliced scallions, and one-fourth of the jalapeño slices. Repeat the layering with the remaining ingredients, ending with a tortilla and cheese.

4 Cover the slow cooker and cook on high for 2 to 3 hours, or until heated through.

5 Remove from the slow cooker with a spatula and cut into quarters.

Per serving: *Calories 400 (From Fat 111); Fat 12g (Saturated 6g); Cholesterol 59mg; Sodium 997mg; Carbohydrate 47g (Dietary Fiber 11g); Protein 28g.*

Classic Vegetable Casserole with French-Fried Onions

Our vegetable casserole creation is based on the granddaddy of all casseroles made with canned green beans and condensed soup — the Classic Green Bean Bake. The original recipe was developed by Campbell Soup Company's home economists in 1955 and has been popular ever since.

We've taken some liberties with the original recipe, replacing the condensed soup with our own homemade mushroom-cheese preparation for the slow cooker. You may substitute 2 packages (10 ounces each) frozen chopped broccoli for the green beans. If you don't have the time or inclination to make our sauce, we also include a variation that uses the familiar condensed soup.

Preparation time: 15 minutes

Cooking time: Low 4 hours

Yield: 6 servings

¼ cup (½ stick) unsalted butter

1 small onion, chopped

¾ cup minced, fresh white mushrooms

2 tablespoons all-purpose flour

1 can (12 ounces) evaporated milk

1⅔ cups grated sharp white cheddar cheese

2 packages (10 ounces each) frozen French-cut green beans, thawed

1 can (2.8 ounces) French-fried onions

1 Lightly spray a 4-quart slow cooker with vegetable oil cooking spray.

2 Melt the butter over medium heat in a medium nonstick skillet. Add the onion and mushrooms and cook for 6 to 8 minutes, or until soft. Sprinkle the flour over the mixture. Cook, stirring for a minute. Stir in the evaporated milk and cook until slightly thickened. Slowly add the cheese and stir to melt.

3 Combine the green beans and mushroom cheese sauce in the slow cooker.

4 Cover and cook on low for 4 hours. Sprinkle with French-fried onions before serving.

Shortcut: Eliminate Step 2 and substitute the homemade mushroom cheese sauce with 1 can (10¾ ounces) condensed cream of mushroom soup and 1¼ cups grated white sharp cheddar cheese.

Per serving: Calories 344 (From Fat 225); Fat 25g (Saturated 15g); Cholesterol 71mg; Sodium 347mg; Carbohydrate 15g (Dietary Fiber 3g); Protein 14g.

Sweet Potato Marshmallow Casserole

The first known recipe for sweet potato casserole dates to the 1920s and has been a popular addition to many a Thanksgiving spread ever since! The version that follows is very similar to it. Marshmallows have been the topping of choice since 1928; the addition of other ingredients such as canned, crushed pineapple or mashed bananas is up to the cook.

Because we never seem to have enough room in the oven on Thanksgiving Day, we decided to enlist the use of the slow cooker in preparing this popular side dish. You'll especially experience the joy of owning a slow cooker on Thanksgiving morning, when your oven is bursting with turkey, stuffing, and pies, and can't hold one more dish.

Preparation time: *15 minutes (if using canned sweet potatoes)*

Cooking time: *High 1 to 2 hours*

Yield: *6 servings*

4 cups mashed sweet potatoes, (2 cans, 18 ounces each, drained and mashed, or 2 pounds, 4 medium sweet potatoes, baked or steamed, and then mashed)

3 tablespoons unsalted butter, melted

1 cup canned, crushed pineapple

2 large eggs, beaten

2 tablespoons sugar

¼ teaspoon ground cinnamon

1 teaspoon salt

1 cup mini-marshmallows

1 Lightly spray a 4- to 6-quart slow cooker with vegetable oil cooking spray.

2 Mix the sweet potatoes, melted butter, pineapple, eggs, sugar, cinnamon, and salt in a large mixing bowl. Spoon half the mixture into the slow cooker. Cover with ½ cup marshmallows. Cover with the remaining sweet potato mixture.

3 Cover and cook on high for 1 to 2 hours, or until hot in the center. Sprinkle the remaining ½ cup marshmallows on top, cover, and cook 5 minutes longer or until melted.

Per serving: Calories 321 (From Fat 72); Fat 8g (Saturated 4.5g); Cholesterol 87mg; Sodium 603mg; Carbohydrate 58g (Dietary Fiber 3g); Protein 6g.

Chapter 11

Desserts and Jams

In This Chapter

- Bringing out the essence of ripe fruit in slow-cooked fruit desserts
- Using the hot water method to make silky smooth custards and puddings
- Cooking sensational fruit butters and jams

*W*e like desserts so much that we have a hard time understanding when people say they don't like a touch of sweetness at the end of a meal. Perhaps, they may have eaten too much and are too full at the moment to have some. But we find it hard to pass up sweets, especially when they're made with tree-ripened fresh fruit and crunchy toppings or silky smooth custards made with farm-fresh eggs. Jams and preserves are also another favorite, especially when fresh fruit is at its peak during the summer months. Crisp, tart apples from local orchards are available in abundance in the fall and ready to be made into mouth-watering desserts and butters. And you can make them almost effortlessly in your slow cooker.

Fruit Desserts

Because the slow cooker heats up slowly and gently, all of the natural goodness and flavor of fresh fruit is slowly extracted as it cooks, making this an ideal method to prepare many fruit desserts. These were the desserts we had to forgo in the dog days of summers past, when — not wanting to heat up an already hot kitchen — we often reluctantly resisted the temptation to turn on the oven and transform tree-ripened summer fruits into delicious baked goods. Then we discovered that we could make some of these homey desserts right in the slow cooker without heating up the kitchen! These desserts hold well and can even be taken with you in the slow cooker to your next potluck or pitch-in supper.

Apple Brown Betty

Although we will never know who Betty was, we can only assume she was a creative, thrifty cook with some day-old bread, butter, and apples on hand. It's amazing how such simple ingredients can be transformed into such a cozy, homey dessert.

Preparation time: *20 minutes*

Cooking time: *High 1½ to 2½ hours*

Yield: *6 servings*

¼ cup (½ stick) unsalted butter

3 cups fresh white bread crumbs

1 cup sugar

½ teaspoon ground cinnamon

¼ teaspoon freshly grated nutmeg

5 medium Granny Smith apples, peeled, cored, and cut into cubes (see Figure 11-1)

1 Lightly spray a 4- to 6-quart slow cooker with vegetable oil cooking spray.

2 Melt the butter in a large nonstick skillet over medium-high heat. Add the bread crumbs and cook until lightly browned and toasted, stirring frequently. Remove immediately from the pan and place in a mixing bowl. Add the sugar, cinnamon, and nutmeg. Stir to combine.

3 Sprinkle one-third of the buttered crumbs on the bottom of the slow cooker. Cover with half the apples. Sprinkle apples with another one-third of the crumbs. Repeat with another layer of apples and the remaining crumbs.

4 Cover and cook on high for 1½ to 2½ hours, or until the apples are tender.

Vary It: *To make Apple and Rhubarb Brown Betty, substitute ½ pound rhubarb, cut into ½-inch slices, for 2 apples. Increase sugar to 1¼ cups and add the zest of one orange.*

Per serving: *Calories 324 (From Fat 81); Fat 9g (Saturated 5g); Cholesterol 22mg; Sodium 291mg; Carbohydrate 60g (Dietary Fiber 3g); Protein 3g.*

Peeling and Coring an Apple

Figure 11-1:
Peeling,
coring, and
slicing an
apple.

Peach Crisp

Some of our favorite desserts are those that we make in the summer using fruit from farm markets at local orchards. Because we really want to enjoy the flavor of the tree-ripened fruit, we prefer to treat them simply, as in this peach crisp recipe.

Preparation time: *20 minutes*

Cooking time: *Low 3 hours*

Yield: *6 servings*

2 pounds ripe peaches, peeled, pitted, and cut into ¼-inch slices

⅔ cup old-fashioned oats

⅔ cup all-purpose flour

⅔ cup packed light brown sugar

½ teaspoon ground cinnamon

¼ teaspoon grated nutmeg

Pinch salt

¾ cup (6 tablespoons) unsalted butter, softened

1 Lightly spray a 4- to 6-quart slow cooker with vegetable oil cooking spray.

2 Layer the peach slices in the slow cooker.

3 Combine the oats, flour, brown sugar, cinnamon, nutmeg, and salt in a medium mixing bowl. Add the softened butter and combine until the mixture is crumbly. Sprinkle over the peaches.

4 Cover and cook on low for 3 hours.

Vary It: *Substitute other fruits, such as apples, pears, or plums, for the peaches (see Figure 11-2).*

Per serving: Calories 441 (From Fat 231); Fat 26g (Saturated 15g); Cholesterol 66mg; Sodium 303mg; Carbohydrate 50g (Dietary Fiber 4g); Protein 5g.

Figure 11-2:
Use fresh and dried fruits in your desserts.

Apple Bread Pudding

We like to eat bread pudding not only as a dessert but also as a breakfast dish. The bread pudding that we share with you is full of sliced apples and doesn't need any added sauce because it makes its own caramel-like topping as it slowly cooks.

Preparation time: 15 minutes

Cooking time: High 2½ to 3 hours

Yield: 8 servings

2 tablespoons unsalted butter, at room temperature

1 cup packed light brown sugar

8 ounces day-old white bread (about 8 to 10 slices), cut into 1-inch cubes

2 Golden Delicious apples, peeled, cored, and sliced very thin

3 large eggs

2 cans (12 fluid ounces each) evaporated milk

1 teaspoon vanilla extract

½ teaspoon ground cinnamon

1 Butter the bottom of a 4- to 6-quart slow cooker.

2 Evenly sprinkle the brown sugar over the bottom.

3 Layer half the bread cubes in the slow cooker. Place the apple slices on top of the bread. Cover with the remaining bread cubes.

4 Lightly beat the eggs in a large mixing bowl. Whisk in the milk, vanilla, and cinnamon. Pour over the bread and press down gently so that the bread absorbs the egg mixture.

5 Cover and cook on high for 2½ to 3 hours, or until a knife inserted in the center of the pudding comes out clean.

Fat Buster: Cut calories and fat by substituting skim, fat-free evaporated milk for whole evaporated milk.

Per serving: Calories 399 (From Fat 113); Fat 13g (Saturated 6.5g); Cholesterol 116mg; Sodium 402mg; Carbohydrate 55g (Dietary Fiber 1g); Protein 17g.

Per serving (made with skim evaporated milk): Calories 284 (From Fat 56); Fat 6g (Saturated 2.5g); Cholesterol 91mg; Sodium 312mg; Carbohydrate 46g (Dietary Fiber 1g); Protein 11g.

Applesauce

Every fall we look forward to making applesauce with locally grown apples. Because Macintosh apples are usually the first available, they're also the first to go into the slow cooker. Some other good choices for applesauce are any Jonathan variety, as well as Gravenstein, Northern Spy, and Winesap.

Preparation time: *20 minutes*

Cooking time: *Low 5 to 6 hours*

Yield: *8 servings (6 cups)*

10 to 12 large Macintosh apples, about 4 pounds, peeled, cored, and cut into eighths	*2 teaspoons ground cinnamon*
1 cup apple cider or juice	*Pinch salt*
1 cup sugar	

1 Lightly spray a 4- to 6-quart slow cooker with vegetable oil cooking spray.

2 Place the apples in the slow cooker with the cider, sugar, cinnamon, and salt. Stir to combine.

3 Cover and cook on low for 5 to 6 hours, or until the apples are very soft.

4 Mash the apples with a handheld potato masher, or process through a food mill for a very smooth consistency. Taste and add additional sugar, if desired.

Vary It: For pink applesauce, add 2 cups of fresh or frozen cranberries, thawed, along with the apples. You may wish to increase sugar by an additional ½ cup.

Per serving: Calories 146 (From Fat 0); Fat 0g (Saturated 0g); Cholesterol 0mg; Sodium 40mg; Carbohydrate 37g (Dietary Fiber 3g); Protein 0g.

Baked Apples

The aromatic smell of apples baking with butter and spices is indeed wonderful, evoking warm thoughts and cozy feelings. This is exactly what you need to smell when you return home after a hectic day!

Preparation time: *15 minutes*

Cooking time: *Low 2 to 3 hours*

Yield: *4 servings*

4 medium Rome apples (about 8 ounces each), cored to within ½ inch of base

3 tablespoons unsalted butter

½ cup pure maple syrup

1 teaspoon freshly grated ginger

4 pieces cinnamon stick, 3 inches long

½ cup apple cider or juice

1 Lightly spray a 4- to 6-quart slow cooker with vegetable oil cooking spray.

2 Peel about 1 inch of skin from the tops of the apples; cut a sliver off the bottom of the apples so they'll stand. Place them in the slow cooker.

3 Cut 1 tablespoon of butter into 4 pieces; fill each apple core with a piece of butter, 1 tablespoon maple syrup, ¼ teaspoon ginger, and 1 cinnamon stick. Place the remaining butter and syrup in the bottom of the slow cooker along with the apple cider.

4 Cover and cook on low for 2 to 3 hours, or until the apples are fork-tender.

Per serving: Calories 298 (From Fat 88); Fat 10g (Saturated 6g); Cholesterol 25mg; Sodium 97mg; Carbohydrate 53g (Dietary Fiber 3g); Protein 0g.

Custards and Puddings

In order to keep custards creamy and smooth, they're always baked in a hot water bath, or *bain marie.* This cooking method involves placing the baking dish with the custard into another pan filled with hot water. Heat is transferred from the hot water to the custard, cooking it gently and slowly so that it doesn't curdle or form a crust. By placing a trivet or cake rack in the slow cooker and filling the bottom with hot water, it becomes a quick and easy *bain marie.*

Creme Caramel

This silky egg custard is covered with a rich, flavorful coating of caramel. When melting the sugar, be sure not to let it cook too long, or it will burn before you know it. ***Note:*** Since the whole milk is mixed with the sweetened condensed milk in this recipe, the possibility of its curdling is greatly reduced.

Preparation time: *20 minutes*

Cooking time: *High 1½ to 2 hours*

Yield: *8 servings*

2 cups boiling water

½ cup sugar

1½ cups eggs (approximately 6 to 8 large eggs)

1 can (14 ounces) sweetened condensed milk

2½ cups of whole milk

1 Place a metal cake rack or trivet in the slow cooker. Add the boiling water to the slow cooker.

2 Melt the sugar in a large nonstick skillet over medium heat. Do not stir. When the sugar is melted and caramel in color, remove from heat immediately. Carefully pour into a 1-quart shallow baking dish that fits in your slow cooker. Swirl the baking dish so that the melted sugar covers the bottom, doing so quickly before the liquid hardens. Place the baking dish on the trivet.

3 Break the eggs into a 2-cup glass measuring cup until you have a total of 1½ cups. Pour into a large mixing bowl and beat lightly. Add the condensed and regular milk. Whisk together until just blended. Pour into the prepared baking dish. Cover the dish with foil.

4 Cover the slow cooker and cook on high for 1½ to 2 hours, or until the custard is set. Remove and cool to room temperature. Refrigerate at least 4 hours or overnight.

5 To remove, set the baking dish in a pan with 1 inch of hot water for 5 minutes. Run a knife around the edge of the pan. Place a large serving plate on top of the baking dish and invert. Custard should release from the baking dish onto the plate. Pour any accumulated caramel over the creme caramel.

Fat Buster: *To lower overall fat content by 3 grams, use fat-free condensed and regular milk.*

Per serving: Calories 336 (From Fat 109); Fat 12g (Saturated 6g); Cholesterol 217mg; Sodium 171mg; Carbohydrate 44g (Dietary Fiber 0g); Protein 13g.

Per serving (made with fat-free condensed milk): Calories 309 (From Fat 81); Fat 9g (Saturated 4.5g); Cholesterol 204mg; Sodium 180mg; Carbohydrate 45g (Dietary Fiber 0g); Protein 13g.

Chocolate Custard

Creamier than traditional chocolate pudding, this chocolate custard is smooth on the tongue and rich in taste!

Preparation time: *20 minutes*

Cooking time: *High 2 to 2½ hours*

Yield: *6 servings*

2 cups boiling water

2 cups milk

1 square unsweetened chocolate

3 large eggs

⅓ cup packed dark brown sugar

⅛ teaspoon salt

½ teaspoon vanilla, or 1 teaspoon dark rum

1 Place a metal cake rack or trivet in the slow cooker. Add 2 cups boiling water to the slow cooker.

2 Heat the milk in a 2-quart saucepan over medium heat. When the milk begins to simmer, add the chocolate. Remove from heat and stir until the chocolate melts.

3 In a medium mixing bowl, beat together the eggs, sugar, salt, and vanilla. Slowly add the hot milk, stirring constantly. Pour into a 1-quart baking dish. Cover the dish with foil. Place in the slow cooker on a trivet.

4 Cover and cook on high for 2 to 2½ hours, or until the custard is set. Remove and cool to room temperature. Refrigerate at least 4 hours or overnight before serving.

Per serving: Calories 130 (From Fat 60); Fat 7g (Saturated 3g); Cholesterol 117mg; Sodium 123mg; Carbohydrate 13g (Dietary Fiber 0g); Protein 6g.

Rice Pudding

We almost always make rice pudding when we have white rice left over from dinner. We trust that you will agree that our custardy version of rice pudding — probably the ultimate in comfort food desserts — is indeed special.

Preparation time: *15 minutes*

Cooking time: *High 2 hours*

Yield: *4 servings*

2 cups boiling water	*2 cups milk*
2 large eggs	*1 cup cooked white rice*
½ cup sugar	*½ cup raisins (optional)*
1 teaspoon vanilla extract	*Ground cinnamon for sprinkling*

1 Place a metal cake rack or trivet in the slow cooker. Add the boiling water to the slow cooker.

2 Lightly beat the eggs, sugar, and vanilla in a large mixing bowl. Whisk in the milk. Add the cooked rice and raisins, if desired. Stir together. Pour into a 1-quart baking dish. Cover with foil and place on the trivet in the slow cooker.

3 Cover and cook on high for 2 hours or until a knife inserted in the center of the pudding comes out clean. Sprinkle with cinnamon. Serve warm.

Per serving: Calories 259 (From Fat 60); Fat 7g (Saturated 3.5g); Cholesterol 123mg; Sodium 93mg; Carbohydrate 41g (Dietary Fiber 0g); Protein 8g.

Fruit Butters and Jams

Fruit butters are a thick and smooth type of fruit spread subtly flavored with spices. A mainstay of most farmhouse pantries, the fruit mixture needs to cook down slowly over a long period of time so that it thickens up to the right consistency without scorching. Jams, with which we are all familiar, are a type of fruit preserve made with mashed up fresh fruits and sugar. Not as smooth as fruit butters, they usually contain small pieces of cooked, whole fruit. We found that the gentle, even heat of the slow cooker makes it an ideal jam kettle for making all kinds of fruit preserves.

Peach Butter

Although the most well-known variety of fruit butter is made with apples, we are particularly fond of this variation made with tree-ripened, late summer peaches. In order to get the best results and the thick consistency of a true fruit butter, we found that we had to start off cooking with the cover on and finish up the last couple hours with the slow cooker uncovered. The delicious results are well worth the small amount of additional attention.

Preparation time: *20 minutes*

Cooking time: *High 7 to 8 hours*

Yield: *About 3½ cups*

5 pounds ripe peaches, peeled, pitted, and cut into eighths

1½ cups apple juice

Juice of 1 lemon

½ cup light brown sugar (repeated as needed)

2 teaspoons ground cinnamon

¼ teaspoon grated nutmeg

¼ teaspoon ground cloves

1 Lightly spray a 4- to 6-quart slow cooker with vegetable oil cooking spray.

2 Place the peaches in the slow cooker with the apple juice and lemon juice.

3 Cover and cook on high for 2 hours, or until very soft.

4 Mash the peaches with a handheld potato masher, or process through a food mill. Measure amount of puréed peaches. Place in slow cooker and add ½ cup light brown sugar for each cup of fruit. Add the cinnamon, nutmeg, and cloves. Stir to combine.

5 Cover and cook on high for 4 hours. Uncover and continue cooking for an additional 1 to 2 hours, or until thick.

Per serving (2 tablespoons): Calories 47 (From Fat 0); Fat 0g (Saturated 0g); Cholesterol 0mg; Sodium 5mg; Carbohydrate 12g (Dietary Fiber 1g); Protein 0g.

Rhubarb and Strawberry Jam

We have always wondered who and why someone decided to combine rhubarb and strawberries. This superb combination appears in pie filling, as well as in compotes and jam. Don't be surprised by the amount of sugar called for in this recipe. Rhubarb is naturally, very, very tart, requiring lots of sugar to tame its flavor as well as to thicken the jam.

Preparation time: *20 minutes, plus 2 hours to sit*

Cooking time: *High 4 hours*

Yield: *5 cups*

2 pounds rhubarb, cut into ½-inch pieces

6 cups sugar

Zest of 1 orange

Juice of 1 orange

2 pounds (2 pints) strawberries, hulled and mashed

1 Lightly spray a 4- to 6-quart slow cooker with vegetable oil cooking spray.

2 Place the rhubarb and sugar in the slow cooker and let sit for 2 hours for the rhubarb to release some of its liquid. Add the orange zest and orange juice. Stir together.

3 Cover and cook on high for 3 hours, or until tender. Add the strawberries and cook for 1 hour longer.

Per serving (2 tablespoons): *Calories 124 (From Fat 0); Fat 0g (Saturated 0g); Cholesterol 0mg; Sodium 2mg; Carbohydrate 32g (Dietary Fiber 1g); Protein 0g.*

Part IV

Jump-Starting Dinner with Your Slow Cooker

The 5th Wave   By Rich Tennant

"I'm using a slow cooker, and all you have out here are minute steaks. Do you have any 8 to 10 hour steaks?"

In this part...

This part contains three master recipes for the slow
cooker. These master recipes can be eaten as they are,
or they can be used to make a total of 34 delicious non-slow-
cooker entrées, quickly and easily, in 60 minutes or less.

Chapter 12

Cooking with a Master Meat Sauce

Cooking in a slow cooker allows you to cook just about anything without having to stir and watch. The only drawback is that it takes about 8 hours — meaning that five in the evening is not the optimum time to start slow cooking if you want dinner at six. Sure you can make a really big batch of slow cooker chili over the weekend and feed that to your family all week. Although they may like it the first day or two, by day three you would most likely have a mutiny at the table.

With just a little organization and 60 minutes of time, however, you can have dinner on the table with minimum effort, whenever you want. We suggest having a master plan along with a master recipe.

A Master Plan, a Master Recipe

Think how convenient it would be to make an extra-large batch of some tasty thing — for instance, pasta sauce — in your slow cooker that you could then freeze in four serving portions, available when needed. And to make your life even easier, what about using some great recipes that enable you to add readily available ingredients — a pinch of this or handful of that — so that the basic pasta sauce takes on a whole new personality in a quick new meal? That's the master plan that we propose.

Our first master recipe is for basic meat sauce that can be served over pasta or turned into Sloppy Joes or a shepherd's pie with mixed vegetables and a golden brown mashed potato crust. And you know what the best part is? Most of the ingredients found in these recipes are probably already in your kitchen, and you can get dinner on the table in about 60 minutes from start to finish.

Master Meat Sauce Cooking and Freezing Tips

Pasta has to be the working man's dream-come-true, especially when the sauce is made in big batches and frozen. Served with a tossed green salad, a dish of pasta with homemade meat sauce is a quick, easy, and delicious dinner to have any day of the week. After trial and error, we've perfected our recipe over the years and are pleased to share with you some tips and suggestions we've come up with to make a good, flavorful meat sauce that can stand up on its own served over pasta, or adapted into many other delicious entrées in less than 60 minutes.

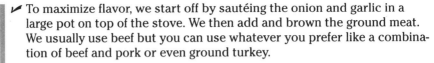

- ✔ To maximize flavor, we start off by sautéing the onion and garlic in a large pot on top of the stove. We then add and brown the ground meat. We usually use beef but you can use whatever you prefer like a combination of beef and pork or even ground turkey.

- ✔ Always be sure that the meat is browned until no longer pink to avoid the risk of *E.coli* bacteria.

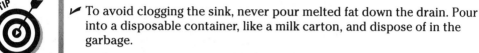

✔ Use the best quality, leanest ground beef possible. By doing so, you won't have to drain off any excess fat before spooning the browned meat into the slow cooker.

✔ If need be, you can cut calories by draining off all the fat and liquid, but we think that you're also throwing out a lot of the flavor. The easiest way to drain fat is to place a large colander over a bowl and spoon browned meat into it.

✔ To avoid clogging the sink, never pour melted fat down the drain. Pour into a disposable container, like a milk carton, and dispose of in the garbage.

✔ Because the main course recipes in this chapter require 4 cups of Master Meat Sauce, freeze the sauce in 4-cup quantities.

✔ Freezer space is always an issue in our homes. We never seem to have enough of it, and plastic containers take up a lot of valuable space. We like to freeze this sauce in 1-gallon resealable plastic freezer bags. Just fill and seal, carefully squeezing out as much of the air as possible. Wipe off any spilled sauce and lay flat in the freezer, stacking the bags on top of each other. You can also, of course, use 1-quart bags.

✔ Label your plastic food storage containers or resealable plastic freezer bags before putting them in the freezer. On the label, write the contents of the container or bag, the quantity, the date it was frozen, and a "use-by" date, which is 3 months after the sauce was made.

✔ To defrost, remove the container or bag of sauce the night before and thaw in the refrigerator overnight, approximately 8 to 12 hours. You can also defrost the sauce in your microwave on the defrost or lowest setting, following the instructions provided by the manufacturer.

The Master Meat Sauce

Although delicious served over pasta, this chunky, thick meat sauce provides the perfect starting place for making other quick and easy dinners with the minor addition of a few other ingredients. Nothing could be easier than having dinner on the table in 60 minutes or less.

Master Meat Sauce

Because the Master Meat Sauce is a master recipe to be used in other recipes, we haven't doctored it up too much with herbs and spices. If you plan to serve this primarily as a pasta sauce, you may want to add ¼ cup each of minced fresh parsley and basil 15 minutes before the sauce is done cooking.

This recipe calls for canned crushed tomatoes, which can vary widely in quality from brand to brand, including some that can be bitter. We recommend that you try experimenting until you find the best brand in your area. Look for a brand that doesn't process too many seeds and tomato peel in with the tomato, because they add no flavor, only bitterness.

You can substitute ground turkey for the ground beef, or a combination of, but beware: Make sure that the turkey is low in fat by checking the package label. Some brands of ground turkey contain ground-up fat and skin.

Preparation time: *35 minutes*

Cooking time: *Low 8 hours*

Yield: *5 quarts, or 20 (8-ounce) servings*

4 tablespoons olive oil	*3 cans (28 ounces each) crushed tomatoes*
2 large onions, finely chopped	*1 cup water*
6 cloves garlic, minced	*1 tablespoon salt*
4 pounds lean ground beef	*1 teaspoon freshly ground black pepper*

1 In a 6-quart saucepan on the stovetop, heat the olive oil over medium-high heat. Add the onions and garlic and cook for 7 to 8 minutes, or until softened, stirring often. Increase the heat to high and add the ground beef. Cook for 8 to 12 minutes, or until the beef is no longer pink, breaking up the pieces with a spoon. Remove from heat.

2 Lightly spray a 6-quart slow cooker with vegetable oil cooking spray.

3 Spoon the browned meat into the slow cooker. Add the tomatoes, water, salt, and pepper and stir well to combine.

4 Cover and cook on low for 8 hours. Adjust seasoning with salt and pepper.

Tip: *If you have a food processor, use it to chop the onions and mince the garlic. Begin by placing the garlic in the food processor container. Press pulse a couple times until the garlic is coarsely chopped. Add the onion, quartered, and pulse a couple times until chopped.*

Per 1 cup serving: *Calories 310 (From Fat 193); Fat 21 g (Saturated 8g); Cholesterol 68mg; Sodium 705mg; Carbohydrate 10g (Dietary Fiber 2g); Protein 18g.*

All-American Chili for a Crowd

Naturally, the premise of the Master Meat Sauce recipe is to be the foundation of other great-tasting entrée dishes. However, you can also add other ingredients in the beginning to make a humongous batch of chili to take to a potluck supper or family reunion, or even just to freeze it as is.

This is essentially the same recipe as the Master Meat Sauce. Changes include lessening the amount of olive oil needed, increasing the onions and garlic, and adding seasonings traditionally found in chili.

Preparation time: *35 minutes*

Cooking time: *Low 8 hours*

Yield: *6 quarts, or 25 (8-ounce) servings (cups)*

2 tablespoons olive oil	*1 tablespoon ground cumin*
4 large onions, finely chopped	*1 tablespoon dried, crushed oregano*
15 cloves garlic, minced	*4 cans (15 ounces each) red kidney beans*
4 pounds lean ground beef	*1 tablespoon salt*
3 cans (28 ounces each) crushed tomatoes	*1 teaspoon freshly ground black pepper*
¾ cup chili powder	

1 In a 6-quart saucepan on the stovetop, heat the olive oil over medium-high heat. Add the onions and garlic and cook for 7 to 8 minutes, or until softened, stirring often. Increase the heat to high and add the ground beef. Cook for 8 to 12 minutes, or until the beef is no longer pink, breaking up the pieces with a spoon. Remove from heat.

2 Lightly spray a 6-quart slow cooker with vegetable oil cooking spray.

3 Spoon the browned meat into the slow cooker. Add the tomatoes, chili powder, cumin, oregano, beans, salt, and pepper and stir well to combine.

4 Cover and cook on low for 8 hours. Adjust seasoning with salt and pepper.

Per 1 cup serving: *Calories 324 (From Fat 163); Fat 18g (Saturated 6.5g); Cholesterol 54mg; Sodium 835mg; Carbohydrate 22g (Dietary Fiber 8g); Protein 19g.*

Recipes Using the Master Meat Sauce

Containers of frozen meat sauce are like having money in the bank. They're ready to use whenever you need them. Here we provide a variety of tasty, satisfying recipes that utilize the Master Meat Sauce. Some of the recipes are variations of ones that live forever in our childhood memories; others are adaptations of ethnic recipes. **Note:** The recipes that follow are *not* slow cooker recipes, but utilize a number of other cooking methods, such as oven baking, stovetop cooking, and so forth.

Johnny Marzetti Casserole

As a baby boomer in elementary school in the mid-1960s, Tom used to look forward to having the hot lunch when this dish appeared on that day's school menu. Originally from Marzetti's Restaurant in Columbus, Ohio, and named after the owner's brother Johnny, this casserole was a party favorite in the 1950s and early '60s.

Preparation time: *20 minutes*

Cooking time: *35 to 40 minutes*

Yield: *6 servings*

4 cups Master Meat Sauce (see recipe earlier in this chapter)	*8 ounces (2 cups) elbow macaroni, cooked al dente and drained*
½ pound mushrooms, coarsely chopped	*12 ounces (5 cups) shredded sharp cheddar cheese*

1 Preheat oven to 350°. Lightly grease a 9-x-13-inch baking dish.

2 Combine the Master Meat Sauce, mushrooms, macaroni, and 4¼ cups cheese in the prepared pan. Scatter the remaining ¾ cup cheese on top.

3 Bake, uncovered, until browned and bubbling, 35 to 40 minutes.

Per serving: *Calories 667 (From Fat 396); Fat 44g (Saturated 24g); Cholesterol 135mg; Sodium 1143mg; Carbohydrate 29g (Dietary Fiber 6g); Protein 39g.*

Shepherd's Pie

Making shepherd's pie is a great way to clean out the fridge and use up odds and ends of leftover vegetables. Most cooks have their own favorite combinations. To save time, try to make this dish the night after you make mashed potatoes. You need about 6 cups of mashed potatoes, so plan accordingly to have enough leftovers.

Preparation time: *20 minutes*

Cooking time: *30 to 35 minutes*

Yield: *6 servings*

4 cups Master Meat Sauce (see recipe earlier in this chapter)

2 cups leftover, cooked vegetables, or frozen mixed vegetables, thawed or, if time is short, rinsed under cold water

1 teaspoon dried thyme

6 cups mashed potatoes, reheated in a microwave if cold, adding milk until smooth and creamy

1 large egg beaten with a teaspoon of water

Freshly ground black pepper

1 Preheat the oven to 400°. Lightly grease a 9-x-13-inch baking dish.

2 Combine the Master Meat Sauce, vegetables, and thyme in the prepared pan. Spread the mashed potatoes on top, all the way to the edges of the pan. Brush with the beaten egg wash and sprinkle with pepper.

3 Bake until the top is golden brown and the filling is heated through, about 30 to 35 minutes.

Per serving: *Calories 483 (From Fat 193); Fat 21g (Saturated 6.5g); Cholesterol 58mg; Sodium 1199mg; Carbohydrate 58g (Dietary Fiber 12g); Protein 19g.*

Stuffed Baked Potatoes

A few years ago, Americans realized that there was more to baked potatoes than butter or sour cream and chives. Suddenly it was fashionable to take an extra-large baked potato, split it in half, and load it up with all sorts of fun toppings like sauces, cheese, olives, and green onions, almost like a baked potato taco.

Preparation time: *15 minutes*

Cooking time: *45 to 60 minutes*

Yield: *4 servings*

4 russet or Idaho potatoes, 9 to 10 ounces each

4 cups Master Meat Sauce (see recipe earlier in this chapter)

Salt

Freshly ground black pepper

Suggested toppings: Shredded sharp cheddar cheese; shredded mozzarella cheese; chopped avocado or guacamole; sour cream; sliced black olives; sliced scallions, white and green parts; sliced, pickled jalapeño peppers; crispy cooked, crumbled bacon

1 Preheat the oven to 400°. Prick the potatoes twice with a fork. Bake for 45 to 60 minutes, or until the potatoes test done when pricked with a fork or skewer.

2 Heat the Master Meat Sauce in a 2-quart saucepan over medium heat until heated through.

3 Split the potatoes in half and squeeze the ends toward the center to plump up. Sprinkle with salt and black pepper to taste. Spoon ½ cup sauce over each potato half. Serve with any or all of your favorite toppings.

Per serving (without toppings): *Calories 530 (From Fat 167); Fat 19g (Saturated 6.5g); Cholesterol 54mg; Sodium 988mg; Carbohydrate 65g (Dietary Fiber 13g); Protein 26g.*

Microwaving your spuds

If you have a large microwave oven, you can save up to 20 minutes cooking time by using it to bake the potatoes. Prick each potato twice with a fork. Place one potato on the center of the glass microwave dish and the others around it. Cook on high power for the amount of time indicated.

✔ 1 potato: 8 minutes

✔ 2 potatoes: 13 minutes

✔ 3 potatoes: 19 minutes

✔ 4 potatoes: 24 minutes

Sloppy Joe Sandwiches

The Sloppy Joe is another one of those 1950s baby boomer specials. If you've ever eaten one, you know why it's sloppy; as far as the Joe part, well, your guess is as good as ours.

Preparation time: *10 minutes*

Cooking time: *20 minutes*

Yield: *6 sandwiches (¾ cup per serving)*

1 tablespoon vegetable oil

1 small onion, chopped

1 small red bell pepper, cored, seeded, and diced

1 large stalk celery, finely diced

1 tablespoon cider vinegar

4 cups Master Meat Sauce (see recipe earlier in this chapter)

¼ cup ketchup

6 large seeded rolls or hamburger buns, split and lightly toasted

1 Heat the oil in a 10-inch nonstick deep sauté pan or chicken fryer over medium heat. Add the onion, red pepper, and celery and cook for 7 to 8 minutes, or until the onion is soft but not browned. Sprinkle with the cider vinegar. Cook until the vinegar evaporates.

2 Add the Master Meat Sauce and ketchup. Bring to a boil. Lower heat to a simmer and cook until heated through.

3 Spoon the Sloppy Joe mixture on the bottom halves of the rolls and cover with the tops. Serve hot.

Per serving: Calories 425 (From Fat 152); 17 g (Saturated 5g); Cholesterol 36mg; Sodium 997mg; Carbohydrate 50g (Dietary Fiber 7g); Protein 19g.

Mom's Baked Rice

This recipe is almost like lasagna but requires less work and contains fewer calories. In fact, this dish, which uses leftover tomato sauce from Sunday dinner, is an adaptation of one that Tom's mother used to make when he was growing up.

Preparation time: *10 minutes*

Cooking time: *30 to 35 minutes*

Yield: *6 servings*

4 cups Master Meat Sauce (see recipe earlier in this chapter)

6 cups cooked white rice

2 cups (8 ounces) shredded mozzarella cheese

¼ cup grated Parmesan or Pecorino Romano cheese

1 Preheat the oven to 400°. Lightly grease a 9-x-13-inch baking dish.

2 Combine 3 cups of the Master Meat Sauce, the rice, 1½ cups of the mozzarella cheese, and the Parmesan cheese in the prepared pan.

3 Spread the remaining 1 cup of Master Meat Sauce over the top and sprinkle with the remaining ½ cup mozzarella cheese.

4 Cover the dish loosely with foil and bake for 30 to 35 minutes, or until heated through.

Vary It: *For a little variety, add 1 cup cooked green peas to the rice.*

Per serving: *Calories 545 (From Fat 196); Fat 22g (Saturated 10g); Cholesterol 69mg; Sodium 775mg; Carbohydrate 60g (Dietary Fiber 6g); Protein 26g.*

The virtues of preshredded cheese

Although there's no comparison to the taste of freshly shredded cheese, one of our favorite convenience foods is preshredded cheese, found in every supermarket from here to Timbuktu. Because cheese is available in a wide variety of types and flavors, have a package or two on hand so that you can turn a so-so meal into something special.

Although usually packaged in 8-, 12-, and 16-ounce sizes, most recipes do not require a full package. Fortunately, shredded cheese freezes well, and most packages have a resealable strip along the top. Simply measure out how much you need and freeze the rest.

The next time a recipe calls for shredded cheese, you'll find it waiting in the freezer, and you don't even have to let it defrost before using it. Just measure out how much you need and put the remaining cheese back before it thaws.

Spanish Rice with Meat

You can approach this recipe in one of two ways, depending on how much time you have and how well organized you are. The easiest and fastest way is to make the rice a couple days ahead, or even the night before, and store it in a covered container in the refrigerator. On the other hand, maybe you're not that well-organized or forgot to make it in advance. In that case, you may want to consider using instant rice or even pre-cooked boiled-in-a-bag rice, which cooks up quickly. Any way you approach it, this is a delicious, simple dish.

Preparation time: *10 minutes*

Cooking time: *15 minutes*

Yield: *6 servings*

2 tablespoons olive oil

1 large green bell pepper, cored, seeded, and diced (see Figure 12-1)

1 large red bell pepper, cored, seeded, and diced

4 cups Master Meat Sauce (see recipe earlier in this chapter)

2 tablespoons brown sugar

1 teaspoon dried, crushed basil

4 cups cooked white rice

1 Heat the oil in a 10-inch nonstick deep sauté pan or chicken fryer over medium heat. Add the green and red peppers and cook for 7 to 8 minutes, or until soft.

2 Add the Master Meat Sauce, brown sugar, and dried basil and bring to a boil. Lower heat to a simmer and stir in the rice. Cook until the rice is heated through.

Per serving: 414 Calories (From Fat 153); Fat 17g (Saturated 5g); Cholesterol 36mg; Sodium 562mg; Carbohydrate 50g (Dietary Fiber 6g); Protein 16g.

How to Core and Seed a Pepper

Figure 12-1: Coring, seeding, and dicing bell peppers.

1. cut out stem

twist and pull out

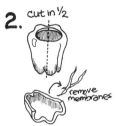

2. cut in ½

remove membranes

3. Cut into lengthwise strips

4. For cubes, hold strips together and cut crosswise

South-of-the-Border Chili con Carne and Cornbread Too

When tummies are empty and time is short, nothing beats a one-pot meal such as this south-of-the-border-inspired chili! You can even reduce the cooking time by "baking" the cornbread right on top of the chili on the stovetop rather than in the oven.

Preparation time: *10 minutes*

Cooking time: *30 minutes*

Yield: *6 servings*

1 package (6½ or 8½ ounces) cornbread mix

4 cups Master Meat Sauce (see recipe earlier in this chapter)

1 can (15 ounces) red kidney beans, drained and rinsed under cold water

1 cup frozen corn kernels, thawed or, if time is short, rinsed under cold water

1 tablespoon chili powder

1 teaspoon ground cumin

1 teaspoon crushed, dried oregano

½ cup (2 ounces) shredded sharp cheddar cheese

2 scallions, white and green parts, sliced thin

1 Prepare the cornbread mix according to the package instructions, but do not bake; set aside.

2 Combine the Master Meat Sauce, kidney beans, corn, chili powder, cumin, and oregano in a covered, 10-inch nonstick deep sauté pan or chicken fryer. Cook over medium heat until hot and bubbly, stirring occasionally. Lower heat to a simmer.

3 Spoon the cornbread mixture around the outside edge of the pan, over the chili, forming a border. Cover and cook for 15 to 20 minutes, or until the cornbread is done.

4 Sprinkle the chili with the cheese and scallions before serving.

Vary It: *If you like your chili on the hot side, add cayenne pepper to taste along with the other spices.*

Per serving: *473 Calories (From Fat 176); Fat 20g (Saturated 7.5g); Cholesterol 47mg; Sodium 1103mg; Carbohydrate 54g (Dietary Fiber 13g); Protein 22g.*

Rice: Types and how to cook it

Rice is generally available in two forms: brown rice, which is the entire grain with only the inedible outer husk removed, and white rice, which has had the husk, bran, and germ removed. For best results, we recommend using white medium- to long-grain or converted rice when preparing any of the recipes in this book. Converted rice means that the unhulled grain has been soaked, pressure-steamed, and dried before milling. Manufacturers treat rice to this process so that it cooks up more fluffy with separated kernels.

The easiest way to cook rice (see accompanying figure) is to bring the appropriate amount of water, as indicated in the following table, to a boil in a saucepan, add 1 cup rice and 1 teaspoon salt, reduce heat to low, and cook, covered, until done. Remove from heat and let stand, covered, for 5 minutes before fluffing with a fork.

The following chart should be your guide to perfectly cooked rice.

Type	Liquid in Cups	Cooking Time in Minutes	Yield in Cups
Converted	2	18	3½
White, long-grain	1½	18	3½
White, medium-grain	1½	23*	3½

How to Make Rice

so easy!

Measure the rice and water. Put them into the pot. Add salt and butter (optional).

Bring to a boil. Stir once. Reduce heat to a simmer. Cover the pot.

Rice is DONE when all the liquid is absorbed. You can see little steam holes on the surface of the rice.

Cuban Picadillo

Picadillo is Spanish for "chopped mixture," which is a good description of what this Cuban dish is all about. Although our version may not be 100 percent authentic, this savory ground beef stew still combines the salty, savory flavors of green olives and spices with the slightly sweet contrast of raisins.

Preparation time: *15 minutes*

Cooking time: *20 minutes*

Yield: *4 servings*

1 tablespoon olive oil

1 small onion, chopped

1 clove garlic, minced

1 small green bell pepper, cored, seeded, and diced

4 cups Master Meat Sauce (see recipe earlier in this chapter)

½ teaspoon ground cumin

½ teaspoon ground cinnamon

¼ teaspoon ground cloves

½ teaspoon dried, crushed oregano

¼ cup raisins

¼ cup sliced pimiento-stuffed green olives

3 cups cooked white rice

4 scallions, white and green parts, sliced thin

1 Heat the oil in a medium saucepan over medium heat. Add the onion, garlic, and green pepper. Cook for 7 to 8 minutes, or until soft.

2 Add the Master Meat Sauce, cumin, cinnamon, cloves, oregano, raisins, and olives. Bring to a boil over medium heat. Lower to a simmer and cook for 10 minutes, or until heated through.

3 Serve over the white rice with the sliced scallions on top.

Per serving: *Calories 562 (From Fat 208); Fat 23g (Saturated 7g); Cholesterol 54mg; Sodium 1033mg; Carbohydrate 66g (Dietary Fiber 6g); Protein 23g.*

Beef and Bean Burritos

Burritos are the ultimate Mexican finger food. Our version consists of a thick meat and bean filling wrapped up in a large flour tortilla. We also add some shredded cheese and onions for added flavor and texture.

Preparation time: *20 minutes*

Cooking time: *15 to 20 minutes*

Yield: *8 servings*

4 cups Master Meat Sauce (see recipe earlier in this chapter)

2 tablespoons chili powder

1 can (15 ounces) refried beans

8 (10-inch) flour tortillas

¼ cup minced onion

½ cup shredded sharp cheddar cheese

Chopped avocado (optional)

Guacamole (optional)

Sour cream (optional)

1 Preheat oven to 400°.

2 Combine the Master Meat Sauce, chili powder, and refried beans in a large mixing bowl.

3 Spoon approximately ¾ cup of the meat sauce mixture on each tortilla, sprinkle with the onion and cheese, and roll up.

4 Place on a baking sheet, cover with foil, and bake until the filling is heated through and the cheese melts, approximately 15 to 20 minutes.

5 Carefully remove with a large spatula to serving plates. Serve with chopped avocado or guacamole and sour cream, if desired.

Per serving: Calories 379 (From Fat) 213; Fat 16g (Saturated 6g); Cholesterol 39mg; Sodium 950mg; Carbohydrate 42g (Dietary Fiber 8g); Protein 17g.

Quick and Easy Greek Pastitso

Although Italians have their baked lasagna and ziti, Greeks throughout the world enjoy *pastitso,* a layered dish of ground meat sauce, pasta, white sauce, and cheese. It traditionally takes almost 2 hours to make this hearty casserole dish, but we simplify the recipe by using our Master Meat Sauce, as well as prepared Alfredo pasta sauce, available in the refrigerated section of most supermarkets.

Preparation time: *20 minutes*

Cooking time: *45 to 50 minutes*

Yield: *8 servings*

1 pound ziti or penne pasta, cooked al dente

2 containers (10 ounces each) Alfredo sauce

2 tablespoons minced Italian flat-leaf parsley

¼ teaspoon ground nutmeg

⅛ teaspoon ground cinnamon

4 cups Master Meat Sauce (see recipe earlier in this chapter)

¼ cup grated Parmesan cheese

1 Preheat oven to 350°. Lightly grease a 9-x-13-inch baking dish.

2 Mix the pasta with one whole container of Alfredo sauce, and ¼ cup of the second container.

3 Add ½ cup of reserved Alfredo sauce, parsley, nutmeg, and cinnamon to the Master Meat Sauce and stir well to combine.

4 Spoon half the pasta into the prepared pan. Cover with all the meat sauce. Cover with the remaining pasta. Cover with the remaining ½ cup of Alfredo sauce, spreading evenly. Sprinkle with the grated Parmesan cheese.

5 Bake for 45 to 50 minutes, or until golden brown on top and bubbly. Let sit 10 minutes before cutting into squares and serving.

Fat Buster: *Use reduced-fat Alfredo sauce to cut fat and some calories.*

Per serving: *Calories 489 (From Fat 164); Fat 18g (Saturated 9g); Cholesterol 49mg; Sodium 761mg; Carbohydrate 59g (Dietary Fiber 5g); Protein 21g.*

Chapter 13

Master Roast Turkey Breast Recipes

....

In This Chapter

▶ Preparing Master Roast Turkey Breast

▶ Using cooked turkey breast in classic favorite entrées

....

*W*hat could be better than slicing up some vegetables and placing them in a slow cooker with a turkey breast? This combination of ingredients will cook up on its own for the rest of the day, giving you enough juicy, tender, flavorful meat for making up to four dinnertime entrées. And if that's not good enough, we also throw in ten surefire non-slow cooker recipes that take less than 60 minutes to prepare! Dinnertime has never been easier!

Master Turkey Recipe to the Rescue

Americans like turkey. In fact, U.S. per-capita consumption of turkey has increased 64 percent over the past ten years to about 18 pounds annually. Part of this increase is due to the new turkey products readily available nationwide. No longer must we purchase a large turkey big enough to feed an army when all we may want is some sliced turkey breast cutlets or a pound of lean ground turkey. Parts like wings, drumsticks, and whole turkey breast on the bone are as commonplace today as the sirloin steak of the 1960s. And turkey is extremely accommodating when cooked in a slow cooker, especially the breast meat, which often comes out dry and stringy when roasted in an oven.

Roasting a golden brown turkey breast

Slow cooking basically braises the turkey breast in its own juices without any browning. For a golden brown breast, follow these steps:

1. Prepare the Master Roast Turkey Breast (see the recipe later in this chapter) as indicated up to Step 3. Do not place the turkey in the slow cooker yet.

2. In a large skillet or Dutch oven, heat 2 tablespoons vegetable oil over medium-high heat. Add the prepared turkey breast and cook, turning with two large kitchen spoons until evenly browned all over, about 10 to 15 minutes. Remove and place in the slow cooker. Proceed with Steps 4 to 6 of the Master Roast Turkey Breast recipe.

Because the slow cooker *slowly* braises — simmers the meat in the cooking liquid — as it cooks, normally dry white meat comes out tender and moist, making it the perfect ingredient for preparing many classic turkey dishes like potpie, croquettes, and Turkey Divan. Simply prepare the Master Turkey Breast Recipe that follows, cut up or slice the cooked meat, and package it for the freezer in 1-pound servings. When you need some turkey, simply defrost and whip up a delicious dinner after a frantic, hectic day, in 60 minutes or less.

Rich turkey broth

We think that the best turkey broth for soup comes from slowly simmering the roasted carcass bones with some veggies like carrots, celery, and onions (a good rule is 2 carrots, 2 stalks celery, and a medium-sized onion). Here's how to make it:

1. After removing all the meat from the carcass, place in a 6-quart saucepan.

2. Add the carrots and celery cut into 1-inch pieces. Peel the onion and add whole.

3. Fill the pot with enough water to cover by 1 inch. Bring to a boil over high heat.

4. Lower heat to a simmer and cook for 1½ hours.

5. When cooled to room temperature, remove and discard the carcass and vegetables.

6. Pour the liquid though a fine strainer. Season the broth with salt and black pepper to taste.

Master Roast Turkey Breast

Roast turkey breast is often dry and stringy. When made in the slow cooker, however, it is extremely moist and tender, perfect to use as the main ingredient in your recipes. Because a 4- to 5-pound breast gives 3½ to 4½ pounds of cooked meat, you'll have more than enough to make three to four dinners, not to mention turkey soup (Chapter 1), using the carcass and bits and pieces of leftover meat.

Preparation time: *15 minutes*

Cooking time: *Low 5 to 6 hours*

Yield: *3½ to 4½ pounds cooked turkey, or 10 servings*

2 carrots, scraped and thinly sliced

2 stalks celery, thinly sliced

3 cloves garlic, peeled and thinly sliced

1 large onion, thinly sliced

1 cup chicken broth

2 bay leaves

1 whole turkey breast, 4 to 5 pounds, bone in, skin on, completely thawed if previously frozen

Salt

Freshly ground black pepper

1 Lightly spray a 6-quart slow cooker with vegetable oil cooking spray.

2 Layer the carrots, celery, garlic, and onion in the slow cooker. Add the chicken broth and bay leaves.

3 Remove any visible fat and excess skin from the turkey breast. Rinse under cold water. Pat dry with paper towels. Rub the cavity and skin with salt and pepper. Place in the slow cooker.

4 Cover and cook on low for 5 to 6 hours, or until an instant-read thermometer stuck into the thickest part of the breast reads 175° to 180° (or when the pop-up thermometer pops up — if one was inserted by the packager of the the turkey breast).

5 Remove the turkey from the slow cooker and let cool for 15 minutes before cutting. Discard the bay leaves. Save the vegetables for making Turkey Potpie (see the recipe in this chapter). Save the cooking liquid to make Quick Turkey Gravy (check out the recipe in this chapter).

6 Remove and discard the skin. Remove the breast halves, one at a time, from the bone. For slices, cut crosswise on a diagonal into thick or thin slices, as you prefer. For cubes, cut crosswise into 1-inch-thick slices. Cut each slice into 1-inch strips and then 1-inch cubes. Save the carcass for making turkey broth.

Tip: If the turkey breast is frozen, you must defrost it before cooking. To do so, leave in its original packaging and place on a baking pan in the refrigerator for 24 to 36 hours, or until thawed.

Per serving: Calories 236 (From Fat 14); Fat 2g (Saturated 0.5g); Cholesterol 132mg; Sodium 310mg; Carbohydrate 3g (Dietary Fiber 0g); Protein 49g.

Quick Turkey Gravy

This very simple, easy-to-prepare recipe uses the accumulated drippings and liquid from the slow cooker after cooking the turkey breast. You should have about 3 cups. If not, make up the difference with water or chicken broth. If you don't plan to make gravy right away, store the accumulated liquid in the refrigerator for up to 4 days, or in the freezer up to 3 months. You can use the gravy when preparing some of the other recipes in this chapter.

Preparation time: *5 minutes*

Cooking time: *15 minutes*

Yield: *3 cups, 6 servings*

3 cups accumulated cooking liquid from cooking turkey breast (see the Master Roast Turkey Breast recipe in this chapter)

1 teaspoon Gravy Master (optional)

2 tablespoons water

2½ tablespoons cornstarch

Salt

Freshly ground black pepper

1 Heat the cooking liquid Gravy Master, if desired, in a medium saucepan on the stovetop until it comes to a boil.

2 Combine the water and cornstarch to make a smooth paste.

3 Whisking constantly, add to the simmering broth. Cook for 1 minute. Season with salt and black pepper to taste.

Tip: *Available since 1935, Gravy Master is a concentrated blend of spices and caramel color blended to enhance the color and natural flavors of meats, fish, poultry, and vegetables. Readily found in most supermarkets where the prepared gravies are sold, it is usually added in a small amount when making gravy.*

Per serving: *Calories 37 (From Fat 23); Fat 3g (Saturated 1g); Cholesterol 2mg; Sodium 303mg; Carbohydrate 2g (Dietary Fiber 0g); Protein 1g.*

Recipes Using the Master Roast Turkey Breast

Our favorite part of Thanksgiving is eating leftovers the next day. Don't get us wrong — we look forward to our annual turkey dinner with all the trimmings, but we also enjoy the following recipes that we make from all that leftover turkey.

With a slow cooker and your freezer, every day can be Thanksgiving at your home. The turkey itself is made in the slow cooker when you're busy doing something else. Eat some of it for dinner or freeze it to make any of the following traditional top-of-stove or oven recipes, any night of the week.

Turkey storage and freezing tips

For us — and hopefully in due time, for you too — our slow cooker and freezer work in tandem in making our lives a wee bit less frantic at dinnertime. Although we don't particularly like to freeze leftovers and reheat them for dinner, components like roasted turkey freeze well (when done properly) to be defrosted later and used as an ingredient in numerous recipes.

Because improper freezing can adversely alter the flavor, the following tips explain how to properly store the cooked turkey in the freezer and defrost it for use.

✔ Let cooked turkey cool to room temperature before storing. However, do not let it sit out more than 1 hour.

✔ If you're preparing any of the recipes in this chapter, store turkey in 1-pound packages. Approximately 3 cups of 1-inch cubes equal 1 pound.

✔ Cooked turkey can be safely stored in the refrigerator in a covered plastic food container or resealable plastic bag, or wrapped in aluminum foil, for up to 4 days.

✔ Freeze cooked turkey in plastic food storage containers or resealable plastic freezer bags.

✔ Cooked turkey can be stored for up to 3 months in the freezer, although it's best used within 30 days.

✔ Label your plastic food storage containers or resealable plastic freezer bags before putting them in the freezer. Write what's in the container or bag, the quantity, the date it was frozen, and a "use by" date, which is 3 months after the turkey was cooked.

✔ To defrost, remove the container or bag from the freezer and thaw in the refrigerator overnight, approximately 8 to 12 hours.

Turkey Potpie

We always eat turkey potpie the Sunday after Thanksgiving. It's almost as important a tradition as having the whole turkey on Thanksgiving Day! This recipe is so simple to make and is a great way to clean up the refrigerator by using bits and pieces of whatever you may have on hand. For convenience sake, we offer a recipe that makes one big, family-sized potpie covered with prepared pie crust from the supermarket dairy case. If you're a frequent pie baker, save any leftover pie crust scraps and use those instead.

Preparation time: *20 minutes*

Cooking time: *20 to 25 minutes*

Yield: *4 servings*

2 cups Quick Turkey Gravy (see the recipe in this chapter) or 2 cans (14-ounces each) prepared turkey gravy

2 cups leftover cooked vegetables (see Step 5 of the Master Roast Turkey Breast recipe in this chapter) or frozen mixed vegetables, defrosted

3 cups (1 pound) cooked turkey (see Master Roast Turkey Breast recipe), cut into 1-inch cubes

1 teaspoon poultry seasoning

Salt and pepper

1 round prepared pie crust (not a frozen pie shell), or homemade pie crust rolled out at least 1 inch larger than the baking dish

1 large egg, well beaten

1 Preheat oven to 400°.

2 Combine the gravy, vegetables, turkey, and poultry seasoning in a large saucepan. Bring to a simmer over medium-low heat. Cook until the turkey is heated through, about 5 minutes. Taste and adjust for salt and pepper. Place the mixture in a round 2½-quart baking dish.

3 Roll out the pie crust on a lightly floured surface until it is 1 inch larger than the baking dish. Cut out a 1-inch circle in the center. Brush the crust lightly with the egg. Place the crust, egg side down, on top of the baking dish. Press around the edges so that the crust sticks to the dish. Trim with a knife or crimp the edges. Brush the top with the remaining egg.

4 Bake for 20 to 25 minutes, or until the crust is golden brown.

Per serving: Calories 444 (From Fat 150); Fat 17g (Saturated 3.5g); Cholesterol 151mg; Sodium 771mg; Carbohydrate 31g (Dietary Fiber 4g); Protein 41g.

Turkey and Dumplings

Here's a baked variation of a hearty farmhouse favorite made quick and simple by using buttermilk baking mix, precooked turkey, and frozen or leftover vegetables.

Preparation time: *15 minutes*

Cooking time: *25 minutes*

Yield: *4 servings*

2 cups Quick Turkey Gravy (see the recipe in this chapter) or 2 cans (14 ounces each) prepared turkey gravy

2 cups leftover cooked vegetables (see Step 5 of the Master Roast Turkey Breast recipe) or frozen mixed vegetables, defrosted

3 cups (1 pound) cooked turkey (see Master Roast Turkey Breast recipe), cut into 1-inch cubes

1 teaspoon poultry seasoning

1 cup buttermilk baking mix, such as Bisquick

⅓ cup milk

2 thin scallions, white and green parts, very thinly sliced

¼ teaspoon freshly ground black pepper

1 Combine the gravy, vegetables, turkey, and poultry seasoning in a medium saucepan with a lid. Bring to a simmer over medium-low heat.

2 Combine the baking mix, milk, scallions, and pepper in a small mixing bowl. Drop by teaspoonfuls on top of the simmering stew. Cover and cook for 10 minutes. Uncover and cook for an additional 5 minutes. Serve immediately.

Per serving: Calories 407 (From Fat 92); Fat 10g (Saturated 3g); Cholesterol 100mg; Sodium 926mg; Carbohydrate 36g (Dietary Fiber 5g); Protein 41g.

Turkey Croquettes

Where would leftover turkey be without turkey croquettes — round or oval-shaped mixtures of ground meat or poultry usually bound together with bread, potatoes, and eggs? Unfortunately, many recipes turn out fried, greasy, heavy versions. Ours, instead, bake up crisp in the oven. To simplify the preparation, plan to make them the day after you have mashed potatoes for dinner. This way, you can make extra potatoes and use the leftovers to make the croquettes.

Preparation time: *20 minutes*

Cooking time: *45 minutes*

Yield: *4 servings*

3 cups (1 pound) cooked turkey, (see Master Roast Turkey Breast recipe) cut into 1-inch cubes and minced

1 cup finely chopped onions (see Figure 13-1)

2 cups dry bread crumbs

1 teaspoon poultry seasoning

2 teaspoons Worcestershire sauce

1 large egg, beaten

Salt

Freshly ground black pepper

2 cups mashed potatoes

½ cup turkey or chicken broth

Vegetable oil cooking spray

Quick Turkey Gravy (see the recipe in this chapter) or canned, prepared gravy

1 Preheat oven to 350°.

2 Combine the turkey, onions, 1½ cups of the bread crumbs, poultry seasoning, Worcestershire sauce, and egg in a large mixing bowl. Season with salt and pepper to taste. Fold in the mashed potatoes and then just enough broth to bind the ingredients together.

3 Shape into 16 equal balls, each approximately 2½ inches in diameter. Roll each ball in the remaining ½ cup bread crumbs. Place on a large, ungreased baking pan. Spray the croquettes with the cooking spray (this makes them crisp).

4 Bake for 30 to 35 minutes or until golden brown, turning over after the first 15 minutes.

5 Serve with Quick Turkey Gravy on the side.

Per serving: *Calories 370 (From Fat 69); Fat 8g (Saturated 2g); Cholesterol 150mg; Sodium 1020mg; Carbohydrate 33g (Dietary Fiber 3g); Protein 41g.*

Figure 13-1:
How to
mince onion
deftly.

Stovetop Turkey Divan

If you've ever been to at least one potluck fund-raiser, we're sure that you've eaten some version of chicken or turkey divan. This 1930s classic is thought to have been the creation of a popular New York City restaurant, Divan Parisien. Although no longer in business, the restaurant is immortalized by this American classic. We hope you enjoy our simplified version.

Preparation time: *15 minutes*

Cooking time: *35 minutes*

Yield: *4 to 6 servings*

1 tablespoon unsalted butter

1 red pepper, cored, seeded, and diced

1 small onion, chopped

1 bunch broccoli, broken into small florets, stems discarded

2 cups chicken broth

1 cup half-and-half

3 cups medium egg noodles, uncooked

3 cups (1 pound) cooked turkey (see Master Roast Turkey Breast recipe), cut into 1-inch cubes

Salt

Pepper

1 In a large nonstick skillet or chicken fryer, melt the butter over medium heat. Add the red pepper, onion, and broccoli. Cook, stirring often, until the pepper and onion are soft, about 6 to 8 minutes.

2 Stir in the chicken broth, half-and-half, noodles, and turkey. Bring to a boil, reduce heat to a simmer, and cook, covered, 20 to 25 minutes, or until the noodles test done, stirring occasionally. Taste and adjust for salt and pepper.

Per serving (based on 4 servings): Calories 419 (From Fat 116); Fat 13g (Saturated 7g); Cholesterol 152mg; Sodium 377mg; Carbohydrate 32g (Dietary Fiber 4g); Protein 44g.

Turkey Chop Suey

We think of Pan-Asian fusion cooking, the combination of Western and Eastern ingredients and cooking methods, as being a 1990s creation — when in reality the first fusion dish made was probably chop suey made by Chinese cooks for American workers laying railroad tracks out West at the end of the 19th century. A mainstay of Chinese-American restaurants for years, chop suey is a creative mix of chopped cooked meat or poultry and vegetables.

Preparation time: *15 minutes*

Cooking time: *15 minutes*

Yield: *4 servings*

2 tablespoons vegetable oil

4 scallions, white and green parts, thinly sliced

3 stalks celery, sliced thin

8 ounces white mushrooms, thinly sliced

3 cups shredded green cabbage

2 cups fresh bean sprouts

3 cups (1 pound) cooked turkey (see Master Roast Turkey Breast recipe), cut into 1-inch cubes

3 tablespoons soy sauce

1 tablespoon dry sherry or white wine

¼ cup chicken broth

1 tablespoon cornstarch

2 cups hot cooked white rice

1 Heat the oil in a large skillet or wok until very hot. Add the scallions, celery, mushrooms, and cabbage and stir-fry until the cabbage is tender, about 3 to 4 minutes.

2 Add the bean sprouts, turkey, soy sauce, and dry sherry and stir-fry until heated through, about 1 to 2 minutes.

3 Combine the broth and cornstarch to make a smooth paste. Add to pan and stir-fry for 1 to 2 minutes, or until the sauce has thickened. Serve with white rice.

Per serving: Calories 284 (From Fat 81); Fat 9g (Saturated 1.5g); Cholesterol 94mg; Sodium 874mg; Carbohydrate 11g (Dietary Fiber 3g); Protein 40g.

Easy Turkey Tetrazzini

A fan created turkey Tetrazzini in the early 20th century for Italian soprano Luisa Tetrazzini, who toured the United States from 1910 to 1913. Combining pasta from Tetrazzini's native Italy with the American turkey, this dish has become a favorite way for generations of Americans to use leftover Thanksgiving turkey. To simplify it a bit, we eliminate the need to make homemade cream sauce by using prepared Alfredo pasta sauce, available in the refrigerated section of most supermarkets. Cook the elbow macaroni *al dente* or Italian style, making sure it is not soft and mushy but has slight chew or bite to it when done cooking in boiling water.

Preparation time: *15 minutes*

Cooking time: *20 to 25 minutes*

Yield: *4 servings*

2 tablespoons butter

1 scallion, sliced thin

½ pound white mushrooms, thinly sliced

1 container (10 ounces) Alfredo sauce

½ cup milk

2 tablespoons dry sherry

⅔ cup freshly grated Parmesan cheese

½ cup diced canned pimientos

3 cups (1 pound) cooked turkey (see Master Roast Turkey Breast recipe), cut into 1-inch cubes

½ pound elbow pasta, cooked al dente

1 Preheat oven to 375°.

2 In a large skillet, melt the butter over medium heat. Add the scallion slices and cook about 1 minute, or until soft. Add the mushrooms and cook about 3 minutes, or until soft. Add the Alfredo sauce, milk, and sherry. Stir well to combine. Bring to a simmer. Remove from heat and stir in ⅓ cup of the Parmesan cheese, the pimientos, and turkey.

3 Lightly butter a 3-quart baking dish. Add the pasta and the turkey mixture. Mix well. Sprinkle with the remaining ⅓ cup Parmesan cheese.

4 Bake, uncovered, until bubbling and brown, about 20 to 25 minutes.

Per serving: *Calories 640 (From Fat 198); Fat 22g (Saturated 0g); Cholesterol 147mg; Sodium 731mg; Carbohydrate 53g (Dietary Fiber 2g); Protein 55g.*

Sliced Turkey with Piquant Tuna Mayonnaise

This is probably the most elegant and easiest to prepare cold entrée that we know. This classic, northern Italian dish is traditionally prepared with poached veal that is sliced thin and then covered with a mayonnaise sauce made with tuna and capers. We have found that we can substitute turkey breast for expensive veal roast, with equally good results. Serve this delicious entrée with some simple steamed string beans dressed with extra-virgin olive oil; sliced, fresh garlic; and salt, and sliced, vine-ripened tomatoes.

If you don't have any capers in your fridge, you should be able to readily find them at your local supermarket where other pickled vegetables are sold. Grown in Mediterranean countries, the tightly closed bud or fruit of the caper bush can be as tiny as a peppercorn or as large as a pea, and add a pleasant but distinct flavor to food. Capers are usually sold in jars with brine, although they are also available packed dry in sea salt.

Preparation time: *20 minutes*

Yield: *6 servings*

1 can (7 ounces) tuna, packed in oil, preferably olive oil, undrained

2 teaspoons freshly squeezed lemon juice

¼ cup extra-virgin olive oil

2 tablespoons capers, packed in brine, rinsed under cold water and drained

1 cup mayonnaise

½ cooked turkey breast (about 2 pounds; see Master Roast Turkey Breast recipe), thinly sliced

Lemon slices (optional)

Whole parsley leaves (optional)

1 Place the tuna, lemon juice, olive oil, capers, and mayonnaise in the bowl of a food processor or blender jar. Process until creamy and smooth.

2 Spread some of the tuna mayonnaise over the bottom of a large serving dish. Cover with a layer of the sliced turkey and another layer of mayonnaise. Repeat layering the turkey and mayonnaise, ending with mayonnaise. If desired, garnish with lemon slices and parsley leaves.

Fat Buster: *You can substitute lowfat or fat-free mayonnaise for regular mayonnaise.*

Per serving: *Calories 422 (From Fat 159); Fat 18g (Saturated 3g); Cholesterol 153mg; Sodium 597mg; Carbohydrate 9g (Dietary Fiber 1g); Protein 54g.*

Cobb Salad

The classic Cobb Salad was the 1937 creation of Bob Cobb, co-owner of the Brown Derby restaurants in Hollywood, California. This brightly colored salad makes for a great main course when served with multigrain bread and fresh fruit.

Preparation time: *20 minutes*

Yield: *4 servings*

1 head iceberg lettuce, finely cut

1 head romaine lettuce, finely cut

1 pint cherry tomatoes, halved

3 cups (1 pound) cooked turkey (see Master Roast Turkey Breast recipe), cut into 1-inch cubes

1 large avocado, halved, pitted, peeled, and sliced (see Figure 13-2)

3 hard-boiled eggs, peeled and finely chopped

6 strips bacon, crisply cooked and crumbled

1 cup bottled, refrigerated blue cheese salad dressing

¼ cup crumbled blue cheese (optional)

1 Arrange the iceberg and romaine lettuce in a large, shallow serving bowl or platter. Arrange the tomatoes in a strip across the greens. Arrange the turkey in a strip along each side of the tomatoes, followed by a strip of avocado and the eggs.

2 Sprinkle salad with the crumbled bacon. Drizzle with the blue cheese dressing. If desired, add the blue cheese to the salad dressing for more of a blue cheese flavor. Toss before serving.

Per serving: Calories 699 (From Fat 446); Fat 50g (Saturated 10g); Cholesterol 272mg; Sodium 955mg; Carbohydrate 18g (Dietary Fiber 6g); Protein 48g.

How to Pit and Peel an Avocado

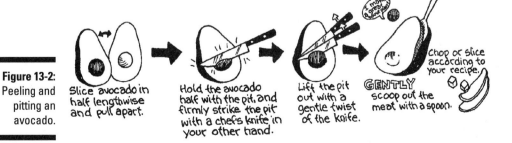

Figure 13-2: Peeling and pitting an avocado.

Slice avocado in half lengthwise and pull apart.

Hold the avocado half with the pit, and firmly strike the pit with a chef's knife in your other hand.

Lift the pit out with a gentle twist of the knife.

GENTLY scoop out the meat with a spoon.

Chop or slice according to your recipe.

Confetti Pasta and Turkey Salad

Hot summer days are the perfect time for one-dish salad dinners, especially when they're chock-full of meat, vegetables, and pasta. One such dish is this confetti salad, aptly named for all the colorful pieces of carrot, celery, and peppers in it.

Preparation time: *45 minutes, including chilling time of 30 minutes in the refrigerator before serving*

Yield: *6 servings*

3 cups (1 pound) cooked turkey (see Master Roast Turkey Breast recipe), cut into 1-inch cubes

4 cups cooked tubetti or ditalini pasta (about 1⅓ cups uncooked)

½ cup finely chopped carrots

½ cup chopped celery

½ cup finely chopped red pepper

½ cup finely chopped green pepper

¼ cup chopped Italian flat-leaf parsley

1½ cups bottled, refrigerated creamy Italian salad dressing

¼ teaspoon freshly ground black pepper

1 large head Boston lettuce, leaves separated into cups, rinsed, and patted dry

1 Combine the turkey, pasta, carrots, celery, red and green pepper, parsley, salad dressing, and pepper in a large mixing bowl. Cover and refrigerate for at least 30 minutes before serving.

2 Spoon the salad into the lettuce leaf cups before serving.

Fat Buster: *Substitute lowfat or fat-free creamy Italian salad dressing for regular salad dressing.*

Per serving: *Calories 482 (From Fat 228); Fat 25g (Saturated 4g); Cholesterol 63mg; Sodium 1073mg; Carbohydrate 31g (Dietary Fiber 2g); Protein 28g.*

Chapter 14

New York Penicillin: Master Chicken Broth Recipes

*H*ungry? Well, if you're in a real rush, you can always go to the cupboard and grab a can of chicken noodle soup. Open the can, pour the soup into a pot, and wait until it comes to a simmer. It smells like soup, but where are the pieces of real chicken and vegetables? Not many to be found, huh? Now if you had been stockpiling rich slow-cooked chicken broth in your freezer, you could prepare delicious homemade soups like the ones in this chapter in less time than it takes to order in a pizza. Sound tempting? We think so!

New York Penicillin

If New York City, the melting pot of the world, had its own dish of culinary distinction, it would have to be chicken soup. As a city made up of hundreds of nationalities, the one common thread amongst them all is some form of soup made with rich, homemade chicken broth. From matzoh ball soup from the Lower Eastside, to lemony Greek *avgolemono soupa* in Astoria, and wonton soup from the hundreds of Chinese takeout restaurants throughout the city, chicken soup stirs up in you memories of feeling good, regardless of your race, creed, gender, and age, especially if you have a case of the sniffles.

In fact, in 1984 the world-renowned Mayo Clinic endorsed the use of chicken soup in soothing cold symptoms. Since then, New Yorkers and others in the know have been affectionately referring to chicken soup and its many different guises as New York penicillin.

Making and Storing Chicken Broth

To make good chicken soup, you need a great broth of slowly simmered chicken pieces and vegetables. Everything else is basically window dressing. Once the broth ingredients are thrown into the pot, hardly any intervention is required, especially if you're using your slow cooker. Go out, play a round of golf, wash the car, have a manicure. And all the while, the diverse flavors of the ingredients will be mingling and combining to make a golden yellow elixir full of depth and body. But hey, don't take our word for it. Try it yourself.

 At least one supermarket has chicken on sale in every town across America, every day of the week, so it pays to shop around. If a cut-up fryer or chicken legs are less expensive than a whole bird, then by all means, use it. Ironically, ever since the Buffalo wings craze, wings aren't as cheap as they used to be. If you're not a wing person (and many people aren't), rather than throw them out, freeze them in a resealable plastic freezer bag and use them when making broth. The same advice holds true with the neck. You paid for it, so if you're not going to eat it, freeze it for making broth later on.

Master Chicken Broth

Having containers of rich chicken broth in the freezer is like having money in the bank. It's always there for a rainy day or whenever the mood strikes you for a steaming hot bowl of homemade soup. In fact, we make sure that we have at least a quart or two in the freezer at all times, and if not, we start another batch in the slow cooker as soon as we can. We recommend making this recipe in a large 5- to 6-quart slow cooker. To find out how to cut up a whole chicken for soup, see Figure 14-1.

You may wonder why our recipe calls for the addition of one chicken bouillon cube to our homemade broth ingredients list. It's our secret ingredient for added flavor and body!

Preparation time: *15 minutes*

Cooking time: *Low 8 to 10 hours*

Yield: *About 3 to 3½ quarts of broth, or 14 to 16 cups*

1 chicken (4 to 5 pounds), cut up	*½ bunch parsley, washed and tied together with string*
4 chicken wings (for added body)	*1 bay leaf*
1 clove garlic, peeled and crushed	*1½ teaspoons salt*
1 large onion, peeled	*½ teaspoon whole black peppercorns*
2 carrots, scraped and cut into 1-inch pieces	*1 chicken bouillon cube*
2 stalks celery, cut into 1-inch pieces	*4 quarts cold water*

1 Place the chicken quarters, chicken wings, garlic, onion, carrots, celery, parsley, bay leaf, salt, peppercorns, and bouillon cube in a 6-quart slow cooker. Pour the water over the chicken and vegetables and stir together.

2 Cover and cook on low for 8 to 10 hours, or until the chicken and vegetables are tender.

3 Remove the chicken from the slow cooker with a slotted spoon. Skin and debone. Set aside the meat, cut into chunks, and freeze for later use. Remove the parsley and bay leaf and discard.

4 Pour the broth and vegetables through a fine mesh strainer, pressing out as much liquid from the vegetables as possible before discarding them. Taste and season with additional salt, if needed.

Vary It: *Add 1 vine-ripened tomato or two canned plum tomatoes that have been peeled, seeded, and quartered, along with the other ingredients. Or for Oriental-inspired chicken broth, make wonton soup by eliminating the celery and onion and adding 1 bunch scallions, trimmed and coarsely chopped, along with a 2-inch piece of fresh gingerroot, peeled and sliced thin.*

Per 1 cup serving: *Calories 25 (From Fat 9); Fat 1g (Saturated 0g); Cholesterol 1mg; Sodium 525mg; Carbohydrate 1g (Dietary Fiber 0g); Protein 3g.*

Cutting Up a Raw Chicken

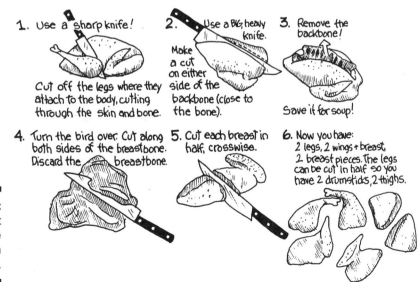

1. Use a sharp knife!

Cut off the legs where they attach to the body, cutting through the skin and bone.

2. Use a BIG, heavy knife.

Make a cut on either side of the backbone (close to the bone).

3. Remove the backbone!

Save it for soup!

4. Turn the bird over. Cut along both sides of the breastbone. Discard the breastbone.

5. Cut each breast in half, crosswise.

6. Now you have: 2 legs, 2 wings + breast, 2 breast pieces. The legs can be cut in half so you have 2 drumsticks, 2 thighs.

Figure 14-1:
How to cut up a whole raw chicken into parts.

Reducing fat content

To reduce fat content, remove and discard chicken skin before placing chicken in the slow cooker. Bear in mind, however, that removing the skin also diminishes the golden, yellow color that's characteristic of rich chicken broth. A good compromise is to leave the skin on and skim the fat from the broth, as shown in Figure 14-2, after it cools. To do so, place the cooled broth in a large shallow bowl or dish and place in the freezer, space permitting, or in the refrigerator overnight. After 15 minutes in the freezer, or the next day if in the fridge, carefully spoon the congealed fat off the top and discard.

Some housewares stores also sell defatting cups. They resemble a miniature watering can with a long spout and no head. To use, you simply pour or ladle the broth into the defatting cup. The fat portion will separate from the broth, making its way up the spout. Pour off the fat and save the broth.

Figure 14-2: Defatting your chicken broth.

Saving and using cooked chicken

Remove any visible fat from the cooked chicken and cut the meat into ¼- to ½-inch chunks. Freeze chicken in 1-cup quantities along with 4 cups of broth to use when making Chicken Rice Soup, Chicken Corn Chowder, or Matzoh Ball Soup, recipes that you can find in this chapter.

Broth storing and freezing tips

Broth freezes easily and stores well for up to approximately six months. Just remember from Science 101 that liquid expands when frozen, so never fill the container all the way to the top. If you do, the container can crack or the top can pop off. The following are some additional tips we want to share with you.

✔ Because you may use anywhere from 6 cups to up to 4 quarts of broth in the recipes in this chapter, we suggest that you package the broth either in various-sized containers or in 2-cup freezer containers or plastic freezer bags.

✔ Freezer space is always an issue in our homes. We never seem to have enough of it, and plastic containers take up a lot of valuable space. We like to use 1-quart or gallon resealable plastic freezer bags. Just fill and seal, carefully squeezing out as much of the air as possible. Wipe off any spilled broth and lay flat in the freezer, stacking bags on top of each other.

✔ Label your plastic food storage containers or resealable plastic freezer bags before filling and putting them in the freezer. Write what's in the container or bag, the quantity, the date it was frozen, and a "use by" date, which is two months after the broth was made.

✔ To defrost, remove the container or bag of broth the night before and thaw in the refrigerator overnight, approximately 8 to 12 hours. You can also defrost the broth in your microwave on the defrost or lowest setting, following the manufacturer's instructions.

Recipes Using the Master Chicken Broth

Picture this: The middle of winter . . . it's cold and raw outside, and the wind is howling. Sleet is pelting everything in its way, including you as you walk through the parking lot to get to your car. Your face is burning from the icy weather. Finally you reach your car only to find that the lock has frozen. After a few desperate minutes of working with it, the lock thaws, you're in the car, and you'd give anything for a bowl of piping hot soup for dinner. Well, dream no more. The quick and easy recipes that follow all use a quart of our Master Chicken Broth, previously made in the slow cooker and frozen — like a squirrel stores nuts for the long winter — waiting for moments just like this one.

Note: Although made from the Master Chicken Broth slow cooker recipe, the soul-warming recipes in this section are intended for quick cooking on the stovetop.

Chicken Rice Soup

What better comfort food can there be than chicken rice soup? It's so reassuring and soothing, just what the doctor (or your mother!) ordered to make you feel better when you have a case of the sniffles. And what could be easier than taking out a container of rich chicken broth from the freezer and sitting down to a bowl of soup less than 60 minutes later?

Preparation time: *15 minutes*

Cooking time: *30 minutes*

Yield: *4 servings*

8 cups (2 quarts) Master Chicken Broth (see recipe in this chapter)

1 cup diced cooked chicken from making Master Chicken Broth

2 carrots, peeled and sliced thin

1 stalk celery, sliced thin

½ cup uncooked enriched long-grain white rice

Salt

1 tablespoon coarsely chopped Italian flat-leaf parsley

1 Combine the Master Chicken Broth with the diced chicken and the sliced carrots and celery in a 4-quart saucepan. Bring to a boil over medium-high heat. Lower to a simmer. Add the rice and cook, covered, for 15 to 20 minutes.

2 Taste and adjust for salt. Add parsley before serving.

Per serving: *Calories 149 (From Fat 18); Fat 2g (Saturated 0g); Cholesterol 2mg; Sodium 1071mg; Carbohydrate 24g (Dietary Fiber 1g); Protein 8g.*

Variations on the Chicken Rice Soup theme

Here are a few of our favorite variations of the classic Chicken Rice Soup recipe:

✔ Add 1 cup fresh or frozen peas along with the carrots and celery.

✔ Instead of rice, add 2 cups uncooked broad egg noodles to the simmering soup and cook until tender.

✔ Add 2 cups fresh or frozen cheese or meat tortellini pasta to the simmering soup and cook until tender. Stir in 2 teaspoons lemon juice, along with the parsley, before serving.

Chicken Corn Chowder

Another American classic, this thick chowder is chock-full of goodness and garden-fresh vegetables. It takes a few minutes longer to prepare than some other soups, but the results are worth it!

Preparation time: *15 to 20 minutes*

Cooking time: *45 minutes*

Yield: *4 servings*

1 tablespoon vegetable oil

1 small red pepper, cored, seeded, and diced

1 small onion, chopped

1 carrot, peeled and sliced thin

1 stalk celery, sliced thin

1 medium potato, peeled and diced

4 fresh ears of corn, kernels sliced from cob (see Figure 14-3), or 2 cups frozen corn kernels

8 cups (2 quarts) Master Chicken Broth (see recipe in this chapter)

1 cup diced cooked chicken from making Master Chicken Broth

1 cup water

Salt

1 cup uncooked broad egg noodles

1 Heat the oil in a 4-quart saucepan over medium heat. Add the red pepper and onion and cook, stirring, until soft, 7 to 8 minutes. Add the carrot, celery, potato, and corn and cook for 2 to 3 minutes, or until heated.

2 Add the Master Chicken Broth with the diced chicken and water. Bring to a boil. Lower to a simmer and cook, covered, 15 to 20 minutes, or until the vegetables are tender. Taste and adjust for salt.

3 Add the noodles and cook until tender, about 10 minutes. To thicken the soup, mash some of the vegetables along the side of the pot with the back of a large mixing spoon.

Per serving: *Calories 232 (From Fat 54); Fat 6g (Saturated 1g); Cholesterol 1mg; Sodium 1072mg; Carbohydrate 36g (Dietary Fiber 4g); Protein 11g.*

Figure 14-3: How to cut fresh corn from a cob.

Matzoh Ball Soup

To make perfect matzoh ball soup (illustrated in Figure 14-4), you have to start with homemade "Jewish" or New York penicillin. If you don't happen to have a Jewish grandmother ("bubbe") or mother available to make you some, do not kvetch. Our Master Chicken Broth is a pretty close substitute.

Matzoh meal is made from unleavened bread or Jewish *matzoh* that has been ground finely into a meal-like consistency. It is readily available in most supermarkets in the specialty foods section or in the section where prepared soups and broths are sold.

Preparation time: *15 minutes*

Cooking time: *30 minutes*

Yield: *4 servings*

3 large eggs, separated	*2 teaspoons salt*
Pinch of salt	*8 cups (2 quarts) Master Chicken Broth (see recipe in this chapter)*
¾ cup matzoh meal	
4 quarts water	*1 cup diced cooked chicken from making Master Chicken Broth*

1 In a large mixing bowl, beat egg whites and salt until frothy. Fold in the egg yolks. Add the matzoh meal. Cover and let rest for 10 minutes.

2 Bring 4 quarts of water to a boil. Add 2 teaspoons salt. Bring the water to a second boil. Roll the matzoh mixture into golf-ball-size balls, and drop into the boiling water. Reduce heat and simmer for 20 minutes.

3 Bring the Master Chicken Broth with diced chicken to a simmer in a large saucepan. Add the matzoh balls and serve.

Per serving: Calories 250 (From Fat 63); Fat 7g (Saturated 1g); Cholesterol 188mg; Sodium 1194mg; Carbohydrate 23g (Dietary Fiber 1g); Protein 23g.

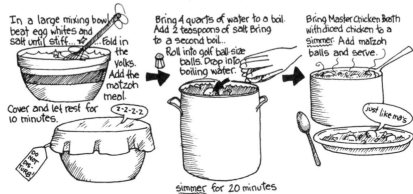

Figure 14-4: How to make matzoh balls.

Greek Egg-Lemon Chicken Soup (Avgolemono Soupa)

In Mediterranean countries like Portugal, Spain, and Greece, cooks often add lemon juice to chicken soup before serving it. The following Aegean version, which dates to the days of the ancient Greeks, also includes beaten egg, which adds body and silkiness to the broth.

Preparation time: *10 minutes*

Cooking time: *25 minutes*

Yield: *6 servings*

6 cups Master Chicken Broth (see recipe in this chapter)	*3 large eggs, separated*
	Juice of 1 large lemon
⅓ cup uncooked rice	*Salt*

1 Bring the Master Chicken Broth to a boil over medium-high heat. Lower to a simmer. Add the rice and cook, covered, 15 minutes. Remove from heat.

2 Beat the egg whites until stiff in a large mixing bowl. Add the egg yolks and beat until light. Gradually stir in the lemon juice. Slowly pour 2 cups of the simmering broth into the egg mixture, stirring constantly.

3 Pour the beaten-egg mixture into the broth, stirring constantly so that the egg does not curdle. Continue stirring for 1 minute. Adjust seasoning with salt. Serve immediately.

Per serving: *Calories 101 (From Fat 27); Fat 3g (Saturated 1g); Cholesterol 107mg; Sodium 751mg; Carbohydrate 10g (Dietary Fiber 0g); Protein 7g.*

Mexican Tortilla Soup

This south-of-the-border soup is probably the best known and most popular of Mexican soups. Although the corn tortilla strips are traditionally fried in oil, we cut back on a few calories by baking them until crisp in the oven. If your local supermarket doesn't carry smooth tomato salsa, either use some of our Holy Guacamole Tomato Salsa (Chapter 6) or purchase your favorite brand of chunky salsa and purée it in a blender or food processor until smooth.

Preparation time: *30 minutes*

Cooking time: *25 minutes*

Yield: *4 servings*

6 (6-inch) corn tortillas

Salt

2 tablespoons olive oil

1 large red onion, diced

3 cloves garlic, peeled and minced

2 cups your favorite brand bottled spicy, smooth tomato salsa

5 cups Master Chicken Broth (see recipe in this chapter)

Juice of 2 limes

1 bunch (½ cup) cilantro leaves (optional)

1 avocado, halved, pitted, peeled, and cubed (optional)

½ cup sour cream (optional)

1 Preheat oven to 350°. Dip each tortilla into a bowl of cold water. Sprinkle lightly with salt. Stack tortillas and cut into ¼-inch strips. Scatter tortilla strips on a large baking sheet and bake until crisp, about 15 minutes. Remove and let cool to room temperature.

2 Heat the olive oil in a 4-quart saucepan over medium heat. Add the onion and garlic, stirring often, and cook for 7 to 8 minutes, or until soft.

3 Add the salsa and Master Chicken Broth. Bring to a boil over high heat. Lower to a simmer and cook, covered, 15 minutes. Taste and adjust for salt.

4 Add the lime juice and crispy tortilla strips. Serve in large bowls. If desired, garnish with cilantro leaves, avocado, and sour cream.

Tip: To easily remove the large pit from the avocado, cut it in half lengthwise, cutting around the pit. Separate the avocado halves. Whack the pit with the blade of a sharp chef's or utility knife. The blade should stick in the pit. As you pull on the knife, the pit should come out easily. See the illustration in Chapter 13.

Per serving: Calories 338 (From Fat 198); Fat 22g (Saturated 0g); Cholesterol 12mg; Sodium 1016mg; Carbohydrate 31g (Dietary Fiber 6g); Protein 9g.

Wonton Soup

Prepared wonton skins — 3-inch squares of prepared pasta dough — make this recipe as easy as folding napkins. They're available in the produce section of most supermarkets or at Oriental food markets. One package will be more than enough for this recipe.

Preparation time: *30 minutes*

Cooking time: *15 minutes*

Yield: *8 servings*

2 tablespoons water

2 teaspoons white wine

½ teaspoon sesame seed oil

1 tablespoon cornstarch

1 teaspoon salt

1 pound lean ground pork

1 tablespoon thinly sliced green scallion tops

48 wonton skins

4 quarts Master Chicken Broth, Oriental variation, if possible (see recipe in this chapter)

2 green scallion tops, sliced thin (optional)

1 Combine the water, wine, sesame oil, cornstarch, and salt in a medium bowl. Add the ground pork and the 1 tablespoon of scallion tops. Blend well.

2 Place a scant teaspoon of the meat mixture in the center of a wonton skin. Moisten the edges with water. Fold the wonton in half diagonally to form a triangle. Pinch edges to seal. Moisten two opposite points and bring together. Pinch to join. (Figure 14-5 demonstrates wonton folding.) Place on a clean kitchen towel and cover with another so that the wonton doesn't dry out. Continue making the remaining wontons.

3 Bring the Master Chicken Broth to a boil in a 6-quart saucepan. Add the wontons and cook until the filling loses its pink color, about 4 minutes. Serve and, if desired, garnish with the scallions.

Per serving: Calories 357 (From Fat 144); Fat 16g (Saturated 5g); Cholesterol 51mg; Sodium 1654mg; Carbohydrate 31g (Dietary Fiber 1g); Protein 20g.

Figure 14-5:
How to fill
and fold
wontons.

Place one scant teaspoon of filling in the center of the wrapper...

Brush the edges of the wrapper with water to moisten.

Fold the wrapper in half to form a triangle and then :pinch: edges to seal.

Pull 2 opposite corners together moisten one corner with egg. overlap with other corner Press to seal.

Italian Egg-Drop Soup (Stracciatella)

Stracciatella drives its name from *stracetti*, which means "little rags" in Italian. When the beaten eggs and cheese are whisked into the hot chicken broth, they break up into small, torn pieces or strands.

Preparation time: *5 minutes*

Cooking time: *15 minutes*

Yield: *6 servings*

8 cups Master Chicken Broth (see recipe in this chapter)

½ cup freshly grated Parmesan cheese

2 tablespoons freshly minced Italian flat-leaf parsley

4 large eggs, lightly beaten

Salt

1 Bring the Master Chicken Broth to a boil over medium-high heat. Lower to a simmer.

2 Whisk the grated Parmesan cheese and parsley into the eggs. Slowly pour the egg mixture into the simmering broth, whisking vigorously for 1 to 2 minutes, or until the egg mixture is broken into fine pieces. Adjust seasoning with salt. Serve immediately.

Per serving: Calories 121 (From Fat 60); Fat 7g (Saturated 2.5g); Cholesterol 150mg; Sodium 1071mg; Carbohydrate 2g (Dietary Fiber 0g); Protein 12g.

Creamy Asparagus Soup

For us, the robin redbreast is not the harbinger of spring. The first asparagus we find at our local farmers market is our proof that spring has arrived! And what better way to finish off a cool, bright spring day than with delicious, bright green asparagus soup for dinner, garnished with spiky asparagus tips.

Preparation time: *15 minutes*

Cooking time: *40 minutes*

Yield: *6 servings*

2 tablespoons olive oil

1 large onion, chopped

2 carrots, peeled and chopped

2 stalks celery, chopped

1 medium potato, peeled and grated

1 clove garlic, peeled and minced

2 teaspoons dried thyme

2 bay leaves

2 pounds asparagus, stems trimmed and sliced into ½-inch-thick rounds, tips set aside

6 cups Master Chicken Broth (see recipe in this chapter)

Salt

1 Heat the olive oil in a 6-quart saucepan over medium heat. Add the onion, carrots, and celery. Cook for 7 to 8 minutes, or until the onion is soft. Add the potato, garlic, thyme, bay leaves, sliced asparagus stalks, and Master Chicken Broth. Bring to a boil over high heat. Lower to a simmer and cook, covered, for 20 minutes, or until the vegetables are very soft.

2 Remove and discard the bay leaves. Purée the soup, in batches, in a blender or food processor until smooth. Return the soup to the pot. Taste and adjust for salt. Add the asparagus tips and simmer for 4 minutes.

Per serving: *Calories 140 (From Fat 60); Fat 7g (Saturated 1g); Cholesterol 1mg; Sodium 565mg; Carbohydrate 13g (Dietary Fiber 1g); Protein 8g.*

French Onion Soup

A far cry from the packaged version in an envelope, real French onion soup is full of slowly cooked, caramelized onions, topped with gooey Swiss cheese. It's almost a meal in itself!

To bring out the sweet, natural flavor of the onions, slowly cook them with a bit of oil and sugar over low heat. Initially, they sweat or release their natural juices. As the cooking liquid evaporates, the onions' own sugars and the sugar that you add combine and caramelize, turning the onions a deep golden brown color.

In order to enhance the flavor of the onion even further, add some balsamic vinegar. Traditionally made in Modena, Italy, balsamic vinegar is deep brown in color. It is thick, almost syrupy, and sweet and sour in flavor. Balsamic vinegar is readily available in most supermarkets in the specialty food section or where the other vinegars are sold.

Preparation time: *15 minutes*

Cooking time: *45 minutes*

Yield: *4 servings*

3 tablespoons olive oil

2 pounds yellow onions, sliced thin

1 teaspoon sugar

1 teaspoon salt

1 teaspoon dried thyme

6 cups Master Chicken Broth (see recipe in this chapter)

1 tablespoon balsamic vinegar

¼ cup freshly grated Parmesan cheese

6 slices French bread, cut diagonally

1 cup grated Gruyère or Swiss cheese

1 Heat the olive oil in a 6-quart saucepan over medium heat. Add the onions and cook for 7 to 8 minutes, or until soft. Add the sugar, salt, and dried thyme and continue cooking, stirring often, until the onions caramelize, about 15 minutes.

2 Add the broth and bring to a boil over high heat. Lower to a simmer and cook, covered, 15 minutes.

3 Stir in the balsamic vinegar and Parmesan cheese.

4 Ladle the soup into heatproof bowls. Top each with a French bread slice. Sprinkle with the Gruyère cheese and place under the broiler. Broil until the cheese is golden and bubbly, about 2 minutes.

Per serving: Calories 369 (From Fat 176); Fat 20g (Saturated 5.5g); Cholesterol 25mg; Sodium 1582mg; Carbohydrate 34g (Dietary Fiber 1g); Protein 15g.

Potato and Leek Soup

Americans unfortunately do not cook as much with leeks as they do with other vegetables. Often referred to as the poor man's asparagus, leeks add a wonderful mellow flavor to foods when they are allowed to slowly sweat and release their mildly onion-like flavor, as in this fabulous French country *pottage,* or soup.

Preparation time: *20 minutes*

Cooking time: *30 minutes*

Yield: *4 servings*

2 tablespoons vegetable oil

3 large leeks, white and light green parts only, washed well to remove all the grit, sliced thin

4 medium, all-purpose potatoes, peeled and very thinly sliced

6 cups Master Chicken Broth (see recipe in this chapter)

Salt and freshly ground black pepper

1 Heat the oil in a 4-quart saucepan over medium heat. Add the leeks and cook for 7 to 8 minutes, or until soft.

2 Add the potatoes and Master Chicken Broth. Bring to a boil over high heat. Cover and simmer for 15 to 20 minutes, or until the potatoes are very soft.

3 Purée the soup, in batches, in a blender or food processor until smooth. Return to the saucepan. Taste and adjust for salt. Season with black pepper to taste.

Tip: *For instructions on how to wash and slice leeks, see the recipe for Moroccan Vegetable Stew with Couscous in Chapter 8.*

Per serving: *Calories 221 (From Fat 77); Fat 9g (Saturated 1g); Cholesterol 2mg; Sodium 804mg; Carbohydrate 28g (Dietary Fiber 3g); Protein 8g.*

Part V
The Part of Tens

The 5th Wave   By Rich Tennant

"It's a microwave slow cooker. It'll cook a stew all day in just 7 minutes."

In this part...

Here, we've assembled some of our favorite top ten lists, which include slow cooking tips we've learned over the years, common stumbling blocks you may encounter (and their solutions), Web sites that we're certain you will find as invaluable as we do, and menu suggestions for twelve months of eating pleasure from your slow cooker!

Chapter 15

Ten Special Occasions for Slow Cooker Entrées

In This Chapter

▶ Suggestions for some of our favorite events, using recipes from this book

*I*t's hard enough to find the time to cook anymore, let alone to figure out what to make for that special occasion, holiday, or get-together. And as if those problems weren't challenging enough, you also have to think of side dishes and desserts that complement and not detract from the event. As we developed the recipes for this book, we made mental notes of what dishes we would consider making for certain occasions and wish to share this information with you.

We chose ten seasonal events that you may celebrate, matched several of our favorite recipes from this book to those events (not an easy task, mind you!), and worked out some additional serving suggestions and foods that complement these dishes.

New Year's Celebration

You'll be surprised how easy it is to get ready for a party and not even have to be at home to cook! That's the joy of a slow cooker. All it takes is a little preplanning, and you'll be ready for the holiday season.

Come November each year, we make a batch of Chunky Chili Sauce and Holy Guacamole Tomato Salsa and freeze them in 1-cup quantities in the freezer for use on demand during the holidays.

When planning a party or get-together, we develop a game plan so that things flow smoothly as we make preparations. For example, if the party is on a Saturday, we might make a batch of the party mix the Monday or Tuesday night before, and store it in an airtight container. Wednesday night we may whip up a batch of the nacho cheese sauce. Thursday or Friday we would make the Asian Chicken Wings and then some Sweet 'n' Sour Meatballs. Naturally, we store the perishable foods, including the nacho cheese sauce, in the refrigerator and then reheat them in the microwave oven.

Many people eat certain foods like lentils and cabbage on New Year's Day as a way of welcoming in the new year with the hope of prosperity and good luck. Why not make our Stuffed Cabbage Casserole or Corned Beef and Cabbage to assure a great year for you, your family, and guests?

Don't forget to use your slow cooker when making beverages, too! Nothing warms you better on a cold winter's night than a hot drink like mulled wine or cider. And for a truly festive-looking beverage, make our Ruby Red Punch. All these drinks can be made and served straight from the slow cooker so that they stay warm.

Here are some savory party foods and beverages to help you and your guests welcome in the new year:

- ✔ Slow Cooker Party Mix (Chapter 6)
- ✔ Chunky Chili Sauce (Chapter 6)
- ✔ Holy Guacamole Tomato Salsa (Chapter 6)
- ✔ Nacho Cheese Sauce (Chapter 6)
- ✔ Sweet 'n' Sour Meatballs (Chapter 6)
- ✔ Asian Chicken Wings (Chapter 6)
- ✔ Ruby Red Punch (Chapter 6)
- ✔ Mulled Wine (Chapter 6)
- ✔ Spiced Cider (Chapter 6)
- ✔ Corned Beef and Cabbage (Chapter 9)
- ✔ Stuffed Cabbage Casserole (Chapter 10)

Super Bowl Chili Party

Be the halftime showstopper when you serve up a batch of our All-American Chili for a Crowd. Begin making the chili the morning of Super Bowl Sunday to be ready exactly at halftime. Because the tantalizing smells will be whetting everyone's appetites, you need to have some munchies on hand. We suggest making a batch of party mix a few days before. And what would Super Bowl

Sunday be without a bowl of nacho cheese sauce for dipping those tortilla chips? How about some requisite mini hot dogs in the form of our Spicy Lil' Piggies, both of which can be made in advance and reheated in the microwave oven? Even if your favorite Super Bowl team loses, you'll still be a winner with these dishes:

- ✔ Slow Cooker Party Mix (Chapter 6)
- ✔ Nacho Cheese Sauce (Chapter 6)
- ✔ Spicy Lil' Piggies (Chapter 6)
- ✔ All-American Chili for a Crowd (Chapter 12)

Weekend Skiing

Nothing warms cold, aching bones (not to mention filling the belly!) after a day on the slopes than a piping hot bowl of thick soup or stew! Prepare it in the morning and let the chili or stew cook in the slow cooker as you head for the ski lifts. For a complete meal, serve these filling one-dish meals with a large tossed salad, crusty bread, and fresh fruit and cheese, like a hearty farmhouse cheddar or Gouda with caraway seeds, for dessert. Here are a few of our favorite one-pot meals:

- ✔ Old-Fashioned Beef Stew (Chapter 8)
- ✔ Coq au Vin (Chapter 8)
- ✔ Provençal Chicken and Potato Stew (Chapter 8)
- ✔ Lemon and Thyme Pork Stew (Chapter 8)
- ✔ Italian Sausage Stew (Chapter 8)
- ✔ Moroccan Vegetable Stew with Couscous (Chapter 8)

St. Patrick's Day

The whole world seems to become Irish every March 17, St. Patrick's Day. And what would St. Patrick's Day be without corned beef and cabbage, which is especially tasty and simple to make in a slow cooker. Pick up some Irish stout and a loaf of soda bread on the way home for a complete Irish meal.

If the seventeenth falls on the weekend, why not have a St. Patrick's Day dinner party one year and lay out a wonderful Irish-inspired spread? You can start off with some delicious Irish smoked salmon served on buttered toast triangles with a squeeze of fresh lemon juice. For a first course, split pea soup, also enjoyed in Ireland, adds a touch of green to the menu. Because lamb and mutton are enjoyed throughout the Irish Isle, why not offer two entrées for your guests to choose from? Two perfect additions to the requisite corned beef and cabbage, are our Rosemary and Garlic Roasted Leg of Lamb or Roasted Lamb Shanks with White Beans and Herbs.

- ✔ Corned Beef and Cabbage (Chapter 9)
- ✔ Rosemary and Garlic Roasted Leg of Lamb (Chapter 9)
- ✔ Lamb Shanks with White Beans and Herbs (Chapter 9)

Passover or Hanukkah

Slowly cooked beef brisket is often the entrée of choice at many Eastern European Jewish family celebrations. Because brisket needs to cook slowly to tenderize, our slow cooker method is ideal.

Our recipe for Cranberry Brisket is perfect for any celebration or family get-together. For Hanukkah, serve it with potato latkes and applesauce. At Passover, accompany the brisket with a side dish of sautéed, tender, spring spinach. And what better way to start off each holiday dinner than with classic Matzoh Ball Soup?

- ✔ Cranberry Brisket (Chapter 9)
- ✔ Matzoh Ball Soup (Chapter 14)

Easter Sunday Dinner

Lamb has traditionally been associated with Easter in both a religious and culinary context for centuries. It is probably the most popular meat — along with ham — to be served on Easter Sunday, and we are especially partial to our meltingly tender, boneless leg of lamb recipe, fragrant with garlic and herbs. We like to make our Easter menu a true springtime celebration by serving locally available produce such as asparagus and tender spinach, simply sautéed. A wonderful and very simple-to-prepare first course could be either our Greek Egg-Lemon Chicken Soup or Italian Egg Drop Soup. The broths for these soups are made ahead of time, requiring only minimal attention before serving. Consider preparing Rosemary and Garlic Roasted Leg of Lamb for your Easter celebration.

- ✔ Rosemary and Garlic Roasted Leg of Lamb (Chapter 9)
- ✔ Greek Egg-Lemon Chicken Soup (Chapter 14)
- ✔ Italian Egg Drop Soup (Chapter 14)

Summer Picnic

Although most people enjoy barbecuing in the summertime, some days are just way too hot for you to be standing over a hot grill. That's when we look forward to some pulled pork barbecue, slowly simmered in the slow cooker and delicious when served on soft rolls. Serve it with some coleslaw on the side, corn on the cob, and plenty of cold, home-brewed iced tea.

A quick and easy to prepare casserole, or two, like Baked Beans and Beef, and Macaroni and Cheese, are also welcome additions to a summer picnic or barbecue. Best of all they can be prepared beforehand and simply reheated before eating. And why not take advantage of locally grown peaches and put together our Peach Crisp for dessert?

These dishes are perfect for summer evening get-togethers:

- ✔ Pulled Pork Barbecue (Chapter 9)
- ✔ Baked Beans and Beef (Chapter 10)
- ✔ Macaroni and Cheese (Chapter 10)
- ✔ Peach Crisp (Chapter 11)

Thanksgiving

Tom's most memorable Thanksgiving was the year his mother decided to surprise the family, break with tradition, and make a ham! As we all know, Thanksgiving just isn't the same without turkey! Because oven space is always at a premium Thanksgiving morning, learn to rely upon your slow cooker. If you have a couple slow cookers, you can also use them for side dishes, such as a sweet potato casserole, or a dessert, such as Apple Brown Betty to serve in addition to the pumpkin pie.

- ✔ Classic Vegetable Casserole with French-Fried Onions (Chapter 10)
- ✔ Sweet Potato Marshmallow Casserole (Chapter 10)
- ✔ Apple Brown Betty (Chapter 11)
- ✔ Master Roast Turkey Breast (Chapter 13)

Christmas Day

Large cuts of meat, like roast beef or turkey, are a tradition for Christmas Day dinner. With all of the hustle and bustle of opening presents Christmas morning, think how nice it would be to slow cook an eye round of beef with potatoes or a juicy, tender turkey breast without having to pay it any attention until it was done cooking. Use the pan drippings to make gravy and serve with our Classic Vegetable Casserole with French-Fried Onions.

For dessert, we would highly recommend something rich and special like Creme Caramel or Chocolate Custard. And for the Christmas toast, prepare Mulled Wine or Ruby Red Punch for the teetotalers.

- Ruby Red Punch (Chapter 6)
- Mulled Wine (Chapter 6)
- Company's Coming Roast Beef with Browned New Potatoes (Chapter 9)
- Classic Vegetable Casserole with French-Fried Onions (Chapter 10)
- Creme Caramel (Chapter 11)
- Chocolate Custard (Chapter 11)

Potluck Suppers

Potluck, pitch-in, or bring-along suppers are the fabric of many community social gatherings in the United States. Local cooks get to show off their talents as they share their offerings. Because most of the dishes are casseroles, slow cookers make potluck suppers a breeze. Add the ingredients, cover, and cook. No need to transfer your hot food to another dish; just take the slow cooker with you. If you have one of the newer models, your slow cooker may even have an insulated carrying case to keep the food steamy hot and protected during the car ride. If not, consider placing the slow cooker in a sturdy box lined with a large plastic bag to protect against spills. You may also want to bring pot holders, too, so as not to burn yourself.

We're sharing with you some of our favorite entrées for potluck suppers:

- Spicy Lil' Piggies (Chapter 6)
- Sweet 'n' Sour Meatballs (Chapter 6)
- Chunky South-of-the-Border Beef Stew (Chapter 8)
- Italian Sausage Stew (Chapter 8)
- Stuffed Cabbage Casserole (Chapter 10)
- Baked Beans and Beef (Chapter 10)
- Noodles Stroganoff Casserole (Chapter 10)
- All-American Chili for a Crowd (Chapter 12)

Chapter 16

Ten Problems and How to Handle Them

In This Chapter

▶ Keeping your cool when things go wrong

▶ Knowing why and how to fix common problems

Slow cookers are relatively easy to use. With no moving parts, they break or malfunction much less frequently than other appliances do. Nevertheless, things can go wrong, be it user error or operational, so we have compiled a list of ten problems that can occur, along with reasons and advice on how to keep the problems from happening again.

If you experience a problem we haven't touched upon, consult the printed materials that the manufacturer provided with your slow cooker. If you still can't find a solution to the problem, contact the company's customer service department. For a listing of manufacturers and their contact information, please see the appendix.

Holy Smoke

Problem: The slow cooker smokes when you plug it in and turn it on.

Reasons:

1. Manufacturing oil on the heating element or metal housing.
2. Spilled food on the heating element or metal housing.

Solutions:

1. Manufacturing oils used in production to protect metal components may cause slight smoking and/or a burning smell the first few times you use your slow cooker. This will dissipate after a couple of uses.

2. Check that no spilled food residue is on the heating element or metal housing. If food happens to spill on the heating element or housing, unplug your slow cooker, let it cool to room temperature, and wipe off the spills with a clean, damp cloth or sponge. Towel-dry before using it again.

Stone-Cold Slow Cooker

Problem: The slow cooker never heats up.

Reasons:

1. Not plugged into a working outlet.

2. If you are certain the electrical outlet is in perfect working order and the slow cooker continues not to operate properly, there may be an electrical component malfunction with the heating element, cord, or plug.

Solutions:

1. Make sure that the slow cooker is plugged in a properly wired and functional 110v, 60hz electrical outlet (the standard outlet found in all homes). If it is but it still doesn't heat up, unplug and plug it into another wall outlet that's on a different circuit.

2. Unplug the appliance and contact the manufacturer for further instructions. If there is uncooked or partially cooked food in the slow cooker, remove it from the crock and continue cooking by using conventional methods if it has been sitting out for under two hours; if the food has been sitting out for more than two hours, discard to avoid the risk of food poisoning.

Just Broke My Tooth on a Potato

Problem: The food is undercooked after the suggested cooking time elapses.

Reasons:

1. Food not placed in proper order in slow cooker.

2. Food pieces too big.

3. Frozen food used.

4. High altitude.

5. Slow cooker not covered, or cover lifted frequently.

6. Slow cooker not heating up hot and/or fast enough.

Solutions and Preventive Tips:

1. Certain foods, such as root vegetables, need to be placed on the bottom and along the sides of the slow cooker so that they are in direct contact with the cooking container. Rather than not be able to eat part of the meal, continue cooking the undercooked portion in a microwave oven or use a conventional stove and cooking methods.

2. Food — especially vegetables, which take longer to cook — should be cut into uniform, bite-sized pieces so that they cook evenly.

3. Never use or add frozen food to the slow cooker, which will add several hours to the cooking time. Thaw or defrost foods before using them.

4. Altitudes over 4,000 feet above sea level can slow down the cooking process. Check with your local cooperative extension office for recommended slow cooker time adjustments.

5. Always cook with the slow cooker cover in place. If you have to remove the lid for stirring, replace it quickly.

6. Consult the Iowa State University Extension Bureau Web site (www.extension.iastate.edu/Pages/families/fs/slowcook.html) for its heat safety test (see Chapter 17).

Uneven Cooking

Problem: The food did not cook evenly.

Reasons:

1. Food not placed in the slow cooker in the proper order.

2. Food pieces not cut to the same size.

Solutions:

1. Certain foods, such as root vegetables, need to be placed on the bottom and along the sides of the slow cooker so that they are in direct contact with the cooking container. If you place some on the bottom and some on top, the ones on top may not cook as quickly and may be undercooked.

2. To assure even cooking, cut foods like vegetables into bite-sized, even-shaped pieces.

Help, I'm Swimming in Liquid!

Problem: Food tastes bland or watery.

Reasons:

1. Underseasoned.

2. Too much cooking liquid.

Solutions and Preventive Tips:

1. Use dried leaf herbs rather than ground dry or fresh herbs because the dried leaf form keeps more flavor during the long cooking time. You can add fresh herbs during the last hour of cooking. Taste and adjust for seasoning before serving.

2. Because little evaporation occurs in slow cookers, you need about 50 percent less cooking liquid than called for in stovetop or oven cooking. If food appears too liquidy, remove the cover approximately 1 hour before it has finished cooking and cook on the high setting so that the cooking liquid can evaporate and thicken.

Probably Done Three Hours Ago

Problem: Food is overcooked.

Reasons:

1. Excessive cooking time.

2. Slow cooker cooks too fast.

3. Faulty thermostat.

Solutions and Preventive Tips:

1. The cooking times provided for all slow cooker recipes allow for safe cooking results during an approximate 6- to 9-hour period. Numerous variables, such as original food temperature and size, can determine how quickly food cooks in a slow cooker. In some cases, especially when you're preparing large cuts of meat or poultry, the food may test done sooner and can be removed and served before the end of the cooking time. Overcooked food can be salvaged as long as it is not burnt. Add small amounts of water to soups and stews that are too thick. Serve an overdone roast with gravy to moisten.

2. Some slow cooker models and brands tend to cook a bit faster than others. If that is the case with your slow cooker, modify the recipe's cooking time until you're satisfied with the results.

3. Perform the heating test found on the Iowa State University Extension Web site at `www.extension.iastate.edu/Pages/families/fs/slowcook.html`. If the water temperature is higher than 185°, discontinue using the slow cooker and contact the manufacturer for technical assistance.

Honey, I Burnt the Roast

Problem: Food burns or sticks.

Reasons:

1. Too little cooking liquid.

2. Food cooked with the slow cooker uncovered.

Solutions and Preventive Tips:

1. With the exception of things like snack mix and granola, you can't dry-cook in a slow cooker. For the appliance to operate properly, you must cook with some liquid; otherwise, the food will dry up as it cooks.

2. Do not cook with the slow cooker uncovered unless you are thickening the cooking liquid toward the end of the cooking process. Otherwise, the cooking liquid will evaporate as it heats. Burnt food usually cannot be salvaged and should be discarded. If something has overcooked a bit and stuck to the bottom or sides of the slow cooker, carefully remove the remaining food without scraping up any of the burnt particles. Let the cooking container cool to room temperature before cleaning. Fill it with warm, soapy water and let it soak until the cooked-on particles can be removed easily.

Get Me a Flashlight!

Problem: The power goes out while food is cooking in the slow cooker or the slow cooker gets unplugged accidentally.

Reasons:

1. Thunderstorm, blizzard, brownout, blackout, and other causes of power outage.

2. Slow cooker accidentally unplugged.

Solutions:

1. Food should not sit out at room temperature for more than two hours. If you're slow cooking at home when you lose power and the power is restored in less than two hours, you can safely continue cooking. If the power comes back on close to the two-hour limit, be on the safe side: Remove the food from the cooking container and finish cooking it by using conventional methods. If the food sits in the slow cooker for more than two hours, avoid food poisoning by discarding the food.

2. If the slow cooker is accidentally unplugged, replug and continue cooking immediately. If the slow cooker has been unplugged for a couple to a few hours, follow same steps as given in the preceding solution.

If you come home and find that you lost power while you were out and the food is not fully cooked, discard it to avoid the risk of food poisoning.

Slow Cookers, Like Cats, Don't Like Water

Problem: Slow cooker base was submerged in water or got wet for whatever reason.

Reasons:

1. Someone decided to break the cardinal rule and used a household appliance outdoors, unattended.

2. Your house was flooded.

3. Someone (heaven forbid) filled the metal base with water to remove cooked-on food.

Solution: Wetting a slow cooker or submerging it in water can damage the electrical components and cause electrical shock. This appliance was meant to be used indoors, where it's protected from the elements. Always unplug the slow cooker before cleaning, and never submerge it in water. Wipe it clean with a damp cloth or sponge and towel-dry before putting it away.

Shattered Lid or Liner

Problem: Glass cover or ceramic cooking container is cracked.

Reasons:

1. Dropping.
2. Setting on a cold counter.
3. Running cold water in the hot liner or placing the hot container in the refrigerator.

Solutions and Preventive Tips:

1. Glass and ceramic can't withstand radical changes in temperature and will crack when hot and exposed to cold rapidly. Never place a hot lid or liner on a cold tile or stone surface; let it cool to room temperature first, or lay a clean, dry kitchen towel on the counter and place it on that.

2. Never run cold water over the hot glass cover or the ceramic cooking container. Also, never place a hot cooking container in the refrigerator or freezer. Allow to cool first.

3. Contact the manufacturer to replace damaged or broken lids and crocks.

Chapter 17

Ten Web Sites to Check Out

In This Chapter

▶ Finding great recipes on the Web

▶ Getting slow cooking advice from the Web

*H*ome computers are playing a significant role in how we cook and eat today. With cents-off coupons for downloading and printing, opportunities to order ingredients and supplies, and recipes galore, numerous sites provide ongoing cooking assistance.

One of the most popular cooking-related categories found on the Internet is slow cookers/Crock Pots. By doing a word search for both terms, we found numerous Web sites that provide information about using this appliance. As we continued our research, we came across several sites that we think are well worth mentioning. However, we want to remind you that Web sites change constantly; what may be great today could very well be passé tomorrow, with something new and exciting just coming into play.

about.com

http://southernfood.about.com/food/southernfood/library/crock/blcpidx.htm

With well over 1,200 slow cooker recipes covering everything from appetizers to main courses to desserts, and even wild game, about.com is the most complete and user-friendly slow cooker site we came across. Arranged by category, the recipes we examined at random were easy to read and looked like they would be simple to make and delicious to eat.

In addition to recipes, this site is a great resource for home cooks who have questions about slow cooking and safety. You can find a reader's forum for questions and answers, as well as links to related sites. In addition to slow cooker recipes, you can find thousands of recipes for other types of cooking, making this site a definite winner!

Allrecipes.com

www.allrecipes.com

This simple-to-access Web site contains recipes of all sorts broken down by type of food, such as appetizer, main course, and dessert. It also provides a brief description of each recipe listed. After clicking on the category that interests you, type **slow cooker** in the Search box. Then click on Search, and all entries for that type of food appear, with brief descriptions.

cs.cmu.edu

www.cs.cmu.edu/~mjw/recipes/crockpot/crkpot-coll-2.html

Cs.cmu.edu is another Web site with an academic touch, this time from Carnegie Mellon University in Pittsburgh. A collection of favorite slow cooker recipes from students, faculty, and staff at CMU and other centers of higher education, this site is fun for its diversity of selections, ranging from beef bourguignonne to vegan dishes like Israeli wheat berry stew.

The Easy Guide to Crockpot Cooking on iVillage.com

http://pages.ivillage.com/fd/debbiens/

The Easy Guide to Crockpot Cooking on iVillage.com is maintained by Debbie Murphy of Nova Scotia. With close to 200,000 hits, this very popular site provides delicious recipes, including lowfat and quick-and-easy dishes, as well as message boards and links to related sites.

exnet.iastate

www.extension.iastate.edu/Pages/families/fs/slowcook.html

Last year, Tom was invited to travel to ten different state fairs to give bread machine baking classes. What really caught his attention was the number of slow cookers being used by the farmers' families in the various animal barns where their prized livestock were being shown — there seemed to be one going in every stall. Because many farms require two incomes, many wives work off the farm in addition to assisting with the day-to-day chores. After long hours, a slow cooker meal is a welcome sight in many farmhouse kitchens!

Because Iowa is such an important agricultural state, we were not at all surprised to find an excellent slow cooker Web site from the Iowa State University Cooperative Extension Bureau, at `www.exnet.iastate.edu`. The ISU site deals with safe cooking practices and the slow cooker. It provides a simple test that you can perform at home to make sure that your slow cooker is getting hot enough. This is extremely important if you have an older slow cooker; you want to make sure that it's still working well. The site provides guidelines for safe slow cooking as well as a direct link to the USDA's site on slow cooker safety (`www.fsis.usda.gov/OA/pubs/slocookr.htm`).

Mega-Zine

`www.Mega-Zine.com/kitchen/crock-pot`

Featuring everything from appetizers to vegetarian dishes, Mega-Zine contains over 100 slow cooker recipes arranged alphabetically. This well-designed site also provides a list of related Web sites as well as active links. There's even a free subscription service to the Mega-Zine recipe club that sends a new recipe daily.

Slow Food

`www.slowfood.com`

Although it's not the same as slow cooking, the International Slow Food Movement, started in Italy a little more than ten years ago, champions the causes of small regional food producers. The Slow Food Web site provides interesting information about the ISF Movement's manifesto, as well as programs worldwide, local activities and programs, and Slow Food–related publications. This site provides some interesting information on getting back in touch with the origins of food, and we have therefore decided to share it with you.

SOAR

`http://soar.berkeley.edu/recipes/crockpot`

SOAR (Searchable Online Archive of Recipes) is an excellent cooking resource with thousands of recipes. The slow cooker site contains 1,001 recipes arranged alphabetically; if you can't find it here, it probably doesn't exist.

Spira Solaris

www.spirasolaris.com/hshp/crockpot.html

Covering a broad range of topics from home/time management to candle and soap making, Spira Solaris contains a Kitchen page that provides a variety of information about slow cookers. Some of the topics covered include recipes sorted by ingredients, descriptions of different styles, and safety tips on use and care.

topica

http://topica.com/lists/crockpot

The e-mail list directory on topica provides a slew of information about various topics, one of which is slow cookers/Crock Pots.

CROCKPOT, a privately owned mailing list, is basically a network of slow cooker uses. The members get in touch with one another to exchange recipes or to provide assistance in answering questions anyone may have in using the slow cooker. With more than 900 members, participants are encouraged to post recipes and questions. To become a member, go to the Web site, scroll down to Subscribe, and click on crockpot-subscribe@ topica.com. You'll be asked to provide your e-mail address and other details, such as your name. Once you join, you will begin receiving information quite frequently.

Chapter 18

Ten Tips for Great Slow Cooking

*B*ecause slow cookers cook differently than conventional methods, you have to rethink some old cooking methods and master a couple new tricks when using your slow cooker, especially if you want delicious results every time. But don't be overwhelmed or perplexed. In this chapter, we share with you what we've learned over the years so that you too can become proficient in cooking with this very simple-to-use kitchen wonder. Slow cooking should be quick and easy with delicious results.

Determining How Much Is Enough

Slow cookers cook with indirect heat. The heat is transferred from the wrap-around electric elements found in the metal housing to the cooking container, which — in turn — heats the food. Because the cooking container does not come in direct contact with the heating elements, the amount of food present in the container is important for the slow cooker to work properly. Slow cookers should always be filled at least one-half to two-thirds full for best results. Too little food and you wind up heating mostly air, which may, in turn, slow down the cooking process.

Because the slow cooker eventually gets hot enough to bring the cooking liquid to a simmer, leave at least 2 inches of space between the food and the top of the container when making receipes with a lot of liquid, such as soups and stews, so that they don't boil over. Very little evaporation takes place when you cook food in a slow cooker. Also bear in mind that foods like roasts release some of their juices, adding even more liquid as they cook.

When converting a favorite recipe to a slow cooker recipe, reduce the liquid called for in the original recipe by approximately 50 percent.

Layering Contents Properly

Strange as it may seem, raw vegetables usually take longer to cook in a slow cooker than meat and poultry do because the cooking liquid simmers rather than boils. To ensure complete doneness of all ingredients at the same time, cut raw veggies into uniform, bite-sized pieces before placing them in the slow cooker, as shown in Figure 18-1.

Figure 18-1: Dice root vegetables into uniformly sized pieces.

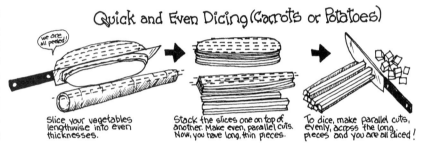

Quick and Even Dicing (Carrots or Potatoes)

Slice your vegetables lengthwise into even thicknesses.

Stack the slices one on top of another. Make even, parallel cuts. Now, you have long, thin pieces.

To dice, make parallel cuts, evenly, across the long pieces and you are all diced!

Also, when cooked with meat, root vegetables, such as white potatoes, sweet potatoes, carrots, turnips, and so forth, should be placed as close as possible to the bottom and sides of the cooking container so that they benefit from close contact with the heat source.

Reducing Fat

Fat adds flavor, color, and texture to food. Even though you hear much talk about reducing fat in your diet, you still need some fat in order to be healthy. If you want to reduce fat in your slow cooker recipes, however, we suggest using lean cuts of meat or trimming excess fat from meat and poultry before cooking. You will be very pleased to see how well lean cuts of beef and pork fare in a slow cooker. Because lean cuts are usually tougher than fattier, marbled cuts, they tend to hold up and cook better.

You can also reduce fat from homemade chicken broth by removing it after the broth has cooled, as discussed in Chapter 14.

Intensifying Flavors by Searing and Browning First

High heat alters the appearance and flavor of food. The natural sugars found in food cause it to brown, making it more appealing to look at because it loses that raw look, while at the same time making it more complex in flavor than boiled food.

We feel that foods such as onions, garlic, and meat benefit tremendously when you take the extra time to either sauté or brown them before placing them in a slow cooker. This may mean spending an extra 15 to 20 minutes in the kitchen, but you'll realize that it was well worth it when you taste the results. In some recipes in which the difference between browning and not browning is negligible, we give you the option, so the call is always yours. For more information on this, refer to Chapter 9.

Cooking with Dairy Products

Although the slow cooking process may tenderize lean cuts of meat, it does a number on dairy products like milk, cream, sour cream, and cheese. The long cooking time and low temperatures cause most dairy products to break down. Milk and cream will curdle, and cheese will become oily-looking as it separates.

To overcome these problems, we suggest using an equal amount of canned evaporated milk for savory dishes, and sweetened, condensed milk for desserts. Processed cheese like American and Velveeta usually gives better results than aged cheese like cheddar, which should be added only toward the end of the cooking time for best results.

Slow Cooking and Frozen Foods

Successful slow cooking depends on maintaining the balance between temperature, amount of food, and cooking time. Frozen foods added at the beginning of the cooking process can add several hours to the cooking time.

Always thaw or defrost frozen foods before adding them to a hot slow cooker. Adding icy-cold food to a hot cooking container will definitely throw things out of whack, and it could also crack the stoneware crock.

Cooking at High Altitudes

If you live at a high elevation (in excess of 4,000 feet above sea level), you probably already know that you need to extend the cooking time when using your slow cooker. For specific recommendations, you can contact your local cooperative extension office, which should be able to tell you approximately how much longer to allow for high elevation.

Keeping It Under Cover

Just as a watched pot never boils, an uncovered slow cooker never cooks. The cover must always be in place during cooking, except perhaps when you want to thicken a sauce before serving (see the following section) or when making such foods as granola or a party mix (see Chapter 6). A slow cooker can take as long as 20 minutes to recover lost heat when the cover is removed, so please trust your slow cooker and refrain from too much peeking. If the recipe calls for stirring, replace the lid quickly after you remove it to stir.

Thickening Sauces and Cooking Liquid

In the event that the recipe you have prepared is too liquidy, or you want to thicken a sauce, remove the slow cooker cover and cook on the high setting for approximately 30 minutes either before the recipe has finished cooking or when it is done.

Always remember to cook with 50 percent less liquid when using a slow cooker so that your dishes don't come out soupy. (Slow cooker recipes call for the right amount of liquid, of course, but you need to do the converting yourself if you're making a traditional recipe in a slow cooker.)

If Your Slow Cooker Cooks Too Slowly

You may be surprised to see how efficient today's slow cookers are. Nevertheless, if, over the course of time, you find that your recipes are taking longer to cook than you anticipated, we suggest that you perform the safety test for heating found at the Iowa State University Extension Web site for slow cookers (www.extension.iastate.edu/Pages/families/fs/slowcook.html).

If your slow cooker passes this test with flying colors and still seems to take too long, reread the suggestions given earlier in this chapter to make sure that you're doing everything right, especially the following:

- Cooking the right amount of food for the size of your slow cooker

- Cutting foods such as root vegetables into bite-sized pieces and placing them at the bottom layer of the foods in the slow cooker

- Thawing or defrosting frozen foods before placing them in a hot slow cooker

- Allowing for additional cooking time at altitudes over 4,000 feet above sea level

- Cooking with the slow cooker covered, except when thickening a sauce at the end of a recipe

Appendix A

Contact Information for Slow Cooker Manufacturers

• •

*O*ccasionally, you may need to contact the manufacturer of your slow cooker. The following list of the most popular brands of slow cookers provides you with the manufacturer's customer service address, phone number, and Web site or e-mail address. Because warranty and return policies vary from manufacturer to manufacturer, we suggest that you always check with the customer service department before sending anything back for repair or exchange.

Some manufacturers offer accessories for their line of slow cookers. If you're interested, we suggest you contact them to see what is available for your specific model.

Corningware

Windmere/Applica
5980 Miami Lakes Drive
Miami Lakes, FL 33014
Phone: 1-800-557-9463

Note: Windmere/Applica is the manufacturer of the Corningware brand of slow cookers.

Hamilton Beach

USA
Hamilton Beach
Receiving Door #6
Attention: Consumer Affairs Center
Washington, NC 27889
Phone: 1-800-851-8900
Web site: www.hamiltonbeach.com
E-mail: customerservice@hamiltonbeach.com

Canada
Hamilton Beach
#10 McFarland Drive
Picton, Ontario
K0K 2T0
Phone: 1-800-267-2826
Web site: www.hamiltonbeach.com
E-mail: customerservice@hamiltonbeach.com

Mexico
Grupo HB/PS, S.A. de C.V.
Gerencia Internacional de Servicio
Blvd. Manuel Avila Camacho No. 2900 Desp. 504
Fracc. Los Pirules C.P. 54040
Tlalnepantla, Edo. de México.
Phone: 01 800 71 16 100 or (52) 53 79 38 11
Web site: www.hamiltonbeach.com
E-mail: mexicoservice@hamiltonbeach.com.mx

Proctor-Silex

Note: Hamilton Beach is the manufacturer of the Proctor-Silex brand of slow cookers.

USA
Hamilton Beach
Receiving Door #6
Attention: Consumer Affairs Center
Washington, NC 27889
Phone: 1-800-851-8900
Web site: www.hamiltonbeach.com
E-mail: customerservice@hamiltonbeach.com

Canada
Hamilton Beach
#10 McFarland Drive
Picton, Ontario
K0K 2T0
Phone: 1-800-267-2826
Web site: www.hamiltonbeach.com
E-mail: customerservice@hamiltonbeach.com

Mexico
Grupo HB/PS, S.A. de C.V.
Gerencia Internacional de Servicio
Blvd. Manuel Avila Camacho No. 2900 Desp. 504
Fracc. Los Pirules C.P. 54040
Tlalnepantla, Edo. de México.
tel: 01 800 71 16 100 or (52) 53 79 38 11
Web site: www.hamiltonbeach.com
E-mail: mexicoservice@hamiltonbeach.com.mx

Rival

The Holmes Group
Customer Service Department
233 Fortune Boulevard
Milford, MA 01757
Phone: 1-800-557-4825
Web site: www.theholmesgroup.com

West Bend

The West Bend Company
Customer Service Department
400 Washington Street
West Bend, WI 53095
Phone: 1-800-821-8821 or 1-262-334-6949
Web site: www.westbend.com
E-mail: housewares@westbend.com

Appendix B

Metric Conversion Guide

• •

*N*ote: The recipes in this cookbook were not developed or tested using metric measures. There may be some variation in quality when converting to metric units.

Common Abbreviations

Abbreviation(s)	What It Stands For
C, c	cup
g	gram
kg	kilogram
L, l	liter
lb	pound
mL, ml	milliliter
oz	ounce
pt	pint
t, tsp	teaspoon
T, TB, Tbl, Tbsp	tablespoon

Volume

U.S Units	Canadian Metric	Australian Metric
¼ teaspoon	1 mL	1 ml
½ teaspoon	2 mL	2 ml
1 teaspoon	5 mL	5 ml
1 tablespoon	15 mL	20 ml
¼ cup	50 mL	60 ml
⅓ cup	75 mL	80 ml
½ cup	125 mL	125 ml
⅔ cup	150 mL	170 ml
¾ cup	175 mL	190 ml
1 cup	250 mL	250 ml
1 quart	1 liter	1 liter
1½ quarts	1.5 liters	1.5 liters
2 quarts	2 liters	2 liters
2½ quarts	2.5 liters	2.5 liters
3 quarts	3 liters	3 liters
4 quarts	4 liters	4 liters

Weight

U.S. Units	Canadian Metric	Australian Metric
1 ounce	30 grams	30 grams
2 ounces	55 grams	60 grams
3 ounces	85 grams	90 grams
4 ounces (¼ pound)	115 grams	125 grams
8 ounces (½ pound)	225 grams	225 grams
16 ounces (1 pound)	455 grams	500 grams
1 pound	455 grams	1/2 kilogram

Measurements

Inches	*Centimeters*
½	1.5
1	2.5
2	5.0
3	7.5
4	10.0
5	12.5
6	15.0
7	17.5
8	20.5
9	23.0
10	25.5
11	28.0
12	30.5
13	33.0

Temperature (degrees)

Fahrenheit	*Celsius*
32	0
212	100
250	120
275	140
300	150
325	160
350	180
375	190

(continued)

Temperature (degrees) *(continued)*

Fahrenheit	Celsius
400	200
425	220
450	230
475	240
500	260

Index

IDG BOOKS WORLDWIDE
BOOK REGISTRATION

Register This Book and Win!

We want to hear from you!

Visit **http://my2cents.dummies.com** to register this book and tell us how you liked it!

- ✔ Get entered in our monthly prize giveaway.

- ✔ Give us feedback about this book — tell us what you like best, what you like least, or maybe what you'd like to ask the author and us to change!

- ✔ Let us know any other *For Dummies*® topics that interest you.

Your feedback helps us determine what books to publish, tells us what coverage to add as we revise our books, and lets us know whether we're meeting your needs as a *For Dummies* reader. You're our most valuable resource, and what you have to say is important to us!

Not on the Web yet? It's easy to get started with *Dummies 101*®*: The Internet For Windows*® *98* or *The Internet For Dummies*® at local retailers everywhere.

Or let us know what you think by sending us a letter at the following address:

For Dummies Book Registration
Dummies Press
10475 Crosspoint Blvd.
Indianapolis, IN 46256

™

BESTSELLING BOOK SERIES